Escape from the Wasteland

Harvard-Yenching Institute Monograph Series, 33

Escape from the Wasteland:

Romanticism and Realism in the Fiction of Mishima Yukio and Oe Kenzaburo

Susan J. Napier

Published by the Council on East Asian Studies, Harvard University,
and distributed by Harvard University Press,
Cambridge (Massachusetts) and London 1991

The Harvard-Yenching Institute, founded in 1928 and headquartered at Harvard University, is a foundation dedicated to the advancement of higher education in the humanities and social sciences in East and Southeast Asia. The Institute supports advanced research at Harvard by faculty members of certain Asian universities, and doctoral studies at Harvard and other universities by junior faculty at the same universities. It also supports East Asian studies at Harvard through contributions to the Harvard-Yenching Library and publication of the Harvard Journal of Asiatic Studies and books on premodern East Asian history and literature.

Publication of this volume has been assisted by a grant from the Shell Companies Foundation.

Jacket illustration by Richard Spencer, based on a print by Clifton Karhu, which was used with the permission of the Tolman Gallery, Tokyo.

Library of Congress Cataloging-in-Publication Data

Napier, Susan Jolliffe.
    Escape from the wasteland : romanticism and realism in the fiction of Mishima Yukio and Oe Kenzaburo / Susan J. Napier.

    p.   cm. —— (Harvard-Yenching Institute monograph series ; 33)
    Includes bibliographical references (p.   ) and index.
    ISBN 0-674-26180-1
    1. Japanese fiction—20th century—History and criticism.
2. Romanticism.   3. Realism in literature.   4. Mishima, Yukio,
1925-1970—Criticism and interpretation.   5. Ōe, Kenzaburō, 1935-
—Criticism and interpretation.   I. Title.   II. Series.
    PL747.67.R64N3   1991

        895.6'3509145—dc20   91-14006
                                                                              CIP

To Ron

Acknowledgments

Many people and institutions helped in the writing of this book. First and foremost I owe my deepest debt of gratitude to Professor Howard Hibbett of Harvard University, who advised me when this book was in its original dissertation form and has continued to offer help and guidance up to its present incarnation. My other important mentor has been Asaii Kiyoshi of Ochanomizu Womens University, whose unstinting support and guidance over the last eight years have been helpful beyond measure.

While it was still in thesis form, my second advisor, Professor Edwin Cranston of Harvard University, was exceptionally thorough and helpful in his comments and criticisms. I also greatly appreciate the encouragement I received at that time from Professor Donald Shively, now at the University of California at Berkeley.

A number of others were very helpful as the work reached its book stage. Professor Thomas Havens of Wesleyan and Professor Harry Harootunian of Chicago each kindly read and commented on a chapter. Mark Oshima was also an extremely thorough and helpful reader. Herman Van Olphen, my chairman at the University of Texas, was very generous in allowing me leave to complete the project.

On the Japan front several other individuals were notably generous with time and effort. I would particularly like to thank my former tutors, Ms. Miyauchi Junko and Ms. Michiko Harada, who were both at Ochanomizu University at that time.

Finally, Mr. Oe Kenzaburo deserves a special message of gratitude for being so unstintingly supportive of this project and for cooking a superb oxtail stew.

Institutionally, this book would not have been possible without two generous grants. The first was from the Japan Foundation, and it allowed me to carry out my initial dissertation research in Japan. The second was a URI grant from the University of Texas, which enabled me to begin the arduous process of turning the thesis into a book.

As always I would like to thank my husband Ron for his endless support, patience, and encouragement.

Contents

Introduction

In Oe Kenzaburo's 1980 novel, *The Game of Contemporaneity* (*Dōji-dai gēmu*), the narrator recounts the legend of some children who disappeared during a village revolt known as the "Fifty-Day War." According to the legend, the children helped the village elders by devising mazes in the forests to trap and confuse the enemy soldiers, ultimately leading them away from their objective. The following day the elders realized that some of the children were missing. Initially, they feared that the children had been taken prisoner by the enemy but another explanation won out: the labyrinths had been constructed so successfully that the children themselves became lost in them. Rather than mourn their loss, the villagers were relieved, for, as the narrator explains:

> "[f]rom the instant the children entered the closed circle of the maze, they had escaped the influence of time and would remain eternally children walking forever through the primeval forest."[1]

Mishima Yukio's 1949 work, *Confessions of a Mask* (*Kamen no kokuhaku*), contains another vision of the relationship between fantasy and reality. The narrator reminisces about "the period of childhood [which] is a stage on which time and space become entangled," and goes on to explain how, as a child, he gave equal weight to three different phenomena: "outside events," the "things that happened before my eyes" and "the fanciful events of the fairy tale world in which I had just then become immersed." He concludes by saying that "I could not believe . . . that the so-called 'social community' which I must presently enter, could be more dazzling than the world of fairy tales."[2]

Each in his own way, Oe Kenzaburo and Mishima Yukio have consistently set up alternative fictional worlds of "closed circles," even of "fairy tales," which are "outside the influence of time," to contrast with the reality of modern Japan. The two writers' alternative worlds are by no means completely alike, but they do share a remarkable number of common elements. They are worlds that are often childish or adolescent in terms of both characters and emotional tone. Appropriate to their youthful focalization, these fictional realms frequently suggest utopian alternatives of infinite plenitude and infinite intensity, larger-than-life realms of action and vivid imagery. They are also literary creations that exist in overt contradiction to most mimetic literature, sometimes containing explicitly fantastic elements, such as reincarnation or supernatural beings. Finally, these fictional alternatives share one further significant ingredient: they are explicit and intense "compensations" for the disappointments of reality resulting from each writer's deep sense of anger and frustration.

This book is a study of Oe's and Mishima's alternative literary worlds; it is also, tangentially at least, a study of postwar Japan, of the troubled reality that the two writers strove to overcome in their writings and in their lives. Fukushima Akira has said of Mishima and Oe that "they are the two Japanese writers most sensitive to the contemporary world,"[3] and this sensitivity leads them to deal with a wide variety of topics and problems in their fiction, including basing novels on actual events such as Mishima's *Temple of the Golden Pavilion* (*Kinkakuji*), and Oe's *Outcries* (*Sakebigoe*). These works are not simply reflections of real events but responses to them, explorations of the society which produced them. It is this variety of topics that gives their writing a range and depth unusual in modern Japanese literature, which even now reflects the long dominant influences of the Naturalist school. Begun in the early twentieth century, this school was influenced by such European Naturalists as Zola but also reflected an indigenous tradition of confessional and diary literature, its most important product being the so-called I novel (*shishōsetsu*), autobiographical novels written in a confessional style. These narratives, with their "privileging of lived experience," as Edward Fowler puts it,[4] tended to restrict that experience to the most limited autobiographical sort, a far cry from the varied materials used by Mishima and Oe, although their works have also included autobiographical elements.[5]

The two men make an interesting comparative study on several other levels. Professionally, Oe and Mishima share a number of important attributes. They are two of the most important and controversial writers of postwar Japan, writing fiction that was sophisticated enough for the critics but, at the same time, entertaining enough to gain a wide readership. Indeed, their works are notable for their action-filled plots on controversial subjects such as sexual and criminal aberrations.

Yet, despite these similarities on the professional level, politically the two writers occupy virtually opposite ends of the spectrum. Mishima's glorification of the emperor system and of the military earned him such appellations as "right-wing," and "fascist," and the excoriation of many left-wing critics. Oe, on the other hand, is almost anarchistic in his conscious hostility toward established authority and is a committed and articulate spokesman for a variety of causes from ecology to human rights. Their politics are not always so simplistically clearcut as they might appear, however, and this surprising complexity provides another important point of comparison.

It is these three elements—their consistent presentation of alternatives to postwar reality, their sensitivity to that reality, and the number of intriguing similarities in their basically differing political viewpoints—that make Oe and Mishima such fascinating subjects for comparison. The differences, however, should not be glossed over, since they include not only the political but also the personal and literary. Consequently, although this book is largely a comparison of the two writers' fictional oeuvres, some mention of their personal and political background sets the framework for a clearer understanding of their fiction.

Mishima, born in Tokyo in 1925 to an upper-middle-class family with aristocratic pretensions, drew on his sophisticated urban background and elite education, first in the Peers School and later on in Tokyo University, to create fictional visions that were appreciated by some critics for their flamboyant beauty, while being criticized by others for their artificiality, a quality not generally admired in modern Japanese literature with its Naturalist heritage. The circumstances of Mishima's own rather bizarre childhood may have played a part in developing that artificiality: As his semi-autobiographical *Confessions of a Mask* reveals, Mishima spent much of his youth separated from his parents and was brought up by his ailing grandmother, whose major pleasures in life seem to have focused on exerting control over her family and going to the kabuki theater. Kabuki, Japanese romanticism, a strong admiration for classical Japanese culture, and later on an interest in German romanticism, all show their influences in Mishima's work, while his own lonely childhood may have contributed to the creation of his many memorable "outsider" characters. Mishima's presumed homosexuality and its effect on his work have also been discussed, ad infinitum, by many critics, both Japanese and Western, sometimes at the expense of more analytical judgments of his writings.[6] Some critics have linked his sexual orientation to the many sadomasochistic fantasies he presents, although the heterosexual Oe also shows a strong preoccupation with sexual violence in his works.

In any case, Mishima's intense sadomasochistic visions were given a political framework in the last decade of his life, as he became increasingly concerned about what he saw as the radical politics and attendant decay of Japanese culture in the 1960s. In response to this presumed degeneration, Mishima developed a comprehensive alternative vision that was considered by many to be fascistic, because of its glorification of the emperor as the center of Japanese culture and of the military who served the emperor. Ultimately, Mishima took his vision beyond the fictional realm in 1970 when he attempted a coup d'etat, ostensibly for the purposes of creating a "Showa Restoration." Following its inevitable failure, he committed the traditional form of suicide known as seppuku.

Oe's background and politics differ widely from those of Mishima. Born ten years later in 1935, Oe grew up in a remote village in rural Shikoku. Although his ancestors had been feudal retainers, his family was running a small shop in the village at the time of his birth. Despite its remoteness, the village was not unaffected by the events of the Second World War, which raged throughout Oe's childhood. The war and the sudden death of his father when he was nine are undoubtedly the most important events of Oe's early youth. Other major influences were the village legends recounted to him by an old woman who was a member of the household, and books in general. Because of an embarrassing stuttering problem, books may have held a particular attraction for the young Oe.

Perhaps as a result of his immersion in literature, Oe, like Mishima, was able to enter the prestigious Tokyo University, where he majored in French literature, writing his thesis on Sartre's imagery. Although

Oe now lives in Tokyo, his fiction has been continuously inspired and empowered by his rural roots, not only in terms of his constantly recurring imagery of a remote valley surrounded by forests, but also by the legends recounted to him and the actual events that occurred while he was growing up, all of which appear and reappear frequently in his fiction.

One event, or rather set of events, which did affect both Oe and Mishima and indeed the entire Japanese nation was, of course, the Second World War, the defeat, and the American Occupation. The war has cast a long shadow over a generation of Japanese writers; but Oe and Mishima are notable for their continued fascination with it, despite decades having passed since the war ended. It is not simply the war per se that preoccupies them but the entire complex of happenings surrounding the watershed year of 1945, which even now divides so much of Japanese culture into a bipolarity of "prewar" and "postwar" periods.

Kataoka Keiji has described the psychology of the ten-year-old Oe in 1945 and the years that followed as that of a split personality.[7] On one side is the "patriotic boy" (*aikoku shōnen*), the boy who trusted implicitly in the imperial house and the imagery and legends surrounding it. In 1945, the "patriotic boy" was supplanted by the "democratic boy" (*minshushugi shōnen*), who developed in Oe's psyche along with the American Occupation and after the emperor's renunciation of divinity. Even now, the conflict between young patriot and young democrat has not been completely resolved, but it is this conflict which has animated some of Oe's best fiction.

Since Mishima was twenty when Japan surrendered, he never received the democratic, American-style education that was instituted during the Occupation. But Mishima's work also highlights a split between pre- and postwar Japanese culture. Most significantly, the two writers share a common concern which grows out of the prewar period, and that is a fascination, some would say an obsession, with the emperor, and with the imperial system in general. In their fiction and their essays, both men return again and again to the era of the war and the influence of the emperor, which they both romanticize—consciously on Mishima's part, almost in spite of himself on the part of Oe—and parody—unconsciously in the case of Mishima, explicitly in Oe's case.

This obsession with the war and the emperor is an ironic one, insofar as neither man served in the military. Indeed, Mishima, the glorifier of military exploits and lost causes, was relieved when he was excused from active duty and even stated that at the time the death of his sister affected him far more profoundly than did the surrender.[8] Oe, of course, was only ten when the war ended, and his most immediate impression was of being amused by the way a classmate imitated the Emperor announcing the surrender.[9]

For both writers this initial lack of response to the surrender changed radically over the years. For Oe and Mishima the emperor is a symbol of continuity, a symbol that helps give meaning, negative or positive, both to their own existence and to the world of postwar Japan. Similarly, the war itself is associated with a time of intense, larger-than-life emotions and actions. In his essay, "The War Within Me" ("Boku jishin no naka no sensō"), Oe reveals his fascination with the "vast sense of solidarity" experienced by the heroes in Western fiction about the Second World War. At one point he even mentions a "peculiar emotion" he experienced when reading war-related works by such authors as Malraux or Hemingway because it felt as if he were reading an "epic poem of a lost Utopia."[10] Oe's point, which he continues to propound in his fiction and essays, is that the old-style wars of yesterday, the "age of heroic battles," as one of his characters calls it, contrast to the grim and utterly unromantic war facing the world in the nuclear age.

Although even in his youth he was clearly affected by the nationalist Japanese Roman-ha (Romantic) movement (in itself related to German nationalist romanticism), Mishima's full-blown obsession with the war and the emperor developed later in his life. Partly in response to the political climate of the 1960s, he began to use the war era as a backdrop for the development of his romantically heroic fictional characters. As will be seen in Chapter Seven, the two writers each devote generous comment to the roles of militarism and the emperor in both their fiction and essays. Despite all their intellectual concerns, however, it seems clear that each author also found an immediate visceral appeal in the notion of war, an appeal that is frankly romantic.

In this regard, the two writers resemble the members of what Samuel Hynes has called the "Auden Generation," the generation of English writers, such as Isherwood, Orwell, and Auden, who wrote after the First World War and felt they had "missed out" on an intense world of experience which was gained during wartime and was no longer available to the post-1918 youth. As Christopher

Isherwood said, "I was obsessed by a complex of tension and longing connected with the idea of war."[11] Although the cultural differences between English writers of the 1920s and Japanese writers of the post-war period should not be minimized, the fact that Oe and Mishima maintained throughout their lives a similar fascination with the war they had "missed out" on, and the emperor who had been its figure-head, is clear in such works as Oe's *The Youth Who Came Late* (*Oku-rete kita seinen*), and *Our Era* (*Warera no jidai*), or Mishima's "Patri-otism" ("Yūkoku") or *Runaway Horses* (*Honba*).

This mutual romantic fascination with the emperor and the war should not, however, lead us to ignore Mishima's and Oe's immense political differences that are revealed in their writing. Mishima's works laud the imperial house as the font of all Japanese culture, in a manner which many Japanese considered blatantly right-wing. In contrast, Oe depicts the imperial system as responsible for some of the worst excesses in Japanese society; and he continuously wrestles with the imperial image in his fiction by satirizing it, parodying it, and even writing an entire book, *The Game of Contemporaneity*, as an attempt to offer an alternative to the traditional emperor-based vision of Japanese history.

As Michiko Wilson points out in her book, *The Marginal World of Oe Kenzaburo*, Oe's primary alternative to the worst aspects of modern Japanese politics and society is a vision of an anarchic world populated by "marginals,"[12] outsiders that range from the demonic gods who inhabit the forest in *The Game of Contemporaneity* to the idiot child whose innocence and vulnerability seem to offer absolu-tion in works such as *The Pinchrunner Memorandum* (*Pinchiranna chosho*) and *The Floodwaters Have Come unto My Soul* (*Kōzui wa wagatamashii ni oyobi*), to the variety of juvenile delinquents, crimi-nals and outcasts who populate so much of his early fiction. These marginal characters are often grotesquely antisocial, but at the same time they are all characterized by a strong awareness of the non-marginal, the "center" world that both repels and fascinates them.

At first glance, Mishima's elitist, emperor-centered world seems far removed from the marginality that Oe espouses. Yet, just as Oe's anti-imperial stance is actually more ambivalent than is initially per-ceived, Mishima's supposed glorification of elitist culture is far more a vision of the destruction of that culture by enraged outsiders, out-casts who cannot or will not conform to the regimens of the society of the center.

It is this constant clash between outsiders (be they romantic or grotesque) and a smug, normal society that creates the tension which animates the works of both writers. In generic terms, both Oe and
Mishima consistently use imagery, motifs and plots that might be
labeled mythopoeic, ranging from the grotesque and the fantastic to
the romantic, but which are, in any case, outside the mimetic tradition. Nevertheless, most of these anti-mimetic elements occur within
texts that are still basically part of the realistic tradition that has
served as the mainstream of Japanese fiction since the Naturalists
began to dominate. This tradition not only "privileged lived experience," the more sordid the better, it also implicitly downgraded or
simply excluded any elements of the romantic or the fantastic.[13]

In this regard, Fredric Jamesons's comment concerning the role of
romance in the nineteenth century is relevant:

> It is in the context of the gradual reification of realism in late capitalism
> that romance comes to be felt as the place of narrative heterogeneity and
> of freedom from that reality principle to which a now oppressive realistic
> representation is the hostage. Romance now again seems to offer the pos-
> sibility of sensing other historical rhythms and of demonic or Utopian
> transformations of a real now, unshakably set in place. . . .[14]

Whether the Japan of the 1960s and 1970s had reached the era of
"late capitalism" is a provocative question, but it is certainly true
that, by the early postwar era, the suffocatingly bleak realism of the
Naturalists had reached an oppressive level. In contrast, Oe and Mishima offered works that mixed mass cultural stereotypes, such as
heroic young warriors or outrageous sexual fantasies that might have
been culled from the pages of a Japanese *manga* (comic book), within
highly realistic descriptions of the bleakness of postwar Japan.

It is this use of heterogeneous genres to suggest Utopian or
demonic possibilities that makes Oe and Mishima so refreshingly distinct from other postwar authors. Their use of romance goes far
beyond an interest in nineteenth-century Romanticism to encapsulate the basic mode of romance which Tom Moylan, echoing Northrop Frye, has identified as "a process of wish-fulfillment or utopian
fantasy that aims at a *displacement and transfiguration* of the given historical world."[15] Although Oe and Mishima do not create full-blown
utopias, their conscious "displacement" and "transfiguration" of real
events and personages (as in "Patriotism" or *The Game of Contempo-*

raneity), within carefully wrought fictional structures, is essentially a romantic rewriting of the "given historical world."

In contrast, most Japanese writers of "pure literature" have, consciously or unconsciously, stayed within the confines of the I-novel tradition, presenting works of a limited scale and setting and often of a semi-autobiographical nature. Other writers, such as Abe Kobo or Ishikawa Jun, also employed fantastic or surreal motifs within largely mimetic settings, but their imaginative grotesques are seldom presented as alternatives to or transfigurations of contemporary reality. Rather, their fantasy creations are used to emphasize and comment on the dreariness of that reality.

Oe and Mishima, on the other hand, consistently present vivid alternate worlds that do not simply criticize what they see as the wasteland of modern Japan but also offer venues of escape from that wasteland. The violently destructive outcast characters who also possess revolutionary agendas serve as one kind of tool to attain this end. These characters may be marginal, but they are not afraid to attack the center, to change the reality that is accepted unquestioningly by their fellow citizens, both in fiction and in Japanese society in general. These confrontational characters, or "heroes of action," animate the narratives of both writers in significant and similar fashion, contributing to the creation of highly colored and exciting narratives that often culminate in violent denouements. Unlike the typical bystander protagonist in much of modern Japanese literature, who usually spends the duration of his role in a solipsistic haze, incapable of anything more strenuous than cynical observation, these "heroes of action" engage in such provocative and amoral activities as terrorism, rape, murder, and arson.

The continual inclusion of such colorful narrative accoutrements might suggest that Oe and Mishima are simply writers of mass-culture fiction; and Mishima, in fact, did write a number of popular works which were serialized in women's magazines. But the complexity of language and ideas in both writers' works immediately elevates them beyond the level of mass literature. Even more importantly, the two authors control the potential excesses of such mass cultural references by their common and frequent use of another kind of hero, the "passive hero." This type of character closely resembles the typical intellectuals of the Naturalist and I-novel tradition, and it is usually through his cynical but perceptive eyes that the reader views the frenetic exploits of the active hero.

Indeed, it is often the relation between passive and active hero that creates the real tensions in each author's work. Thus, Mishima's *Forbidden Colors* (*Kinjiki*), ostensibly a revenge fantasy conceived by an old man who uses his handsome young protégé to seduce and betray women, draws its literary strength from the developing jealousies and frustrations that are experienced by the older man as he monitors his young protégé's exploits. Similarly, Oe's *The Silent Cry* (*Man'nen gannen no futtoboru*), is animated not only by its series of bizarre riots and rapes but, on a deeper level, by the psychological struggle between the passive and cynical older brother and his pathological younger brother. In most of these relationships, the passive hero is characterized by his lack of desire, typical of the modern antihero, as Rene Girard suggests,[16] while the active hero, who is a throwback to the one-dimensional protagonist of earlier romance, usually desires too much and ends his life tragically as a result.

The deeper tragedy, however, often befalls the passive hero who not only lacks desire but also fears it because on another level it attracts him. He therefore attempts to destroy it, both in himself and in those people around him. Ironically, in his attempt to destroy desire, he may achieve his own self-destruction, often in as romantic a fashion as that of the despised active hero. For often both active and passive heroes in Mishima's and Oe's work are actually romantics or would-be romantics. In this regard they resemble their creators, both of whom, I would argue, are frustrated romantics, not only in their use of the romantic literary mode but also in their overall visions of life. While Mishima may have turned his romanticism towards an elitist emperor worship, whereas Oe has grown increasingly anarchistic in his search for revolutionary alternatives to central culture, the attitude that engendered those searches for alternatives in real life and fiction is essentially a romantic one.[17]

The two writers themselves were aware of this similarity, at least in regard to their respective fictional works. In a revealing discussion with the two authors that was arranged by the literary magazine *Gunzō* in 1964, the interviewer makes a point of emphasizing that, within a literary world where Naturalism still predominates, the readers of Oe and Mishima are finding something new and different. During the course of the discussion, the authors differentiate themselves from what they call genre literature, with Oe even admitting that his writing is a form of "compensation" (presumably for the problems and disappointments of modern life), and stating that "I have no choice but to establish my characters as beings who would appear strange to the ordinary person."[18] At the end of the conversation, when asked why he avoids writing about normal life, Oe places the blame on his exposure to French literature, "where the world of the novels was always a different one from the ordinary, limited world."[19]

It was Mishima, however, who delivered the discussion's strongest statement concerning writing in relation to ordinary life. In a contemptuous final note he asserted:

"The words 'ordinary life' describe a particular dream which is expressed in lower middle class romanticism, [a dream] filled with such rubbish as a little loneliness and a little idealism. That's my vision of ordinary life and I don't have the slightest desire to put that stuff into a novel."[20]

Both Oe's and Mishima's romanticism differ sharply from the lower middle class "stuff" that Mishima despised, but their popular success indicates that the violent, grotesque, and intense literary visions they offered struck a responsive chord in much of the postwar reading public. At a time when many Japanese writers were still recycling their war experiences or returning to Naturalist modes, Oe and Mishima offered visions that were distinctly original.

But among modern Japanese writers, are Mishima and Oe really unique in the bitterness of their disappointment and the strength of their romanticism? They are certainly not unique in the depths of their disappointment or in the type of concerns and criticisms they voiced—many Japanese intellectuals, writers and readers shared the same views. In terms of the vividness and the consistency of their compensatory alternative visions, however, their literary response to these points *is* unique.

Many writers in the periods following the Meiji Restoration and Second World War have chronicled the loss and destruction of Japanese culture. Indeed, the basic theme of much of modern Japanese fiction is that of the continuing power of the past, both a fictional character's individual history and the past of his entire culture, to cast a shadow on the present. This shadow is often one from which the protagonist tries to escape.

It is not surprising, therefore, that several classics of early modern Japanese fiction centered on two basic narrative structures—a son's relationship with his father, or a young man's departure from home to discover a new identity in either an alien country or the almost equally alien big city of Tokyo. In such works as Shimazaki Toson's *Broken Commandment* (*Hakai*) or Natsume Soseki's *Kokoro*, the two structures are combined in what might be regarded as the Japanese version of the *Bildungsroman*. The youthful protagonist defines himself first by his separation from the father, an action that is often followed by, or attendant on, his journeying to an urban, "modern" place, where he frequently finds a new, "modern" father.

This drama of separation and search for identity is a basic theme in all civilizations, but in modernizing Japan it was an especially problematic one. To borrow Jacques Lacan's terminology, Japan's leaders after the Restoration were trying to impose a new "Word of the Father," which was the discourse of modernization, in order to destroy the old Word of the Father, the patriarchal feudal system that characterized premodern Japan. Not only did Japan have to deal with the loss of the traditional Word of the Father, it also had to cope with the problems presented by the fact that there were in reality two new fathers: the Meiji emperor, in whose name the Restoration was carried out, and the alien "father" of the West. It was this new and powerful discourse of the alien father, the discourse of Western culture, which flooded Japan after 1868 and with which Japanese writers had to deal.

Consequently, it is not surprising that one of the classic novels of this period, Soseki's *Kokoro*, revolves around the relationships between a son and three father figures, his own father in the country village he has left, the Meiji emperor, and his new mentor/father figure in Tokyo. By the novel's end all three "fathers" are killed off, while the reader's final glimpse of the son/inheritor is as he rides a train, in itself signifying the progress of modernity, towards an uncertain future in Tokyo.

The defeat in 1945 only intensified this problem of the search for identity vis-à-vis a lost or inadequate father. Fukushima Akira has written that Oe's characters "exist in a fatherless world,"[21] but this "fatherlessness" is not confined to Oe's protagonists. The loss of the war and the emperor's renunciation of his divinity intensified the sense of being potentially orphans of history. This sense of loss, indeed of abandonment, is sharply highlighted in Japanese postwar fiction.

Not only did the emperor renounce his divinity in 1945, but the Western father became a concrete and overwhelming presence with the arrival of the American Occupation. For a time, many Japanese followed Oe in becoming "democratic youths" who looked toward the new father as a repository for the absolute trust many had previously felt towards the emperor. In terms of the Japanese psychoanalytical discourse developed by Doi Takeo, the Japanese nation looked toward a new superior figure for the purpose of *amaeru* (dependence).[22] Inevitably, however, the new "father," being both alien and transient, could not be nearly so effective as the old. The broken world that the Japanese of the Meiji period initially inherited was even further fragmented by the country's loss in the Second World War. Even now, over forty years later, it is unlikely that another unified vision of such proportions will ever again take hold of the collective Japanese consciousness.

It is this broken world of modernity that the postwar Japanese writers have made their special fictional territory. Overall, this territory is characterized by a sense of loss, betrayal and anomie. Thus, the fiction of Sakaguchi Ango and fellow writers of the Decadent school in the late 1940s shows characters wandering aimlessly through the garbage heap of postwar Tokyo, coupling with idiots in a nightmare vision of a meaningless world, while Ishikawa Jun wrote of a demonic Jesus-like figure, who appears in the ruins of postwar Japan only to run away mockingly. And it is surely no accident that during the same period a group of poets after the war named themselves the Wasteland Group to reflect their impressions of their seemingly arid and degraded culture.

This vision of modern Japan as a wasteland continued, perhaps unconsciously, in the fiction of later postwar writers. Abe Kobo's most famous novel, *Woman in the Dunes (Suna no onna)*, is the story of a man trapped in a sandpit with a mysterious, anonymous woman, his only satisfaction deriving from a trickle of clear water at the novel's end. In the 1982 literary sensation *Somehow Crystal (Nan to naku kurisutaru)* by Tanaka Yasuo, Tokyo has become a desert of materialism, a morcellized universe of fashionable brand names and one-dimensional characters.

Oe and Mishima are also master chroniclers of the postwar wasteland. The absent or inadequate father serves as a central motif in many of their writings, while much of their narrative action takes place within a framework of abandonment and betrayal, sometimes climaxing in a trial, as characters attempt to blame each other for the degraded world around them. Imagistically, their work abounds in bleak cityscapes that offer ironic refuges, such as the coffee houses where the homosexuals huddle in *Forbidden Colors,* or the train which offers both asylum and stimulation to the perverts in Oe's *The Sexual Human* (*Seiteki ningen*). Furthermore, as the plots of these novels suggest, both writers are brilliant explorers of the sexual wasteland of the modern world. Degraded sexuality, most prominently voyeurism, is highlighted. Indeed, it is the literally and spiritually impotent voyeur who is often the primary character in their visions of the fallen postwar world. Not surprisingly, the overall atmosphere is one of constriction and suffocation, while the dominant emotional tone is one of bitterness, loneliness, and frustration.

Oe and Mishima are brilliant in their depictions of this claustrophobic postwar wasteland but, as previously noted, these bleak visions are simply part of a larger view of the world that is shared by many Japanese writers. Nosaka Akiyuki's black-humored accounts of sexual deviance come to mind as examples of this degraded sexuality, while the works of both Tanizaki Jun'ichiro and Kawabata Yasunari made extensive use of the voyeur figure, which in itself was an important element in premodern literature as well. What is unique to Oe and Mishima is their willingness to provide alternatives by mixing genres within the overall realistic frameworks of their texts. As the two quotations at the beginning of this chapter indicate, their works offer visions of worlds consciously set apart from the disappointing real.

These fantasy worlds are, however, more than simply the compensation for reality that Oe described. They are also confrontational—conscious confrontations with actual society, even with history, as H. D. Harootunian says of Mishima.[23] It is this defiant aspect that makes Oe and Mishima's fiction so exciting from an extraliterary point of view.

Not content simply to chronicle bleakness or to show characters turning to focus on their inner selves, Oe and Mishima consistently show characters who attack reality and then try to set another world in its place. How that alternate reality differs between the two writers will become clear in further chapters through the analyses of their various works, but certain common elements deserve specific mention.

As noted previously, these alternate venues are often youthful worlds in terms of both characters and emotional tone. In contrast to the monotony and fragmentation depicted in their mimetic descriptions, the alternative worlds are exciting and appealing environments, signposts toward the transcendent unity that their characters desperately crave. In some ways, they compare with the Lacanian realm of the Imaginary, the prelinguistic realm of the infant who is yet unaware of his independent existence away from his mother. As the individual develops into the realm of the Symbolic, he or she is still unable to forget the earlier world of wholeness and identity with the mother.[24]

In more traditional literary terms, these worlds compare to the prelapsarian realms of pastoral innocence. Indeed, pastoral, or at least aesthetically pleasing elements, abound, offering implicit contrast to the ugliness of the postwar urban world. Most importantly, these features are frequently related to traditional Japanese culture, although Mishima's creations reflect images of the elite, whereas Oe returns to the village, as Yamanouchi Hisaaki points out.[25] In Mishima's famous *Temple of the Golden Pavilion*, the temple stands as an almost threatening signifier of an impossible world of traditional Japanese beauty, while Oe's recent *Letter to a Nostalgic Year* (*Natsukashi toshi e no tegami*), celebrates rural folk learning. In contrast, when either writer confronts the "real world" of modern Japan, words such as "decay" and "decadence" occur frequently.

It is fitting that these descriptions should make the two writers' works sound to some extent didactic: Oe and Mishima are original and highly imaginative writers; but they are, in some ways at least, political writers as well, and political writers have a "message." This message is conveyed through creative and complex fictional structures, but it is a message nonetheless.

In this regard, it is useful to compare their work with what Susan Suleiman has called the *"roman à thèse"* or ideological novel. In her book, *Authoritarian Fictions*, Suleiman dissects a number of overtly political and, therefore, rather simplistic right-wing French novels of the 1920s and 1930s and discovers a variety of literary formulas by which their ideological messages are conveyed. These include such devices as narrative redundancy, the use of an "apprenticeship" plot structure and the highlighting of characters who are obviously "good" or "evil."[26]

All of these elements occur to some extent in the works of Oe and Mishima. Obviously, the writings of Oe and Mishima are far more complex than a simple ideological novel; but they do contain a message that can be reduced to two basic components: The first is that contemporary Japan is, if not evil, at least disappointing; the second, corollary point is that this lamentable state of affairs can be avoided.

Thus, although the average reader is unlikely to be seized with the desire to go out and burn down an ancient temple or engage in a shootout with Japan's Self-Defense Forces after completing a novel by Oe or Mishima, he or she will have experienced an articulate and memorable criticism of modern Japan and will also be offered a vision of characters who do more than criticize.

The fact that both writers have been politically active also merits attention. As early as 1960, Oe visited China as a member of a writers group sympathetic to the Communist Revolution's ideals; since then, his concern for and commitment to a variety of causes, such as the discrimination against Hiroshima bomb victims and Koreans in Japan or the destruction of the environment, has made him an exemplar of the thoughtful and dedicated activist.

Mishima's "political" activities are infamous to the point of damaging his literary reputation. Starting in the mid 1960s when he began assembling his own private army—the so-called Shield Society—in order to "protect" the emperor and culminating in his attempted coup and ritual suicide, his bizarre, emperor-centered solution to the political problems of the 1960s was well known. Although many Japanese would prefer to dismiss these activities as simply a crazy fanaticism, it is interesting to note the fact that his exploits were countenanced and indeed encouraged by members of the conservative Japanese government including former Prime Minister Yasuhiro Nakasone, as Henry Scott Stokes has chronicled.[27]

Neither Mishima nor Oe is simply a lonely voice crying in the wilderness, a point that is supported by their sustained popularity among a variety of Japanese readers. Even today, when young readers are increasingly turning away from pure literature, however, the two writers' concerns, their fears, and their desires are echoed by a wide range of Japanese. Reading Oe and Mishima, then, is not only an introduction to two powerful Japanese writers; it also constitutes an introduction to some of the key problems, concerns, and even obsessions that make up postwar Japanese culture.

Memushiri was a dream world, emphatically separated
from the wretched smell of reality that filled so many Japanese novels,
reeking as they did with wormy Naturalism.
—Matsubara Shinichi[1]

1 · The Lost Garden: Beginnings of a Mythic Alternative

Among the writings of Oe and Mishima are three works that consciously separate themselves from the reality of postwar Japan. These
narratives offer some of the most all-encompassing and appealing
alternatives to the wasteland of modern Japanese society that either
writer has ever presented, a set of explicitly pastoral dream worlds
that surprised and captivated the Japanese reading public, enervated
by the dreariness of the 1950s. The works in question, Oe's "Prize
Stock" ("Shiiku") and *Pluck the Buds, Shoot the Kids* (*Memushiri kouchi*), both written in 1958, and Mishima's *Sound of Waves* (*Shiosai*),
written in 1954, not only were written around the same period but
also share a quality of almost hyperpastoralism, in significant contrast to the reindustrializing economy that was emerging at that time.

Far from being celebrations of the changing economic environment, the three works are almost deliberately anti-modern, even anti-
capitalist. *The Sound of Waves* celebrates a traditional seafaring community full of hardy types who would be acutely uncomfortable in
the complicated world of 1950s modernity. Oe's two narratives are
more complex: Although both are set in idealized mountain villages,
reality in the form of war frames the two stories and also ultimately
forces its way into the narratives, undermining the idyllic ambiance
that is carefully created in each work. The very intrusion of the technological machine of war, however, makes Oe's pastoral "dream
worlds" an all the more attractive contrast, as Matsubara's comment
suggests. Mishima's *Sound of Waves* was a particular surprise to readers familiar with his fondness for the grotesque and the sexual, while

Oe's works, which were published just as he was beginning his career, charmed the critics with their very freshness.

Although Mishima and Oe are among the Japanese writers most aware of contemporary events, these three works are notable for being either virtual refutations of the contemporary (Mishima's *Sound of Waves*), or else attempts to transcend or escape the contemporary through a complicated and compensatory form of mythmaking (Oe's two works). Most Japanese writers in the mid 1950s were either still grappling with the war, as evidenced by Kawabata Yasunari's *Sound of the Mountain* (*Yama no oto*) of 1952, or else developing an avant-garde but often deeply pessimistic form of narrative, such as the writing of Ishikawa Jun or Abe Kobo. Mishima and Oe, on the other hand, present almost fairy-tale worlds of extraordinary charm, immune, at least in the short term, from the "influence of time." In fact, the worlds in Oe's early work are virtually Edenic, as one Japanese critic suggests,[2] and Mishima's *Sound of Waves* has an innocent, almost prelapsarian quality.

The term *pastoral* is perhaps a more appropriate description than *Edenic;* for these works are, among other things, celebrations of primitive nature and innocence that are surprisingly close to the Greek pastoral tradition.[3] Indeed, Mishima's novel is explicitly based on the Greek pastoral romance Daphnis and Chloe, while Oe himself has referred to his 1950s stories with the Japanese term *bokkateki,* which means "pastoral." Besides their ties with Greek myths, the narratives also take part in the traditions of Japanese and Western fairy tales, and even children's adventure stories in the classic *Swiss Family Robinson* mode. In their uninhibited celebration of nature and sexuality, the works also draw on Shinto, the earliest of Japanese religious traditions. In terms of theme and imagery, then, the three works are fascinating hybrids of ancient and contemporary modes and Western and Japanese tradition; and, in their fundamental role of providing romantic alternatives to contemporary reality, the hybrids succeed remarkably well.

This success may partly result from another important element common to these works, a quality of youthfulness, which is applicable for three reasons: First, each work was written at a relatively early point in the author's career and thus represents a truly young writer's novel; second, each work contains a kind of exuberance and lightness not found in either writer's more mature fictions; and third, and most importantly, their narrative focalization is through either the eyes of a child or those of a young adolescent.

This youthful focalization is one of the most crucial elements behind the effective depictions of the pastoral theme in the three works. After all, the pastoral is inherently a child's world of innocence. An adult focus would only tarnish the fairy-tale like appeal of the texts, as indeed does occur in Oe's works when the focus shifts briefly to the adult world. Although lacking adult sophistication or complexity, the narratives provide a fresh vision of a lost youthful paradise, a vision notable for its absence in much of modern Japanese literature.

To create these worlds, both writers consciously apply fantasy and myth in combination with a fictional environment which, although still credible, is carefully set outside of contemporary urban society, the normal venue of most Naturalist novels. Their protagonists also differ in marked degree from the typical characters populating an I novel. Thus, Mishima's protagonists are notable for their "flatness"; they are stock fairy-tale creations who help to anchor *The Sound of Waves* firmly inside the world of romance. Oe's protagonists are usually drawn from a more realistic mode but, in the case of the black soldier in Oe's "Prize Stock," the man's characterization is so removed from quotidian reality as to be a deliberate icon of the Other, a surreal being whom the protagonist both admires and fears. Oe's work never drifts into the total fantasy world of the fairy tale, however. In both of his texts, realism and romance contest each other throughout the narrative to produce a strangely disturbing, but extremely memorable, effect.

All three of the works are based on an outwardly directed, action-filled narrative structure, which also differentiates them from naturalist novels where much of what happens occurs inside the characters' minds. Indeed, the three stories correspond closely to Jerome Bruner's paradigm of myth as an externalization of the human psyche. As opposed to an internalization, that is, the inward mental journeys of numerous heroes in modern novels, the myth actually develops around external events: a war, a journey, a death.[4] It is not surprising that in these three externally oriented works, passive intellectual heroes are absent. This is a world where intellect is not yet a necessity, where successful, spontaneous action is still possible. This is also a fictional world in which the narrative structure closely resembles what Joseph Campbell has called the "monomyth," the archetypal story of the hero's adventure.

In the paradigm of the monomyth there are three basic elements:

separation, initiation and return. As Campbell explains, "A hero ventures forth from the world of common day into a region of supernatural wonder; fabulous forces are there encountered and a decisive victory is won. The hero comes back from this mysterious adventure with the power to bestow boons on his fellow man."[5] Other elements of the monomyth include the hero's crossing of a threshold (separation in psychological terms), supernatural aid, the orphaning of the hero, and a "road of trials" by which the hero is initiated into manhood or achieves glory. But at its most basic level, the monomyth is the story of the regeneration of the Wasteland as set forth with a definitive explication in Sir James Frazer's *Golden Bough*.

Classical Japanese literature is notable for its relative lack of mythic quests, in comparison to both the West and to such Chinese classics as *Journey to the West*, perhaps because goal attainment has been traditionally less important in Japan than the maintenance of the collectivity through continued endurance. Nor does modern Japanese literature focus much on action-filled quests. This absence may be due to Japanese literature's traditional lack of emphasis on Western-style linear narrative with a clear-cut beginning, middle, and end, and due also, of course, to the predominance of the I-novel confessional mode. In contrast to the I novel's privileging of intellectual ruminations, Mishima's novel is an action-filled romantic quest, while Oe's stories are striking examples of a young boy's initiation into manhood through a series of trials. In addition, since all three stories deal in such obviously fairy-tale discourse, they exemplify a sampling of the most comprehensive features of each author's alternative to the wasteland.

FESTIVAL DAYS: *THE SOUND OF WAVES*

Because Mishima's *Sound of Waves* is the simplest and purest in form of the three works, it can serve as a useful foil to the more complex and perverse visions that characterize Oe's stories. *The Sound of Waves* is an alternative to reality in its purest form; it is virtually a fairy tale that ends on a highly optimistic note. This upbeat aspect is not the only unusual characteristic of the novel. It is, as John Nathan comments, "the only love story that Mishima ever wrote that was not perverse."[6] Another unusual aspect of the novel is its explicit base in the fourth-century Greek myth of the shepherd boy Daphnis and the nymph Chloe. Interestingly, Mishima has ignored the fact that most versions of the myth end tragically and given his own work an unambiguously happy ending.

Literary influences aside, the setting of *The Sound of Waves,* although technically in Japan, differs greatly from the resurgent urbanizing and industrializing Japan of 1954. The story takes place on a beautiful island called Utajima (Song Island), far from the urban world in terms of culture and setting. The text opens with a long description of the physical environment, enumerating first the island's geographical position vis-à-vis the Japanese mainland and then highlighting its spiritual isolation with descriptions of such landmarks as "Yashiro Shrine" at which the island's inhabitants are "devout worshippers," a religious characteristic seldom found among modern Japanese.

More than manmade artifacts, however, the novel emphasizes the natural world and the mutually fruitful relationship maintained between the island and its human inhabitants, most of whom are fishermen attuned to the rhythms of nature and the traditions of the past. In particular, Shinji, the novel's protagonist, exemplifies these characteristics, plus a number of others that are appropriate to a hero of myth or fairy tale: diligence, semi-orphanhood (his father is dead), and kindness to his elders, most notably in his filial piety to his mother. Unlike Oe's young heroes who are forced to create their own community of outsiders, Shinji is already happily ensconced within an outside community—a literal island isolated from the mainland/wasteland of Japan. Indeed, the only description of the mainland in the novel occurs when Shinji's younger brother travels over on a school excursion and returns raving about such material delights as pinball parlors. This brief contrast, however, only serves to underscore the island's idyllic isolation from reality.

The actual narrative itself is also largely separated from reality. The basic plot conforms to the structure of the monomyth in which the hero must prove himself through a series of trials before returning to reinvigorate the community. In *The Sound of Waves,* the physical trials revolve around Shinji's strength and endurance while the emotional tests gauge his courage and purity of heart, a set of trials very similar to those suffered by a hero of a medieval European romance.[7] The plot is simple: Shinji falls in love with a beautiful village girl named Hatsue, who returns his love but dares not question her socially prominent father, who insists that she marry a man of similar social status to her.

Shinji and Hatsue endure a number of trials before their love wins out, including such climactic moments as Shinji's fight with the wealthy village bully, who also covets Hatsue; an attempt by the bully to rape Hatsue, which is foiled by the near miraculous intervention of an angry hornet; and a difficult moment when Shinji is afforded the opportunity to take advantage of Hatsue but manages at the last minute to overcome his baser urges. In the end, Hatsue's father devises one last test: he assigns Shinji and the bully to work on one of his boats and has the captain report on their behavior. Shinji triumphs easily, not only because of his obviously superior character, but from his sheer physical endurance when he successfully performs the task of swimming through stormy seas to secure the ship to a buoy.

The Sound of Waves is untainted by even a hint of realism. Shinji both fights his battles and receives his rewards within the romantic framework, finally achieving the "rights of manhood" in the eyes of Hatsue's father, who represents Utajima's fixed patriarchal structure. Mishima develops explicitly fantastic creations such as Hatsue's miraculous rescue by the hornet, or her dream in which she sees that Shinji is the reincarnation of Prince Deki, the former ruler of the island, without even attempting to ground them in a realistic framework. The romantic quality extends even to his description of the unconsummated sexual encounter between Shinji and Hatsue, a scene which is both charming and rather unlikely, since the two protagonists display a virtuousness that seems more natural to the purehearted young adolescents in Christian fables than the youth in traditional Japanese folk tales. In the following passage, for example, Mishima builds up a state of pleasurable erotic anticipation only to crush the reader's expectations by having his young lovers behave in a remarkably disciplined way:

The white chemise in the girl's hands had been half covering her body from breast to thigh. Now she flung it away behind her. The boy saw her and, standing just as he was, like some piece of heroic sculpture never taking his eyes from the girl's, untied his loincloth.

"Jump across the fire to me. Come on, if you'll jump across the fire to me" . . . They were in each others arms. The girl was the first to sink limply to the floor, pulling the boy after her.

"Pine needles, they hurt," the girl said.

The boy reached for the white chemise and tried to pull it under the girl's body.

She stopped him. Her arms were no longer embracing him. She drew her knees up, crushed the chemise into a ball in her hands, thrust it down below her waist and, exactly like a child who had just thrown cupped hands over an insect in the bushes, doggedly protected herself with it.

The words that Hatsue spoke were full of virtue.

"It's bad. It's bad . . . it's bad for a girl to do that before she's married."[8]

To readers familiar with Mishima's normally highly perverse view of sexuality, this passage must seem ironic in the extreme, especially the words "full of virtue." Mishima quite obviously is not trying to paint a realistic portrait of adolescent sexuality; rather he is trying to present a beautiful picture of two aesthetically perfect creatures. Shinji, in particular is described in artificial terms, such as "heroic sculpture"; he is an icon of young male beauty, rather than a three-dimensional character. In the context of aesthetic eroticism, then, unconsummated passion is perhaps more satisfying than explicit sexuality. In the context of the pastoral form, this almost exaggerated emphasis on innocence simply underlines the implicit difference between the pastoral alternative and the fallen real world.

The Sound of Waves was a tremendous popular success; and although in later years Mishima referred to it as his "joke on the public,"[9] the slightest hint of irony is absent from the text itself. Perhaps the entire work, with its celebration of youth and optimism, stood as an ironic gesture to the world by Mishima (always a possibility in Mishima, as will be seen in the discussion of "Patriotism"), but, at least in terms of the readers' enthusiastic response to the novel, it can be taken and appreciated on an unironic level as well.

Besides adolescent virtue, other key features play roles in this early alternative world. Not surprisingly, beauty in all forms—manmade, natural, and human—is a major element. For example, the novel introduces Shinji with an aesthetically pleasing passage:

"After the sun had completely set, a young fisherman came hurrying up the mountain path leading from the village past the lighthouse . . . Mounting the flight of stone steps, he went on beyond Yashiro Shrine. Peach blossoms were blooming in the shrine garden, dim and wrapped in twilight."[10]

The image of peach blossoms recalls classical Japanese poetry as well as the "peach blossom village" of Taoist writings, a primitive utopia which exists only in the poet's imagination. The depiction of nature, traditional architecture, the shrine, and the traditional occupation of fisherman combine to make this a stock scene from virtually any classical East Asian painting. The opening thus serves as an invitation to an aesthetic, romantic, and finally historical escape; for this is a world where capitalism, modernization, and westernization play no part.

Another aspect of the alternative world is intensity, of both nature and emotion, which is in stark contrast to the brooding haze of apathetic despair that often surrounds the protagonist in the I novel. In a later passage, for instance, Mishima describes Shinji anticipating his next encounter with Hatsue:

> Shinji looked up at the pouring rain, beating upon the eaves and spreading wetly against the windowpanes. Before, he had hated days when there was no fishing, days that robbed him both of the pleasure of working and of income, but now the prospect of such a day seemed the most wonderful of festival days to him. It was a festival made glorious, not with blue skies and flags waving from poles topped with golden balls, but with a storm, raging seas and a wind that shrieked as it came tearing through the prostrate treetops.[11]

The language of this passage underlines the emotional excitement within Shinji, the feeling of intense anticipation metaphorically expressed in the raging storm and the sea. This excitement is not confined to natural objects, however, but is related to another aspect of Mishima's alternative world, sexual intensity. The passage precedes the previously quoted amorous encounter between Hatsue and Shinji, which despite (or perhaps because of) its rejection of the sexual act is one of Mishima's most erotic. Indeed, in contrast to Mishima's bleak portrayals of empty, manipulative sexuality in his more realistic works, such as *Forbidden Colors,* the erotic subtext of *The Sound of Waves,* with all its anticipation, naiveté and fundamental innocence, is a highly charged one.

The stereotypically beautiful imagery, the flat characterization, and the heightened tone of emotional intensity are all effective elements by which to compose a romantic vision, but even more important is the characterization of the overall setting. The term *characterization* is used advisedly here, because the island of Utajima and its community are as much a character as any of the actual protagonists. In discussing Frye's privileging of the hero in romance, Jameson makes the point that, rather than the hero himself, it is usually the "world" of the romantic hero that leaves the most permanent effect on the reader.[12] In Oe's "Prize Stock" and *Pluck the Buds,*

Shoot the Kids, as well as in *The Sound of Waves*, the setting matches the importance of the action; and in Mishima's work, the setting overwhelms virtually all other elements.

The text begins with a two-page description of the island before focusing on Shinji, the nominal protagonist who, in his very flatness, is an obvious precursor of later Mishima heroes of action, the stalwart alternates to the realistic, complex and usually miserable protagonists who serve as his human symbols of the postwar wasteland. Far more important than Shinji is the community in which he lives, a nostalgic evocation of a simple, wholesome society. Obviously, such a society could never actually exist, but the nostalgia of the modern writer for that otherworldly pre-industrial community is not limited to the Japanese.

In this regard, it is especially significant that Mishima makes this community a sea-based village; for, even today, seafaring work is one of the few tasks in postindustrial society that still maintains ties to the *Gesellschaft*, the community existing before the alienation of human beings from their products. The sea is also of course the ultimate romantic icon, the place of mystery and potentiality in a world with little of either. Throughout his oeuvre, Mishima consistently highlights the sea, both in terms of its otherworldly quality but also, perhaps surprisingly, as a place of work; for one part of Mishima's alternative vision is the primitive collectivity exemplified by the fishermen. This is featured unironically in *The Sound of Waves* and thoroughly ironically in the later *The Sailor Who Fell from Grace with the Sea* (*Gogo no eikō*), and finally, problematically, in the final volume of Mishima's tetralogy, where Toru "falls" from the relatively wholesome life of lighthouse keeper into the depraved world of upper-class Japanese society.

In a discussion of Conrad's *Lord Jim*, Jameson underscores the importance of the author's depiction of his hero as a sailor and his placing him at the vast reaches of empire and on the surface of "the place that is a non place," the sea, "the space of the degraded language of romance and daydream, of narrative commodity and the sheer distraction of 'light literature.'"[13] Of course, Mishima's setting of *The Sound of Waves* on an island can be seen as having a realistic base, since a peripheral island community is more likely traditional than an urban area; but the other textual elements noted previously tend to subvert any possible thread of realism. In any case, this primitive community, where all know their place and are united through their work and in their fellowship (Hatsue herself is a pearl diver, and the best in the village, but her skill never engenders jealousy or rivalry), is an almost textbook example of an idealized precapitalist society. In its idealization of simple physical labor, it is also, of course, an implicit contrast to the empty work that so many of Mishima's intellectuals produce.

The notion of a "non-place" such as the sea, is vital to both Mishima's and Oe's imaginary realms, but *The Sound of Waves* is one of the few occurrences of the "non-place" being presented at face value, with no disturbing overtones. Although there are ironies in the fact that this atypical story was the first of Mishima's works to be translated in the United States, its very success there as well as in Japan suggests that its celebration of youth, innocence, and beauty generates universal appeal.

REPLETION AND RHYTHM: "PRIZE STOCK"

In contrast to Mishima's unalloyed vision of a fairy-tale world, Oe's two texts subvert their essentially romantic and mythic qualities by introducing a realistic focus at climactic points in the narratives, thus making their initial pastoral visions even more enticing. However, more so than in the atypical *Sound of Waves*, these alternative pastoral communities, isolated in the mountains from the rest of Japan, became the staple environment of many of Oe's fictional products. They are consistent, spiritual reference points, yearned-for "non-places," where his characters retreat in times of crisis in order to escape the alienation of modern Japan, by drowning themselves in the all-encompassing sense of *kyōdōtai* (communality), a word and a feeling that are usually associated in Oe's works with primitivism, violence, and nature.

"Shiiku," which was translated into two English versions—"Prize Stock" and "The Catch," won Oe his second Akutagawa prize in 1958. The critics were enchanted by it. In both subject matter and narrative style, it is an original and affecting story. Its basic outlines are realistic, comprising the development of a friendship between a young village boy and a captured black American soldier during the Second World War. But this is not the sentimental story of a cross-cultural friendship such a summary would lead one to expect: The boy is a country child living in a remote part of Japan; to him and his friends, the soldier becomes something between a god and a pet

animal. Furthermore, far from having a sentimentally upbeat conclusion, the story has the soldier turn on the boy and take him hostage
when villagers come to deliver him to the authorities. The townsfolk
manage to kill the soldier and save the child, but the cost is great—his
father is forced to smash the boy's hand with a hatchet in order to
free his child from the soldier's grip.

Of course, far more is lost than the boy's hand; it is his innocence
which is sacrificed. "I was no longer a child,"[14] the boy states at the
end of the novella; but, as one Japanese critic notes, the child is not
an adult either.[15] Rather, he has become an outcast, and he has far
more in common with the dead soldier than he does with any of the
members of his previously idyllic country community.

"Prize Stock" brilliantly explores the problematic relation between
innocence and primitivism throughout the story by outlining the relationship between boy and soldier, and soldier and village, only
through the child's eyes. The soldier and the village children form a
positive kind of primitive community, while the supposed adults, in
their war-engendered violence and slyness, come across as barbarians
of a particularly vicious kind. The story also plays on the archetypal
pattern of the transition from innocence to experience; like *The Sound
of Waves*, it narratively limns a boy's initiation into manhood. In chilling distinction from Mishima's story, however, where the initiation
ends on a positive note, "Prize Stock" leaves its protagonist longing
emptily for the pre-initiation days of childhood innocence.

The story begins in a world of death, although its young protagonists are not consciously aware of this, as is clear in the striking opening lines, "My kid brother and I were digging with pieces of wood in
the loose earth that smelled of fat and ashes at the surface of the crematorium . . ."[16] These lines serve to introduce the unnamed narrator,
who initially serves a bystander function similar to the roles played in
other Oe stories by the ubiquitous older, passive intellectuals. Here,
the boy's first function is to observe and to mythicize his observations,
transforming an unusual wartime experience into a mythic allegory
through his consistent association of the black soldier with the Other.
His second function is more participatory—to undergo a rite of passage from innocence to experience. Thus, "Prize Stock" functions on
two levels: It uses its mythic and romantic trappings to create an alternate world and thus compensate for the ugliness of reality; and,
through the narrative of the young boy's loss of innocence, it sends out
an unambiguous ideological message that war is evil.

For both structural and didactic reasons, it is not surprising that the story begins in a crematorium, a pit of death. The image of the pit recurs in Oe's later writings (once in "Teach Us to Outgrow our Madness," twice in *The Silent Cry*), and acts as an obvious metaphor for a mythic "threshold," the place the hero must enter before he begins his journey. Structurally, the pit suggests a narrative movement upward and out, a kind of rebirth reinforced by the womblike aspects of the pit. As it turns out, however, the rebirth is a degraded one, an emergence into the unwanted agonies of adult perception, the realm of the Symbolic: rather than an outward movement, the story ends in yet another pit of death. The pit is also linked with war, because the innocent boys are digging for bones to use in making medals. Thus, on the very first page, "Prize Stock" sends out an insistent ideological reminder, while at the same time preparing the reader for a journey, although it is a largely psychological rather than physical excursion.

After the opening in the crematorium, the narrator's entrance into the "adventure" part of the narrative occurs through the medium of the black soldier. Upon leaving the pit, the boy sees the pilot's plane crash and rushes to the village to await the coming of the soldier, an arrival that is portrayed in highly dramatic terms. After a period of suspenseful anticipation, just when the narrator feels he will "go mad with waiting," the soldier appears encircled by his captors. The narrator continues:

> With the other children I ran out to greet them and saw a large black man surrounded by adults. Fear struck me like a fist.
> Surrounding the *catch* solemnly as they surrounded the wild boar they hunted in winter, their lips drawn tightly against their teeth, their backs bent forward almost sadly, the adults came walking in. The *catch* . . . wore a khaki jacket and pants, and on his feet, ugly heavy-looking boots. His large, darkly glistening face was tilted up at the sky still streaked with light, and he limped as he dragged himself along. The iron chain of a boar trap was locked around both his ankles, rattling as he moved. We children fell in behind the adults as silent as they were.[17]

Here is the Other incarnate, in all its fearsome aspects. Not only is the man a soldier and an American, he is black, which makes him almost insuperably alien to Japanese village children in whom "fear strikes like a fist," perhaps an omen of the boy's crushed hand. His alienness is emphasized in the opening description: "a large black man surrounded by adults." The soldier is not an adult. Rather, the narrator immediately equates him with the untamed and dangerous animal world of the boar hunt and the catch, noting that his ankles are bound by a boar trap.

The black soldier's associations are not only with the animal world, they are with myth. For example, in the above passage the soldier's face is "tilted up to the sky," reminding the reader and perhaps the observers that he does not come from some dark lair, like a wild boar, but from the heavens, like a god. Finally, the entire tableau itself—the following of solemn adults and silent children, the tall, isolated man in chains, and the sense of fear that surrounds the entire procession—evokes images of ritual sacrifice.

The black soldier is consistently inarticulate throughout the narrative (except when he sings what appears to be a soulful Negro spiritual), reinforcing both his nonhuman nature and his total belonging to the preverbal world of the Imaginary. It is precisely this genuine primitivism (as opposed to the degraded barbarism of the evil adults) that makes him the object of such fascination to the innocent children.

For the children do not remain permanently in fear of the soldier, and the first part of "Prize Stock" can be read as a monomythic story of a boy going through trials and learning to conquer his fear of the unknown. In fact, the fear seems to change to something close to a blend of worship and patronizing affection. The narrator's father assigns him the task of looking after the black soldier; and, after much initial hesitation, the boy finally becomes friendly with and even makes a "pet" out of the "catch."

Deciding that the soldier is "as gentle as a domestic animal,"[18] and even "like a person"[19] (thus reinforcing the soldier's essential ambiguity), the narrator and his friends liberate the prisoner from the cellar keep; and it is this liberation which ushers in the high point of the story, a vision of primitive pastoral plenitude, as the description of the scene at the village swimming hole illustrates:

Wet and reflecting the strong sunlight, his nakedness shone like the body of a black horse, full and beautiful. We clustered around him, splashing and shouting . . . Suddenly we discovered that the black soldier possessed a magnificent, heroic, unbelievably beautiful penis. We crowded around him bumping naked hips, pointing and teasing, and the black soldier gripped his penis, planted his feet apart fiercely like a goat about to copulate and bellowed.

. . . How can I describe how much we loved him, or the blazing sun above our wet heavy skin, that distant splendid summer afternoon, the deep shadows on the cobblestones, the smell of the children, and the black soldier, the voices hoarse with happiness, how can I convey the rhythm and repletion of it all?

To us it seemed that the summer . . . would continue forever and never end.[20]

Aside from its own intrinsic beauty, the above passage is a reminder of certain similarities between Greek and early Shinto myths. Both religions interweave gods and nature; and the gods themselves occupy a problematic space between divinity, humanity, and animal nature. The sheer ecstatic celebration of nature, however, in particular the water imagery, is distinctively Japanese, if not necessarily consciously Shinto. In addition, the imagery of bright sunlight and luxuriant water suggests an intensity of experience that can only be appreciated by children or by adults who have not been corrupted by the realities of the war and modernity in general. The children's matter-of-fact acceptance of the soldier's sexuality suggests a world of joyous primitive innocence, a pagan rite somehow transposed to the twentieth century, a point that is supported in the text's reference to the children as "woodland gods" or "Pans."[21]

The ending of "Prize Stock" also suggests a pagan rite of dark sacrificial violence, but it is a ceremony that forces the narrator back into the realities of the twentieth century. The day following the pastoral idyll at the swimming hole, the adults come to take the soldier hostage. Transformed from the half god, half animal to the shockingly human, the panic-stricken soldier takes the narrator hostage in an attempt to save himself. Instead, both the narrator and the soldier are sacrificed. In a scene where the savage but slow-motion violence recalls a ritual killing, the boy watches paralyzed as,

> [f]rom the midst of the bunched adults my father stepped forward dangling a hatchet from his hand. I saw that his eyes were blazing with rage and feverish as a dog's. The black soldier's nails bit into my neck and I moaned. My father bent down over us and seeing the hatchet being raised I closed my eyes. The black soldier seized my left wrist and lifted it to protect his head. The entire cellar erupted into a scream and I heard the smashing of my left hand and the black soldier's skull.[22]

The screams that erupt through the cellar suggest the agonies of birth, but on the part of the narrator, who must leave the wordless realm of the Imaginary for the pitiless realm of the Word of the

Father. Conversely, the soldier is once and forever removed from the realistic realm. Indeed, at the story's end he returns once again as the negative, fearsome Other, an angry ghost back to haunt the village through the relentless odor of his cremated body: "The odor fountaining furiously from the black soldier's heavy corpse blanketed the cobblestone road and the buildings and the valley supporting them, an inaudible scream from the corpse that encircled us and expanded limitlessly overhead as in a nightmare."[23]

In this story, language, in its simplest form, is the stuff of nightmares, expressing a world of fear and pain with no way out. The soldier's inaudible scream will ring forever in the narrator's ears.

The events in "Prize Stock" are believable, once the unlikely possibility of a black American pilot dropping from the heavens into a rural Japanese village is accepted. The overall impression left by the narrative is of a romantic pastoralism similar to that of *The Sound of Waves*, however. The three most important elements that create this effect are, first, the isolation and anonymity of the setting (as Shinohara Shigeru points out, since none of the characters have proper names and are identified only by nickname or family relationship, the village could occupy any country, any time, or even an alternate mythic world;[24] in other words, it is a "non-place"); second, the use of the child's perspective; and, third, the exalted language surrounding the black soldier. The children's excitement and awe at the soldier are effectively conveyed in such scenes as at the swimming hole. The soldier himself is conveniently mute, an icon to be interpreted, rather than a realistic human character.

The final effect of this romanticism and mythicization is not to let the reader escape from reality, but to make the final awakening to reality, the smashing of the boy's hand, all the more traumatic. Ultimately, "Prize Stock" employs romantic and mythic modes that both evoke the imaginary and serve to highlight the horrors of the real world, a place where fathers smash their own sons' hands. The story begins in one pit, the crematorium, ascends to the heavens from which the soldier comes, and ends in another pit, the cellar where the soldier dies, to underscore the fact that real escape is impossible. In fact, the narrative's actual ending, a rather curious coda in which the boy's one adult friend Clerk is killed while indulging in the overtly childish sport of sledding, seems designed merely to emphasize once again that there can be no return to the Eden of childhood.

THE SACRIFICE OF THE INNOCENT WRIT LARGE:
PLUCK THE BUDS, SHOOT THE KIDS

The elements of isolation and child focalization also contribute importantly to the superbly unreal world of Oe's *Pluck the Buds, Shoot the Kids* and again serve to make the ideological point that war grotesquely distorts the adult and sacrifices the innocent. Again, what makes this less than startlingly original point so refreshing is the richly depicted utopian world of the children that is offered up to the sacrifice. As Oe's first long novel, *Pluck the Buds* offers a comprehensive vision of what Isoda has called Oe's "Garden of Eden": a pastoral community more fully realized than the village in "Prize Stock," and one more perfect, because initially there are no negative adults to ruin it, a condition that enables the young inhabitants to band together in a shared sense of *kyōdōtai*.

Oe's version of *kyōdōtai* is an important ingredient in his alternative to postwar reality; it suggests a simpler world of beings grouped together for a common good and is resonant of both childhood game-playing and the *Gesellschaft*. Unlike Mishima in *The Sound of Waves*, however, who creates a contemporary *Gesellschaft* through placing it on an isolated island, Oe in *Pluck the Buds*, as in "Prize Stock," uses the artificiality of war with its deforming and destructive qualities to create a temporary community that exists in reality only under these exceptional circumstances. Also, as in "Prize Stock," the text forces reality in at the end of the novel to destroy the carefully wrought pastoral atmosphere.

Like "Prize Stock," *Pluck the Buds* is set in an isolated village in the mountains and focuses on children who have been damaged by the adult world. In further structural similarity, this novel also skirts a thin line between fantasy and reality, although once again all the depicted events slip just within the bounds of plausibility. Even more than "Prize Stock," however, it creates a quintessential children's, or at least boys', world of adventure and liberation in a "non-place." In this regard, *Pluck the Buds* bears a certain resemblance to *Huckleberry Finn*, especially when Huck and Jim enjoy themselves in the "non-place" of the raft on the river; this similarity is probably not fortuitous since Oe is a devoted fan of Twain's book, as evidenced by his essay, "Huckleberry Finn and the Problem of the Hero."[25]

Pluck the Buds, however, is more overtly "mythic," in the sense of explicitly exalting its characters and its setting to an otherworldly level, while remaining as morally engaged as Twain's story. The heightened descriptions in the introduction are particularly romantic, evoking a world sharply estranged from normality. Thus, an early section of the novel sets the scene: "It was a time of killing people. Like an endless flood, the war had poured its collective craziness into every fold of human emotion, into every corner of the body, into the trees, the road, and the sky."[26]

Various clues suggest that the war mentioned in the passage is the Second World War, but this is never specifically stated in the novel. Rather, the text simply introduces the reader to "a time of killing people," with the emphasis on the special character of the "time" signaling that the work is not primarily realistic and its events should be seen through an allegorical lens. Thus, the passage goes on to speak of the young boys who make up the little group of protagonists, who are described in romantic, generalizing terms: "During that period, when adults lost their senses and rushed around the town, it is probably sufficient to record that there was a strange passion to continue the imprisonment of youths who possessed nothing more than smooth skin and shiny hair, who had performed some trifling misdeed, and who were simply judged as possessing anti-social tendencies."[27] Even more than the narrator in "Prize Stock," these boys are characterized as anonymous victims who, because of some "trifling misdeed," are being sacrificed by society.

Once the text establishes the rather unworldly innocence of its protagonists, much of the remaining action is described in brutally realistic terms. These boys are not mythic heroes but are in fact a group of abandoned juvenile delinquents, marginals. Indeed, they are abandoned three times: First they are renounced by their parents (in a touching early scene, the narrator is overjoyed to see his father and younger brother, whom he assumes have come to claim him from the institution where he has been incarcerated, only to discover that his father is actually handing his younger brother over to the institution since he feels incapable of caring for him). The second abandonment occurs when the officials of the institution turn them out and force them to journey through the mountains in search of a village that will accept them as laborers. Finally, the villagers in their new home abandon them. Upon discovering that plague has broken out in the village, the residents flee to the next hamlet, leaving the boys to take over the village and do as they please.

The themes of abandonment and betrayal are important ones in modern fiction; but in many modern novels the betrayal is carried out by the protagonist, often on political grounds, as is the case with the intellectual heroes of Sartre and Camus. This atmosphere of political treachery relates to the anxiety of the intellectual who feels incapable of contributing to society, but who feels guilty at his incapacity, and is a theme clearly evident in much of Oe's later fiction. But the betrayal here is on the deepest level, by what should be an allknowing father of his own son. Of course, in *Pluck the Buds* it is not only the father per se but the authorities in general, those who make up the patriarchal order, who suddenly and inexplicably (from the boys' point of view) turn on their own children.

In *Pluck the Buds,* the "hero" is basically a collective entity, the group of abandoned youths, although the narrator remains the focalization point. The basic elements of the story, orphanhood (in this case figurative), the journey (in this case quite literal, since a good part of the text narrates the details of the boys' painful progression through the mountains), and, above all, the various trials of endurance, both physical and emotional, which the boys must endure, all compose a monomythic narrative. Furthermore, much of the novel's structure mirrors a generic adventure story, such as *Swiss Family Robinson* or the Enid Blyton adventure stories, in which children lost on a desert island or in the wilds learn to live off the land until rescued. In the case of *Pluck the Buds,* however, the "rescue" turns out to be a sham, because the adults destroy the world made by the children.

The war rumbles only on the margins of this adventure story, making it perhaps even more effective when the text occasionally throws up reminders of the battles and other elements of the real world. These reminders include a diverse group of characters, who also function as companions to the heroes on their mythic journey. One, a Korean boy named Chin, whose settlement has also been abandoned by the Japanese villagers, becomes the narrator's good friend after an initial fist fight—another obvious ritual trial on the road to growing up. At the same time, the presence of Chin, whose Korean background renders him an alien even among outsiders, also serves to remind readers of the racist aspects of Japanese society, a culture that permits the sacrifice of Koreans along with delinquents. The other companions include a deserter from the army (within Oe's antiwar ideology a "good" adult), a stray dog named Leo, whom the narrator's younger brother adopts, and a little girl who becomes the narrator's first love.

For a brief time, these outsiders band together in a surprisingly harmonious community that is complete with such pleasures as hunting and a "festival amid the snow." The exhilaration reaches its peak after a snowfall that sends the boys temporarily mad with joy, in a sort of winter counterpart of the idyllic summer captured in "Prize Stock." As the narrator describes it: "Outside was a totally fresh and silent dawn. The fallen snow had hidden the textures of the trees and bushes, giving them a plumpness like the rounded shoulders of animals. The snow glittered and sparkled in the limitless brilliance of the sun. 'Snow,' I thought, letting out a warm sigh. 'Snow.' In all my life I had never seen such abundant, luxurious snow."[28]

This vision of plenitude is the novel's most thorough alternative to the wasteland that lurks just outside the borders of the village. After the snowfall, the boys participate in their "festival of the snow and the hunt," where they sing Japanese and Korean folk songs, feast on a pheasant they have trapped, and get drunk on the beauty of the snow and the special fortune of their situation. The childlike appeal of the adventure is underscored by its resolute masculineness; all the characters are male except for the little girl; and all, once abandoned by the villagers, engage in traditional masculine pursuits of hunting and trapping, unthreatened by female sexuality. These pursuits are also strongly group-oriented, suggesting the attraction of a collective, nondifferentiated form of bonding in this imaginary realm.

Sexuality does exist, of course; but it is a spontaneous and basically innocent sexuality, as was also the case in "Prize Stock" where the children gaze in open wonder at the black soldier's penis. In *Pluck the Buds* sexuality advances to the adolescent stage of *The Sound of Waves* when the narrator attempts to make love to the abandoned girl. In Mishima's story, actual consummation is avoided; here it is problematic, if not quite a failure, and the encounter is described in direct and simple terms, although with a most un-Mishimaesque sense of humor, as the following passage illustrates:

> Excitement was stirring inside me. Suddenly it welled up, making me dizzy. I grasped the girl's arm roughly and pulled her up ... I could no longer see her pale little face. Like a chicken scampering helter-skelter to escape its pursuers, I gripped the girl's body tightly in my arms and rushed into the dark storehouse. Not stopping to take off my shoes, I climbed onto the bed, which was in total darkness.
> Still silent, I hurriedly pulled at my trousers and lifted up her skirt. Then I fell down on top of her. I moaned. My penis, as erect as a stalk of

asparagus, was caught in my underpants and felt as if it was about to break off. And then, the contact with the panic-stricken girl's cold genitals, like dried paper. And then, after a slight trembling, the withdrawal. I let out a deep sigh. And that was all.[29]

Judging from the boy's description, it does not appear to be a particularly enjoyable sexual encounter, especially for the girl; yet the narrator, at least, is content. In Oe's early fictional worlds, the satisfaction of the female characters is unimportant as long as the male protagonist achieves his connection with bliss.

This sense of contentment also occurs when he breaks off another encounter with the girl to see the spoils of a hunt:

[A]s I rushed towards the woods where my little brother was watching for me among the rose thickets, I felt as if I might go crazy with the feelings of pride and delight that were rising up in me. I had my very own fine and adorable love and nobody knew but me. Breathlessly, I climbed up the slope tumbling often in the snow. I heard the sound of snow falling softly behind me as I ran through the laden trees towards the manly bounty of the hunt.[30]

This sense of post-sexual exultation and omnipotence parallels the following passage from *The Sound of Waves,* which occurs after the aforementioned unconsummated encounter between Shinji and Hatsue:

From time to time the dying fire crackled a little. They heard the sound and the whistling of the storm as it swept past the high windows, all mixed with the beating of their hearts. To Shinji it seemed as though the unceasing feeling of intoxication and the languid booming of the sea outside and the noise of the storm among the treetops were all beating with nature's violent rhythm. And, as part of his emotion there was the feeling forever and ever, of pure and holy happiness.[31]

In each example, the erotic meeting brings to the young man a simultaneous sense of peace and exultation that is translated into a feeling of oneness with the natural world. This diverges sharply from the ugly and manipulative encounters described in the two writers' more realistic texts.

In Oe's fiction the sexual and nature-inspired euphoria does not last. In the midst of the festival, the narrator hears that the girl is dying of the plague, having been bitten by Leo, the younger brother's

dog. She dies in agony; the younger brother (who is even more innocent and even more of a sacrifice) runs away and is accidentally
killed; and the villagers return in a grim scene, which signals the
triumph of the wasteland: "The mist was clearing, and we could see
the cloudy sky low on the horizon, filled with the damp gleam of
morning and softening the newly refrozen dirty snow mixed with
mud. My companions and I were led out of our temporary shelter.
And all around, gradually growing in number, the villagers encircled
us, grasping bamboo spears and hunting rifles, their faces stiffened
into expressionless masks."[32] Once again, the Edenic world is shattered; and the boys' adventure story ends on a note more appropriate
to *Lord of The Flies* than to *Swiss Family Robinson*, with the difference
being that it is the adults with their spears, rifles, and "masks" who
revert to barbarity, like the children in Golding's novel.

In romance the hero triumphs over physical odds and human dangers; but in realistic novels, especially the novels of the twentieth century, the hero does not even dream of such triumphs and, if he does,
his awakening is painful. The fantasy kingdom of the boys' alternative world, where even violence is simple and regenerative, is
destroyed by the formalized violence inherent in the adult world of
war, hypocrisy and betrayal. Within the imaginary world the youths
prove victorious over all trials but, with the advent of the realistic
denouement, they are reduced once again to sniveling children.

The hypocrisy and reversal of values that are standard to the real
world are brutally evident in a "trial" which the boys are forced to
undergo as the villagers cast accusations against them for breaking
into the village houses. Confused, the boys turn on each other and
eventually agree to the villagers' wishes: They will not inform the
authorities about their abandonment by the villagers if the villagers,
in turn, agree not to press charges against them. With this twist, the
rightful accusers become the accused, and the carefully built up
atmosphere of *kyōdōtai* is totally destroyed; the boys have acquiesced
to the false Words of the Fathers. Only the narrator refuses to
comply with this sell-out and in the end is forced to flee the village,
leaving behind his friends, his dead younger brother, his dead love,
and his dead dreams. The novel's last lines illustrate the full impact of
encroaching reality: "I wasn't sure if there was any strength left in me
to start running again. I began to sob tears of rage and exhaustion.
After all, I was only a child trembling with cold and hunger. Suddenly

a wind sprang up and brought with it the sound of the villagers' pur-
suing footsteps from somewhere nearby. I gritted my teeth and stood
up and ran in search of refuge in among the still deeper trees toward
the still darker grasses."[33]

Refuge, however, is elusive in *Pluck the Buds*. The text makes clear
that this final escape is an escape into darkness. In formal terms, both
Pluck the Buds and "Prize Stock" can be seen as warped rite of passage
stories, stifled *Bildungsroman,* in which a boy leaves behind his innocence but not necessarily in order to enter the world of experience.
Rather, once their mythic worlds are shattered, these heroes are left
to wander miserably, with nowhere to go except into the outer darkness of reality. In Lacanian terms they are sacrificed from the Imaginary into the world of the Symbolic but are unable to accept their
new circumstances. Unlike Mishima's Shinji, who in the intact
romantic world of *The Sound of Waves* can adjust to the Word of the
Father (in his case, Hatsue's father), Oe's characters are expelled into
fragmented new worlds where the Word of the Father is false. Within
the mythic confines of each Oe narrative, the heroes succeed: The
boy in "Prize Stock" finds courage to befriend an alien Other, while
the narrator of *Pluck the Buds* survives abandonment in the cold to
create his own mythic kingdom and win the love of a young girl. At
the moment success is attained, however, the romantic genre abruptly
stops, forcing the heroes and the readers out of the comfortable fantasy land that the texts' evocative descriptions make momentarily
believable. The wasteland cannot be reinvigorated. All that remains
are brief visions of plenitude.

Based on their generic discontinuities, Oe's novels can be interpreted as nihilistic visions of romance's inevitable subjugation to realism. The works can also be read in terms of Suleiman's concept of the
ideological novel. Although very different from a typical *roman à
thèse* in style and subject matter, both works contain a number of
elements that suggest the presence of an ideological message. These
indications include an essentially black-and-white value system, a
structure that uses the rite-of-passage/*Bildungsroman* style for didactic purposes, and a reliance on redundancy.

Similar to the ideological novel with its Manichean value system,
both *Pluck the Buds* and "Prize Stock" establish a major cleavage
between "good" and "bad" characters, usually children and outcasts
versus adults/fathers/authority, with very little ambiguity of interpretation possible. Imagery also serves to enhance this dichotomy—sun-

shine, water, spontaneous sexuality, and luxuriant snow, compare with various types of pits, muddy snow, mist, and the darkness into which the narrator runs at the end of *Pluck the Buds*.

Structurally, too, the subversion of the traditional happy ending of the monomyth underlines the stories' bleak message. In the mono-myth the protagonist learns by trial and error to be a hero. Oe, how-ever, plays on the reader's expectations of the monomyth or even of its nineteenth-century development in the *Bildungsroman* and then shatters these projections by revealing the lessons learned by the hero: War is bad and adults, or at least society, are evil. To grow up and fit into that society is an immoral, ideologically reprehensible act. Thus, the protagonist must escape at the end, rather than return to help regenerate the wasteland.

On the positive side of the message, the hero and the reader are allowed a glimpse of an alternative world, a childish realm close to nature, that completely contrasts with adult reality. The similarity between Oe's works and a true *roman à thèse* ends here, however. Unlike a more overtly ideological novel, Oe's work does not contrast liberal humanism to fascism in any explicit terms. The reader must make the final interpretation, which is a simple task if the reader responds to the power of the text. Furthermore, even if the boys are "sacrificed" in the story, they—or at least the narrator—retain their innocent nobility, which produces an ending that is not totally pes-simistic. As Suleiman says of an apparently failed hero in the *roman à thèse*, "if the hero is defeated, he can nevertheless claim a spiritual or moral victory, *since he is right.*"[34] And, as far as the ideological mes-sage of Oe's narratives is concerned, these heroes are unquestionably "right."

Mishima's *Sound of Waves* is even less overtly ideological than the two Oe works. No immediate links can be drawn between the simple natural beauty of Utajima and the aesthetic militarism that animates his later, more genuinely ideological novels. However, the privileging of the simple seafaring community, at ease with itself and its tradi-tions, is an obvious swipe at the prosaic pinball parlors of modern Japan. The stalwart, beautiful, and unthinking "good" protagonists are prototypes of his later characters who are cast into a more rigid political framework.

In these early works of Oe and Mishima, the underlying philoso-phy which they are trying to promote is less distinguishable than in later stories; but no question arises that a "wrong" and a "right" way to behave exist and that the heroes have conducted themselves in the "right" way. The boy's willingness to warn the black soldier in "Prize Stock," the narrator's unwillingness to go along with the morally reprehensible villagers and his turn-coat comrades in *Pluck the Buds*, and Shinji's determination to win Hatsue in a fair competition in *The Sound of Waves* are all examples of a superior moral vision, while Shinji's handsomeness and strength suggest what was probably even more important to Mishima, an aesthetic image superior to common mortals.

These works also deserve to be examined in terms of redundancy, an area that covers everything from simply verbal repetitiveness and recurring themes and characters to a clear, constantly reiterated authorial interpretation. Redundancy occurs naturally in all discourse, but it is a particularly significant aspect of the ideological novel. Since a *roman à thèse* is a novel with a thesis, a message that must be communicated or taught, it is not surprising that one of its key stylistic elements is redundancy.

A closer examination of Oe's and Mishima's texts reveals a fairly high degree of redundancy in at least two areas—character formation and interpretive commentary. In terms of characters, one notable aspect of both Oe novels is the strong emphasis on the group. Suleiman's statement that "the members of the group merge into a single collective hero,"[35] is applicable here, although the narrator does have his own specific feelings and does experience his own personal suffering. But it significant that these emotions—fear and awe in "Prize Stock" and fear, exultation and the sense of abandonment in *Pluck the Buds*—are also experienced on a collective level as well by the other children in "Prize Stock" and by the other juvenile delinquents in *Pluck the Buds*. Moreover, the character of the younger brother, while distinctive to Oe's literature, as Wilson points out,[36] is also a "redundancy," in that the younger brother is truly innocent, not merely symbolically, and he, too, is sacrificed.

This collectivization of the subject strengthens the ideological message by emphasizing that it is not just a single individual who suffers, but a large number; and it also serves to underscore the sense of *kyō-dōtai*. Finally, the fact that both stories end with an expulsion/voluntary withdrawal from the group serves to emphasize how the wasteland has helped to degenerate the previous shared joy of *kyōdōtai*.

Redundancy of character does not exist only in the doubling or tripling of the number of heroes. It also appears in terms of the types of heroes represented. Thus, in *Pluck the Buds,* the reader is introduced to unfairly treated juvenile delinquents and Koreans, an oppressed army deserter, an outcast little girl (it may be significant that the one "good" villager is female), and finally, an unwanted stray dog! The fact that these undesirables are morally upright people, as opposed to the villagers who are inhuman to the point of having faces characterized as "masks," only underscores Oe's message concerning the sacrifice of the innocent. Similarly, although less overtly ideologically, Mishima's text presents us with two protagonists who are virtually mirror images of each other. Both Hatsue and Shinji, though of different sex, have several typically mythic virtues. They are stalwart, upright, strong, and filially pious, superior to anything the real world could offer.

The second type of redundancy that frequently occurs in both novelists' writing is redundancy of interpretation or description. For example, the above-mentioned attributes that Hatsue and Shinji possess are not limited to cameo illustrations, they are returned to repeatedly.

Redundancy of action offers another means of driving the point home, as is clear in *Pluck the Buds* when the boys are abandoned in quick narrative succession, not once, not twice, but three times. In the coda to "Prize Stock," the boy's only adult friend, Clerk, is killed, significantly while playing on a sled, in other words, in a moment of youthfulness, reinforcing one last time the story's point that youthful pleasures must be sacrificed to the wasteland of reality.

The boy's reaction to this episode is an example of interpretive redundancy: "To avoid being surrounded by the children I abandoned Clerk's corpse and stood up on the slope. I had rapidly become familiar with sudden death and the expression of the dead, sad at times and grinning at times, just as the adults were familiar with them."[37]

This passage represents an expansion of the boy's brief statement after the killing of the black soldier that "I was no longer a child" and, although certainly useful in projecting the message, is perhaps stylistically unnecessary. Neither Oe nor Mishima are usually as clumsy as the *roman-à-thèse* authors; but as the above passage suggests, their desire to make their points sometimes interferes with literary effect.

These works trace the beginnings of an alternate and highly attractive vision of society that, given the consistency with which it is presented throughout the two writers' works, might legitimately be labeled the beginnings of an alternative romantic ideology. In Oe's works, this alternative vision includes youth, freedom, and nature, while in Mishima's story, it is inscribed with youth, beauty and archaism. In later writings by both writers, the protagonists are exiled from their worlds of romance, which thereafter occur only in flashes—a vision of the sea, the reflection of a temple in a pond, an unusually satisfying sexual encounter, a dream of Africa, or the ultimate alternative of beautiful death. But in these early works, the two writers created entire worlds of beauty and freedom.

"I used sex to shock people, to disturb them, to wake them up."
—Oe Kenzaburo[1]

"As a novelist I wanted to relate to the world only in an erotic sense. And my early novels did relate to society only on erotic terms, very much like those of Oe Kenzaburo, I think."
—Mishima Yukio[2]

2 · The Wasteland of Sex

In 1962, Oe made the surprising announcement that he would no longer write "pastoral novels";[3] and, to a large extent, the works which followed that statement present worlds that are indeed distant from the appealing environments in which *Pluck the Buds, Shoot the Kids* and "Prize Stock" are set. Mishima as well, although the change in his works is less clear-cut, never again created such a rose-tinted work as *The Sound of Waves*. Far from the realm of the Imaginary, where wholeness and plenitude still appeared possible and where language was less important than visceral experience, most of their other works are firmly entrenched within a realistic discourse. This is not to say that the Imaginary, usually expressed in romantic terms, is no longer a part of Oe's and Mishima's works, but rather that it has gone underground in the form of dreams and desires that stand in implicit contrast to the repressive order of postwar realism.

This chapter leaves the imaginary countries of the pastoral novels to enter the world of modern Japan. To put it in imagistic terms, the movement is from a child's focalization to an adult vision, and, in general, from the country to the city, for the wasteland of modern Japan is very much an urban one. In these dreary urban settings, the little marginal worlds of summer plenitude and winter abundance that centered *Pluck the Buds* and *The Sound of Waves* exist largely by absence, or else as fragmentary objects of desire, dreamed of by the adult protagonists who understand, intellectually, that unity and wholeness are no longer possible, but who still cannot emotionally accept the overwhelming presence of the broken world around them. The literary

43

expression of this fragmentation is evident through one of the most powerful of its metaphors—sexuality and the degradation of desire.

EROTICISM IN POSTWAR LITERATURE

The works with this sexual focus are from a thirty-year period, ranging from Mishima's immediate postwar *Confessions of a Mask* to Oe's "The Swimming Man" ("Oyogu otoko") of 1983; but they all share two important common factors: First, to capture the fragmentation of the postwar world, they overtly depict non-procreative and illicit sexual behaviors—autoeroticism, homosexuality, voyeurism, adultery, rape, and sadism. Second, to probe the relations and connections that do operate in society, they make sexuality itself a key element in narrative after narrative.

Michel Foucault has said, "We know now that it is sex itself which hides the secret parts of the individual: the structure of his fantasies, the roots of his ego, the forms of his relationships to reality";[4] and this assertion holds true for literature as well. In the case of modern Japanese novels, it is not simply the individual's secrets and relationships that are mediated through sex, but the secrets and relationships of an entire society—the world of postwar Japan. Inscribed in the erotic discourse of Oe, Mishima, and a number of other postwar writers' works is a microcosmos of humiliation, chaos, and loss, in which sexuality serves as a redemption, a compensation, an escape, or a means of control. Or it can be the most extreme expression of the lack of redemption, the absence of compensation, the closing off of escape, and the loss of control, all of which are epitomized in Oe's bleak paradigm of 1950s Japan, the humiliating triangle of a prostitute, her Japanese lover/pimp and her American client.[5]

The paradigm is not limited to Oe: Mishima's *Temple of the Golden Pavilion* contains an even more explicit version of this pattern in its depiction of a Japanese priest trampling on a pregnant prostitute at her American boyfriend's behest, directly in front of the Golden Temple, one of the most important cultural treasures of Japan. Other examples of this paradigm exist in other writers' works: For example, a later story by Nosaka Akiyuki, the black-humored "American Hijiki" ("Amerikan hijiki"), revolves around a middle-aged Japanese man's attempt to come to terms with his youthful pimping for the American forces by taking a new American friend to a live sex show, only to have the male partner of the sex act become impotent at sight of the American. Humiliation, impotence, and voyeurism all combine to suggest a shattered society, uncontrolled and powerless, dependent on an alien Other.

The sexuality of much postwar Japanese literature—obsessive and antagonistic to social norms—is not necessarily a product of the country's defeat in the war nor even peculiar to the literature of Japan. As Tony Tanner points out, in the typical European bourgeois novel, the absence of pleasure and thus the degradation of desire is a key theme related to the development of late-capitalist industrial society and the attendant reification of human intercourse.[6] Indeed, degraded sexuality was also an important aspect of prewar Naturalist fiction's tortured confessions of desire, as expressed in the incestuous relationship described in Tayama Katai's infamous *Futon* and the adultery in Shiga Naoya's *Dark Night's Passing* (*Anya koro*), both of which are significantly different from the largely positive celebrations of sexuality in premodern Japanese literature, where the lyric erotic delights of the Manyoshu or even the humorous satires of Saikaku were far more the norm. In fact, it is in what often comes close to an obsession with degraded sexuality that the two writers come closest to the Naturalists in their writings.

They also follow the Naturalists in the explicitly confrontational aspect of their portrayals of sex. Thus, the leading Naturalist writer Tayama Katai called his fellow Naturalists "war correspondents in the battlefield of life."[7] This sense of "confrontation" is very much a part of both writers' consciousness, as is clear from Oe's statement that he used sex to "shock people."

Whereas sex in premodern literature was accepted as both pleasurable and natural, much of early modern fiction describes sexuality in negative and usually antisocial terms, often using a tortured sexual relationship as a means of isolating the protagonist vis-à-vis society. This isolation contrasts with the compartmentalized but still communally accepted sexuality of the Tokugawa pleasure quarters and may be seen as a form of ego or identity development on the part of the Japanese writer as he attempts to separate himself from the strictures of family or tradition. In the I novel, this kind of sexuality was finally encapsulated and neutralized in the confessional form, a means by which the writer/protagonist confessed his, usually sexual, misbehavior. Through his action, he was able both to purge himself and demonstrate the sincerity of his suffering, thereby gaining absolution and reentry into the collective fold. Thus, "confessional" literature performed as a mediator both for expressing the views of the new society and ultimately for transcending that very newness, by providing a vehicle for a return to the traditional collectivity. As Katai said, the writers were *correspondents* on the battlefield, they were not the actual soldiers.

In the postwar period, such a comforting resolution of sexuality/ identity problems was no longer possible. In fact, the expression of sexuality in the era's literature is both even more explicitly anti-social than the darkest imaginings of the Naturalists and, in a perverse way, far more aggressively celebratory of this antisocial quality. This is true not only of the writings of Sakaguchi Ango and his immediate postwar "Decadents" group, who turned their anger and despair into grotesque celebrations of a Bacchanalian nightmare world where men copulated with animals and with idiots, but also of such long-established writers as Tanizaki Jun'ichirō and Kawabata Yasunari, who eclipsed their own prewar erotic masterpieces by such later works as Tanizaki's *The Key* (Kagi), and "Bridge of Dreams" ("Yume no ukihashi"), which unabashedly celebrated voyeurism and a kind of incest, and Kawabata's *House of the Sleeping Beauties* (*Nemureru bijo*) and *The Lake* (*Mizūmi*), which highlighted voyeurism, prostitution, and sexual perversion.

A key difference between the older masters' treatment of sexuality and that of postwar writers, however, is in the issue of control. When Tanizaki and Kawabata deal with such themes as impotence and voyeurism, their impotent or voyeuristic protagonists maintain control of their sexual lives or at least believe that they do. The dying father in "Bridge of Dreams," for example, explicitly arranges for his wife to seduce his son (her stepson), while the elderly protagonist in *House of the Sleeping Beauties* discovers a place where his withered erotic desires can still be satisfied, for a fee. Tanizaki and Kawabata create tightly manipulated worlds, pleasurable "non-places," where sexuality is by and large controllable.

Neither control nor pleasure is much in evidence in the many sexually explicit works of the postwar generation of Japanese writers. Far from the private spaces of Kawabata or Tanizaki, which themselves are related to the compartmentalized sexual worlds of Edo society, sex in postwar works often takes on a quasi-public air, from the live sex show in Nosaka's story, and the train perverts of Oe's *The Sexual Human*, to the voyeurs watching couples groping in the park described in Mishima's last novels. Perhaps the most obvious examples of out-of-control sexuality occur in Abe Kobo's works: places that normally represent science and order, such as hospitals or laboratories, become the scenes of wild orgies such as the extraordinary high-tech bacchanalia of *Secret Rendezvous* (Mikai), where a man watches as a woman who may be his wife is strapped to a machine that measures orgasms and is then forced to have intercourse with a series of anonymous men.

If a private erotic world remains in postwar fiction, it is usually in the solipsistic pleasures of masturbation; but even here, the fantasies are notable for their very banality. In a famous scene from Mishima's *Confessions of a Mask,* the hero masturbates within an exceptionally romantic setting (sun, sea, and sand) but has as his object of desire his own armpits; the scene evokes a world of total solipsism, where the objects of erotic focus are not only morcellized but only barely belong to an Other. Even more banal is the description in Oe's "Seventeen" ("Sebunchin") of the pathetic adolescent hero masturbating in the bathroom while recalling an article in a woman's magazine about a bride developing peritonitis on her wedding night. Not only are the objects of desire (armpits, disease), displaced and degraded ones, the act of masturbation itself symbolizes a fragmented sexuality between one object, the penis, and a series of fragmented images—an ironic undercutting of the ecstatic wholeness that the practitioner supposedly seeks. It is also an act that was frowned upon by Japanese society, as is clear in both books from the shame the protagonists feel and their fear of having their "secret" revealed.

Oe and Mishima are not alone in their use of aggressive and shocking sexuality as a social and political statement. But they are perhaps the most self-conscious in their use. As the opening statements in this chapter demonstrate, both writers were highly aware of the confrontational aspect of their sexual themes. An even more important similarity is that, despite the fact that they are master chroniclers of the absence of sexual desire, many of their works actually treat certain kinds of sexuality positively.

Where desire does appear as a topic, it is no longer the spontaneous simple desire of the pastoral novels, but rather desire in its most extreme form. Because *Pluck the Buds,* "Prize Stock," and *The Sound of Waves* were essentially romances, they could still limn a positive kind of sexuality in a tone typified by the children's delighted laughter in "Prize Stock" over the black soldier's erection. Within the realistic genre that frames most of the works in this chapter, such innocence is no longer possible. At best, or at worst, the way out of the wasteland of alienation is not back through innocence, but down into a world of intense experience, the darker and the more grotesque the better, which is why sexuality and violence often occur in tandem. Conventional sexual intercourse can never fulfill the protagonists; and, by its very unfulfillment, it only reminds the participants of the inadequate world around them.

Consequently, truly satisfying sex in Oe's and Mishima's works can only exist either in the utopian fantasies of the pastoral novels or in what one commentator on Oe calls "moments at odds with reality,"[8] apocalyptic and unlikely situations achievable only through perversion or violence, whether individual or collective. No longer part of the natural order, satisfying sex can now only be found through unnatural means.

However society in the novels may judge these acts, it is usually true that the perpetrator of them does finally experience a sense of fulfillment. Unlike the grotesque fantasies of Abe Kobo's novels, where sex is almost uniformly despairing and mirrors the fundamental meaninglessness of the world in general, the works of both Oe and Mishima contain many passages where sex serves as the path out of the wasteland rather than the means of attacking it. The works in this chapter may therefore be characterized (but only barely) as ideological novels in that they do present a "message," but the message is more diffuse than in the pastoral novels and is presented with more complexity than the pastorals' monomythic structures can offer.

The final, major similarity in the two writers' treatment of sexuality is their tendency to use dual protagonists, passive and active heroes. Unlike the pastoral romances where the protagonists were basically united in terms of style and abilities, the more realistic works tend to express the fragmentation of the world by literally fragmenting the role of the protagonist. Thus, one character may be the thinking half. This "brain," or passive intellectual, is frequently impotent and always jealous of his doppelganger, the active hero who is the other half of the combination. The active hero is unthinking, often handsome, and usually erotically successful, perhaps because of his very lack of ratiocinative powers.

The most obvious paradigm of this interaction is the aging writer Shunsuke and the beautiful young homosexual Yuichi in Mishima's *Forbidden Colors*. In this bleak work, the embittered Shunsuke attempts to extract his revenge against every woman who has rejected him, by using Yuichi to seduce and then reject them. The scheme is only partially successful, however, because Yuichi's conquests only stir Shunsuke's jealousy, eventually turning Shunsuke as much into the manipulated as he is the manipulator. *Forbidden Colors* may be read as a revenge fantasy against women and "straight" society, but the homosexual underground it depicts is scarcely more agreeable. The novel's real interest lies in the increasingly intimate but twisted relationship between Shunsuke and Yuichi as each seeks to control the other, before each gives up in frustration.

Overall, this entangled relationship between intellectual and "man of action" in *Forbidden Colors* hints at Mishima's profound despair about postwar Japan, still groping to recover itself from a prewar romantic ideology where "spirit" and "action" had been touted as a way of conquering superior Western technology. The intellectuals in his postwar world know the ultimate futility of such ideas but simultaneously are romantically drawn to them, while dreaming of controlling this "spirit" through their own superior intellects. Ultimately, the futility of this dream is always exposed, and one or the other type of hero is "sacrificed," a victim of a postwar society where thought and action are always divided. Often, it is on the "battleground" of sexuality where the sacrifice takes place.

ABSENCE AND DESIRE:
CONFESSIONS OF A MASK AND *OUR ERA*

The role of "degraded sex" is perhaps one of the best signifiers of absence, because of the emotional expectations built around eroticism. Degraded sex comprises the absence of intensity, of love, of connection, and, most of all, of desire. Tanner and Girard's tracing of the absence of pleasure in the nineteenth- and twentieth-century Western novel explains how the absence of desire becomes a major signifier in itself of the industrialized and commodified world of the realistic novel. In Mishima's *Confessions of a Mask* and Oe's *Our Era,* the nonexistence of sexual desire, at least desire for the socially approved object, becomes both a reflection and a criticism of the society that has spawned this absence. As is appropriate for young men's novels about young protagonists, the two works also deal with the problem of identity as the two protagonists work their way towards an understanding of what they are and what they are not, through sexual and other means of exploration.

Oe's 1959 work, *Our Era*, stands as one of his most controversial novels partly because, as Oe himself commented, it "contains a sexual reference on virtually every page,"[9] but also for its overall atmosphere of anomie and despair. The sexuality in the novel may be shocking but it is never titillating, because the main protagonist, a French literature student named Yasuo, never enjoys it. He is only aware that "[t]he one pleasure he got out of sex was the tiny little shiver that ran over his skin just when coitus was about to end. At that instant he would experience his trembling flesh as something without relationship to himself. That felt good."[10]

Indeed, Yasuo is virtually "without relationship" to anything. He is bored with his girlfriend Yoriko, a prostitute who services Americans, tired of the university, and largely indifferent to his younger brother Shigeru, the novel's active hero who, in contrast to Yasuo, is full of desires and whose romantic, as opposed to realistic, adventures, will be dealt with more thoroughly in Chapter Four. While Shigeru is active and emotional, Yasuo is the classic modern antihero, an intellectual who can only brood abstractly about the problems of the world. In his attempt to dissociate himself from all feeling, he rushes desperately into intellectual activities, immersing himself in bookish fantasies and constantly abstracting his individual plight into a representative one of his "era" (hence, the novel's title). Yasuo even turns intercourse into an abstract act by making it an occasion for intellectual analysis and calculation. This predilection is exemplified by the following passage where he begins to think abstractly, while having intercourse with Yoriko: "'Let's see, sex . . . If you and I have sex three hundred and sixty five times over twenty years, adding five for leap years, that amounts to five liters of sperm.'"[11]

Different in style, Mishima's *Confessions* is also a more complex exposition of the problems of desire and of the lack of desire. Written in 1949, *Confessions*, like *Our Era*, was the author's first major work and was also highly controversial, for it describes the development of a young intellectual as he becomes aware of his homosexuality. The anonymous narrator of the book also subjects his sexuality to intense intellectual analysis, quoting from such learned authorities as "Hirschfield," to dissociate his sexuality from his own despairing self. Unlike Yasuo, the unnamed narrator of "mask" harbors strong sexual desire, but not toward the socially "correct" object. Instead, he is obsessed with a collection of bloody homoerotic fantasies which both torment and stimulate him.

Another major difference between them is that Yasuo simply wants to escape into a variety of "non-places" that his "era" and his French studies have revealed to him, while the mask attempts to escape his sexuality by donning a new persona, that of the heterosexual. Where *Our Era* degrades sexual desire by showing its futility within the alienating "era" of the novel's title and was therefore highly controversial, *Confessions* chronicles the unsuccessful attempt to create desire for the socially sanctioned "normal," and in some ways this makes it even more implicitly subversive. It was not just the novel's highlighting of the theme of homosexuality that disturbed the public. More subtly, the novel shows an implicit contempt for society and for the "normal": its "confession" parodies the Naturalists' purgative absolutions by showing that the narrator, who supposedly removes his mask, is even more isolated from society at the end of the novel than before his confession.

This experience may also reflect the position of the author himself, since *Confessions* is widely considered to be an accurate account of Mishima's childhood and adolescence and consequently can be seen as a gauntlet thrown down before Japanese society. Even more confrontational than the presumed autobiographical implications, however, is the contrast within the novel between the bland emptiness of bourgeois courtship, romantic love, and marriage as sanctioned by society and the intensity and vividness of the narrator's gory visions.

The emptiness of Japanese society is unveiled in the novel's second half when the mask attempts to enter conventional society, only to realize his fundamental lack of desire for it. This portion of the book has been faulted by critics, both Japanese and American, because of its very blandness compared to the early intensity of the mask's developing awareness of his homosexuality. Even if *Confessions* fails as a novel, however, thematically, this second half is necessary to show how thoroughly absent pleasure has become.

Thus, the mask, turning reluctantly from his secret visions of blood and ecstasy, tries to imitate the courtship of a normal young man, an imitation which, although outwardly successful, is inwardly unfulfilling because of his lack of passion for Sonoko, the woman he courts. Although he enjoys his "act" intellectually, it cannot provide him the pleasure of his earlier fantasies of the dying soldier or the female entertainer that the first half describes. The "sugary novels"[12] that he congratulates himself on choosing for Sonoko differ sharply from his own private fantasies of a "murder theater," where young men are butchered and eaten, or of "a death among strangers, under a cloudless sky."[13]

Although the contrast between desire and its lack may be stronger in *Confessions of a Mask*, the contrast between an unfulfilling bourgeois society and romantic dreams is clearer in *Our Era*. In Oe's novel, Yasuo endlessly laments that he was born too late for the "age of heroic battles" (his idealized perception of the Second World War)[14] and dreams of going to Africa to fight on the side of the Arabs against French imperialism. Both he and the mask are similar, however, in their fascination with alternative worlds, which, though hardly pastoral environments, share some affinities with the realms discussed in Chapter One. Their visions contain more brutality than the pastoral romances, but they resemble the more innocent "nonplaces" in those works in their simplicity and masculinity. In the dream worlds of Yasuo and the mask, the complex problems of heterosexual adult society are reduced to images of heat, light, and death.

It is towards these worlds that genuine desire appears in both novels, and the protagonists' desire is fundamentally a yearning to escape, not simply from society but from their own overly intellectualized selves. Mishima's hero even looks forward to the landing of the American army: "I was hoping—no, it was more than mere hope, it was a superstitious certainty—that during that month the Americans would surely land at S bay and we would all be sent out as a student army to die to the last man . . ."[15]

In this regard, the two protagonists are also archetypal intellectual egotists who share the hope that external change will somehow sweep away their personal problems, the desire, as Victor Brombert says of the French intellectuals of the 1930s, to "merge personal tragedy with collective disaster."[16] Unable to take action themselves, they simply wait passively for some deus ex machina to save them. This passivity is translated sexually into impotence; for, towards the end of each novel, each protagonist has unsatisfactory sexual experiences with women, which underline their failure in dealing with the "real world."

Yasuo, however, is given a genuine opportunity to escape from his humiliation and from the dreariness around him, when his thesis wins him a scholarship to study in France. The opportunity comes at a particularly advantageous time, because Yoriko has just announced her pregnancy—another indication, in Yasuo's eyes, of the suffocating nature of sexuality. Yasuo's thoughts on winning the scholarship indicate his conflation of sexuality with all his other problems: "The hope of escaping Japan, of escaping from a disagreeable life that mixed sexuality with humiliation, from the saffron smell of cleaning fluid, from the 5 liters of semen, from 7,305 ejaculations into dirty water, from dying with a senile smile on one's face, from all that was the opposite of an active heroic life, that was what Yasuo had bet his thesis on."[17]

Yasuo's unfitness for an "active heroic life" becomes even clearer when, at the novel's end, he attempts to have intercourse one last time with Yoriko and fails. His impotency is not only literal but is symbolically related to the wider issues of postwar Japanese life, most notably dependence on America. Thus, when Yasuo thinks of "sexuality mixed with humiliation," it is clear from his constant association of himself with his generation that this feeling is not just on a personal level but on a national scale as well. Occupied, subordinate Japan has only powerless male defenders incapable of protecting her from the threatening American Other—the father who castrates the male whose only recourse is acceptance of the Symbolic order on the alien Other's terms. Yasuo's almost parodic intellectuality and his insistence that he is a representative of a "generation" or an abstract "era" are inevitable responses to a world where the father is so utterly alien that the child can hardly imagine competing with him in the theater of the Real. Consequently, he must resort to intellectual competition, where he can hope to win by manipulation.

With Mishima's novel, such political concerns are less explicit, but the relative textual absence of the war, almost inconceivable for a novel published in 1949, so soon after its end, is a clue to the war's underlying importance. The war does lap at the borders of *Confessions,* but it is focalized entirely through the narrator's egotistic preoccupations with his own problems. At one point, for example, the mask joins his supposed girlfriend Sonoko and her family on a farewell outing for her soldier brother, an event that would be a call for some form of sentimentality or at least acknowledgment of the looming presence of destruction in most narratives. The mask, however, can only say fastidiously that, "I regret to say that no matter how I looked I could find no beauty in the scene."[18]

The narrator's egotism is not the only reason for the war's textual absence. The mask's refusal to acknowledge his kinship with the rest of humanity in the face of adversity and his egotistical conflation of the war with his own troubles is an attitude shared by other postwar authors. As in the writings of Ango and the other Decadents, the cataclysm of destruction has freed the mask to admit to and even highlight what he calls his "inversion," for society is now no longer rigid enough to constrain him. The touches of decadence appearing in *Confessions of a Mask,* especially the fantasies of a murder theater where young men are sacrificed and eaten, hint at an outer environment where young men are victimized in a depraved fashion.[19] Although it may not be the case that Mishima consciously equated these images of sacrifice with the destruction of Japan, the fact that his own private sexual preoccupations came to the fore so strongly in 1949 is surely related to the destruction of the traditional, compartmentalized Japanese culture wrought by the defeat.[20]

The political elements are far more clear-cut in Oe's novel than in *Confessions,* both in terms of Yasuo's obsession with his "era" and in the humiliating triangular relationship with Yoriko and her American lover. In addition, Yasuo's romantic preoccupation with war reflects the reverse side of the mask's patronizing dismissal of it and also, ironically, stands as a precursor to Mishima's similar glorification of war in his later works. Yasuo's "era" looks nostalgically at war precisely because it is such a peaceful period. The Japan of 1963 had largely rebuilt itself and renounced war, thus making it safe for Yasuo to fantasize about it, just as the mask occasionally fantasizes about the American invasion, as long as it is still safely in the distance. The fact that both books rely so heavily on fantasies is also important. In a world that can no longer be controlled, fantasies of escape or of power that promotes the butchery of young men (as in the mask's "murder theater") may be inevitable.

Japanese novels written by men who served in the war rarely dabble in fantasy, except the pedestrian dream of a safe return home. Most soldiers understood too well that control was something they could never have. It was to the noncombatant intellectuals that the luxury of such wishful thinking was granted.

Significantly, both books end with the vision of a young man's death and an episode of impotence followed by thoughts of suicide. The death of the young man is in some ways a kind of sacrifice of the nonintellectual alter ego. In *Our Era,* this sacrifice is of Yasuo's younger brother Shigeru, the "romantic" active hero of the story, whose antic attempt to assassinate the emperor will be discussed in

Chapter Four. Shigeru is never as three dimensional a character as Yasuo. He exists, like so many of Mishima's and Oe's young, unthinking heroes, as an object of sacrifice, to force his brother into an awareness that he can never reach the imaginary days of "heroic battles" and to clarify to Yasuo that he and his era are prisoners of postwar history. To underline Yasuo's powerlessness even further, his pregnant girlfriend leaves him for one of her American clients. At the end of the novel, it is little wonder that the totally isolated Yasuo contemplates suicide, while standing in front of a poster that vividly proclaims "Young men, this is your era!"

Yasuo does not himself sacrifice Shigeru. He is merely an onlooker to his brother's life and death. To the end of the book, he remains locked in the total passivity that his impotence has brought to the surface, knowing that he can never be a man of action. His only genuine action throughout the novel has been to turn down the scholarship to France because of his solidarity with the Arab cause. After this one attempt at self-definition, the void reemerges and the reader's last glimpse of him is as he stands unable to decide whether to kill himself and thinking in typical rationalizing fashion: "But there will always be the opportunity for suicide ... even though usually we can't get up the courage to kill ourselves, so we go on living, always looking for that omnipresent chance for suicide and that is the era we live in."[21]

Confessions also ends on a note of despairing self-realization, although this self-realization may have more positive, even galvanizing consequences. Despairing over his impotence after he fails to make love to a woman, the narrator seriously considers suicide; like Yasuo, however, he is unable to carry it out and ends up, also like Yasuo, finding an alter ego, a young man of action to metaphorically "sacrifice.'

This development occurs in the final scene, where the protagonist has gone to a dance hall with his former girlfriend Sonoko, who is now safely married and thus unattainable, and consequently slightly more interesting again. In this scene, however, the protagonist finally realizes his inescapable attraction to young men when he watches a handsome young tough in the dance hall:

> I had forgotten Sonoko's existence. I was thinking of but one thing: of his going out into the streets of high summer just as he was, half naked, and getting into a fight with a rival gang. Of a sharp dagger cutting through

that belly band, piercing that torso. Of that soiled belly band beautifully dyed with blood. Of his gory corpse being put on an improvised stretcher, made of a window shutter and brought back here . . .[22]

The young tough is not simply the object of his desire but the Other, whom the mask wants to be but cannot be because of his intelligence, background, and personality, as he suddenly realizes:

At this instant something inside of me was torn in two with brutal force . . . I felt as though I had witnessed the instant in which my existence had been turned into some sort of fearful non-being.[23]

Although the narrator has been split into two and forced, like Yasuo, to recognize his fragmentation from the whole, he is still far from non-being. Rather, he is beginning to "be." Thus, although at the novel's end, he sees glittering empty reflections that prove that he can never return to what Lacan calls the mirror stage of the imaginary (he can never "be" the handsome young tough), he has finally begun to recognize his identity vis-à-vis society. In the mask's blatantly erotic fantasy of the young man's death, the Other is "sacrificed" so that the homosexual I can finally be born, and he can finally acknowledge himself. Mishima himself called Confessions a form of "reverse suicide,"[24] and this is a fitting description for both protagonist and writer. The protagonist discovers what he is and what he can never be in the final scene, while, for Mishima, the very writing of the novel, and the consequent inscribing of himself into language, was a form of new life. Indeed, it was the success of Confessions that allowed him to become a full-time writer.

For Yasuo, standing in front of the poster which presumes to tell him what he is ("Young men, this is your era!"), the awareness of his isolation and impotence is almost too overpowering for his fragmented emotional state. The near realization of his fantasy of escape has caused him more misery than his desire for it. In contrast, the mask in Confessions seems to have regained his desire, even if for a socially non-approved object. Yasuo's end is thus more tragic since even fantasies no longer seem possible alternatives to the wasteland in which he is enmeshed.

Both of these works were considered controversial upon publication, initially because of their explicit sexual imagery and themes. In the long run, however, the narratives' antisocial sexuality is less problematic than the traits it masks, an underlying contempt for, and despair of, normal society. Yasuo seems to have given up all hope of escape even through fantasy, while the narrator of *Confessions* appears to have become increasingly enslaved to fantasy as, perhaps, was the case with the novel's creator.

FROM FANTASY TO REALITY: "THE LOCKED ROOM" AND "THE SWIMMING MAN"

In neither *Confessions of a Mask* nor *Our Era* does the protagonist ever act on his fantasies: Yasuo never goes to France or fights in Algeria; Mishima's narrator only dreams of sadistic homoeroticism and death (when *Confessions'* protagonist is actually called up for military service, he is enormously relieved when he is disqualified). The violent sexual fantasies in two other works, Mishima's "Locked Room" ("Kagi no kakaru heya") and Oe's "Swimming Man" ("Oyogu otoko"), do, however, come close to being realized. In fact, they are realized, but not by the fantasists, and perhaps not quite in the way the dreamers had originally expected, since both protagonists are ultimately left frustrated: The fantasies are fulfilled by someone or something else. This frustration is not surprising; for, even more so than Yasuo and the mask, they are essentially passive heroes; and although they do eventually discover desire, it is initially unfocused. The four works are similar, however, in that each revolves around the contrast between the bleakness of outer reality and the intensity of the protagonist's perverse inner visions.

In "The Swimming Man" and "The Locked Room," these visions initially seem haphazard but, in their violence and brutality, ultimately suggest a profound anger at the world. Consequently, although hardly "romantics" in the traditional sense of the word, the protagonists share the romantics' dissatisfaction with reality and a longing for some more intense experience. The fact that the two never do actually commit the crimes about which they fantasize heightens the nihilistic quality of both works.

The passive nature of fantasizing reveals another common element of sexuality in Mishima and Oe: the voyeuristic element. While Oe's hero is an unconscious voyeur, unwilling to admit his suppressed excitement as a perverse relationship unfolds before him, Mishima's hero is perhaps the ultimate voyeur, a creator of a dream world where he can listen avidly to the sadistic fantasies of others. Mishima's hero perhaps dwells on his sick fantasies because of the chaotic nature of the world around him. Written in 1950, "The Locked Room" is set against a background of postwar nihilism; and its hero epitomizes the fashionable lack of desire imputed to the new antihero. Although written largely in a drearily realistic style, the story, like *Confessions*, still contains "romantic" or at least escapist overtones, with its garish visions of aestheticized blood and brutality.

The story's protagonist, Kodama Kazuo, initially seems far from any form of romanticism. An employee in the Citizens Savings Section of the Finance Ministry, Kazuo spends his days preparing reports on runaway inflation and wondering idly if spiraling prices might lead to a revolution. Since the story is set only two- and-a-half years after Japan's surrender, such concerns are hardly surprising. What is surprising is that Kazuo appears indifferent to matters of inflation or the possibility of revolution. If anything, he is pleased by the "chaos and corruption"[25] he sees around him and takes pride in being a solitary individual with no ties to anyone, delighting in his own "inner disorder."[26]

Even Kazuo's sexuality has a solitary, apathetic quality to it. The text describes him at work when "trying to ward off sleepiness, he leaned against his desk and consequently had an erection."[27]The text goes on to describe how, for Kazuo, "To be called from his seat at such times was very embarrassing. When he was on a moving bus he always got an erection. Perhaps this was the same thing. He put his hand in his pocket and lightly caressed himself. There was no particular feeling of pleasure."[28]

Like Yasuo, Kazuo's sexuality at first seems only marginally related to desire. If anything, Kazuo gets more pleasure out of watching the woman next to him knitting yarn dolls: "Yarn was good. No matter how many times a yarn doll was pierced, it would stay the same shape. Kazuo thought of the straw dolls in bayonet practice which fell apart when pierced."[29]

Kazuo's fascination with piercing an object that can retain its shape suggests a search for unity in the fragmented postwar world. At the beginning of the story, it appears that he has found that elusive unity, a place that cannot be penetrated, that will shield him from the outer chaos of society. It also seems that he has found a vulnerable victim over whom to assert control. The place is the "locked room" belonging to Kiriko, a woman he meets at a dance hall who becomes the "partner in his inner disorder."[30] Kiriko is a married woman who apparently makes a practice of inviting attractive young men to her home on the many evenings her husband is away. Whether the transgression of society through adultery adds spice to Kazuo's pleasure is uncertain, but it is clear that he finds his relationship with Kiriko highly satisfactory. Appropriate for an alternative to reality, it excludes the outer world completely and literally through the medium of the living room door which Kiriko locks the first night Kazuo visits her. As the text states, "The sound of the key locking the door adroitly excluded the outer world," but it also adds enigmatically, "It was important that it should be the woman who locked the door—it had to be that way."[31] Kazuo appears to understand subliminally that it is woman as caretaker/womb/mother who holds the "key" to the desired realm of the imaginary.

The outside world does eventually invade the lovers' "tiny crystal chaos preserved in the small locked room"[32] (note how the room encompasses all boundaries from the rigid "crystal" to the formless "chaos"), and it does so in the form of death: Kiriko suffers a sudden heart attack while they are making love and Kazuo leaves the house never to see her again. He does return to the locked room, however, and the remainder of the story follows his relationship with the little girl who now occupies it and the grotesque fantasy she inspires.

Kazuo is unsure why he is drawn back to the room, but one day he does return and is entertained therein by the maid Shigeya, and by Fusako, Kiriko's coquettishly sophisticated nine-year-old daughter. Fusako also locks the door; but this time the sound of the key in the lock frightens Kazuo, although he is not sure why.

It is probable that Kazuo's fear results from his awareness of his loss of control over the situation. When Kiriko was alive, he could indulge himself in the fantasy world protected by a door locked by a mother figure. With Kiriko's death, he realizes such a refuge has vanished or perhaps never existed, and the image of a nine-year-old girl attempting to reassert that false fantasy only makes the impossibility of refuge even more obvious.

Kazuo's fear may also be related to a strange dream he had the night before he returned to the locked room, in which he found himself walking down a cold empty road "encircled by groves of trees and high walls," and in search of a bar called "The Club of the Covenant" which he knows the government has opened in order to "lend a hand to disorder."[33] He is unsure of his reasons for going there; and when he finally finds the club, he sees no one nor any of its wares. Only as he leaves does he notice a wine bottle, but it is lying in the street dripping "something that looked like black blood."[34]

The dream world, far from being an escape fantasy, is both an encapsulation of the narrative's basic sadistic dream and of outer reality, the "cold" and "empty" world that Kiriko's death has revealed. The emphasis on the fact that the government has "lent a hand to disorder" highlights the dreamer's unconscious awareness that the disorder is both inner and outer. The long road "encircled by deep groves of trees" suggests both a feminine symbol, the passage back to the womb, and a sense of entrapment—the combination of womanhood and entrapment often occurring together in Mishima's and Oe's fiction. The sense of encirclement also suggests the corresponding need to escape, to pierce through into some outside place; but Kazuo is not yet willing to break out, for he is still searching for something. In this dream he does not find it but only perhaps a fragment of it, the bottle from which "black blood" seeps. The bottle could represent either a feminine or masculine symbol, but the liquid that it emits, be it semen or menstrual fluid, will not regenerate the surrounding wasteland but rather drip uselessly onto the empty road.

The sadistic elements underlying the dream become clearer as Kazuo begins to fantasize in waking life about the body of the little girl, Fusako, thinking about the weight and feel of her flesh and wondering why it "aroused in him the desire to commit profane and wicked acts."[35] It is after this daytime dreaming that he is successful in finding the Club of the Covenant no longer closed to him in his night dreams. The Club of the Covenant, not surprisingly, turns out to be a group of sadists, with the important qualification that these are sadists in word only. As one of the members explains, "Unfortunately we have never had any real experiences. So our method is to speak about our fantasies as if we had actually experienced them."[36]

The club members then go on to relate their fantasies as Kazuo listens eagerly in a scene that combines voyeurism with the author's swipe at himself (and the reader) for enjoying the fantasies of "others," all the time denying that they are actually his own. The members are simply Kazuo's "active" alter egos who at least dare to admit their fascination with blood and humiliation, as is clear from the content of their fantasies. Thus, one club member, a fabric dyer, tells of using the entrails of a murdered woman to create the perfect color for a particular piece of cloth. Another tells of tattooing a "dress" onto a living woman, the dress being correct in every detail, down to such touches as a "pocket" for a compact, for which he provides a real compact, placing it in the slit until it becomes covered with blood. He finishes his story by saying, "The woman died in five or six hours."[37]

Kazuo then asks the story teller an important question:

"In the compact's mirror, what was your face like reflected there?"
"There is no relation between ours and a devil's features. But that is the biggest misconception that the world has about sadists. I . . . if I had to, I'd say it was an extremely gentle face."[38]

Like the mask in *Confessions,* Kazuo is beginning to develop his identity in relation to others, even if the others are products of his own imagination. Thus, while he has yet to admit his own sadism and is still far from acting on it, he is at least willing to ask about his alter ego's face in the mirror. The fact that it is "gentle," however, is perhaps not totally reassuring, suggesting the impossibility of ever truly knowing one's real self. For example, later on in the story, Kazuo takes the little Fusako to a dance hall and is relieved when, catching a glimpse of them dancing in the mirror, he sees that the mirror simply reflects "a sentimental young man dancing with a little girl."[39]

The mirror is also the perfect symbol for the confusion that exists in the story between fantasy and reality, which Kazuo at times seems to enjoy and at other times wants to cut through. Thus, when the dream members of the club ask him for his fantasy, he responds with a brutally direct and unromantic one, "I raped a little girl. I ripped her. The little girl bled a lot and died."[40] Kazuo's unembellished words pierce the grandiose fantasies of the others, just as his fantasy action pierces the little girl.

Kazuo's blunt response also suggests a lurking dissatisfaction with grandiose fantasy and empty romantic language and the story's suspense builds around whether Kazuo will decide to substitute action for voyeuristic visions. But Kazuo does not rape Fusako. Instead, when he visits the locked room for the last time, determined to bring his sadistic impulses to their logical conclusion, he is informed by the maid that Fusako has begun to menstruate. Kazuo suddenly feels as if "the room had been stained bright red with blood"[41] and flees the house. Behind him, Shigeya, who has revealed herself to be Fusako's real mother calls out, "Are you going now? You really mustn't."[42] He ignores her words, while behind him, for the last time, he hears the sound of the door being locked.

"The Locked Room" operates on many levels to suggest finally a world from which there is no possibility of escape or control except in the form of fantasy or in the form of sexual violence. Thus, the members of the Club of the Covenant are content with their erotic dreams, which are more grotesque but still akin to the erotic fantasies of Edo-period authors or even those of Tanizaki or Kawabata. For Kazuo, however, such fantasies are no longer enough. He desires to break through the walls of reality, not through fantasy, but through an attempt to turn fantasy into reality and to create a world that conforms more truly to the inner and outer chaos.

This concern with turning dreams into action is reminiscent of Kazuo's creator. It is almost as if the Mishima of 1950, himself a recent employee of the Finance Ministry and just beginning his writing career, was finally beginning to work through the problem of the emptiness of the "word," as in the exaggerated language of the members of the club, versus the real power of action. It is perhaps for this reason that Kazuo's fantasy is so brutal and stripped of romanticization, far from the aestheticization of so many of the sadomasochistic visions in Mishima's work.

Kazuo, at least, never fulfills his fantasy, his attempt to control and perhaps even gain revenge on the real world, for again reality stops him. In this case, the real world is represented jointly by women and nature.

The association of women with natural reproduction is hinted at early in the story as Tanaka Miyoko points out,[43] by a scene where Kazuo gazes at a bottle on which the label has the picture of a woman holding a bottle on whose label another woman is shown holding a bottle, and so on. Women are thus associated with an endless cycle of reproduction. Kazuo's intent gaze into the bottle also reminds us of his concern with mirrors. Here, however, in the world of women, which represents the unified wholeness of the locked room, there is no reflection of Kazuo's face. He can never enter that particular world.

The locked room that only women can control serves thus as an escape from the outer world and an ironic reminder that the outer world is always there. Even in the artificial "crystal chaos," nature/ reality intrudes in the form of menstruation which stains Kazuo's safe haven bright with blood, and it is not blood shed at his whim. Rather, as Tanaka has commented,[44] nature has taken away from Kazuo the privilege of violating the little girl, of asserting his control;

and neither the reader nor Kazuo will ever know whether his "senti-mental" face is actually that of a sadist or not.

The hero of Oe's novella "The Swimming Man," is also caught in a world of fragmented identities where dream mixes with reality, but he finds an alter ego for himself not in dreams but within the real world itself. Like Kazuo, the unnamed narrator of "The Swimming Man" is a passive hero, although a writer rather than a bureaucrat; but, in contrast to "The Locked Room," Oe's story contains a genu-ine man of action. The stories also share another important common element, however, and that is that the pivot around which Oe's pro-tagonists devise their fantasies or actions is the same as in "The Locked Room," a provocative but ultimately unknowable woman.

Although lacking the breadth of contrast found in "The Locked Room" between the small locked room and the outer "chaos" of immediate postwar Japan, "The Swimming Man" achieves an almost suffocating atmosphere of sexual tension and frustrated desire, as it chronicles the increasingly bizarre relationship among three people: a woman, the man of action, and the passive intellectual. Like "The Locked Room," most of the action in "The Swimming Man" occurs inside a small room, but in Oe's story the protagonist is unable to flee from it; the room even returns to him in dreams.

As in "The Locked Room," the room in "The Swimming Man" contains a sexually charged atmosphere; but, in this case, the protag-onist is unsure whether his awareness of this tension is correct. This is because the room is the sauna room of a posh swimming club, a family-oriented place in which it is unlikely that incidents of a bla-tantly sexual nature would occur. Furthermore, the tension, if it does exist, does not initially include the narrator but instead appears to emanate from the two others: a young student named Tamari, who is an exceptional swimmer, and a youngish woman whom the narra-tor initially refers to as "the OL" (office lady). The pair are in the sauna when the narrator finishes his swim; but at first they exchange no conversation, although the narrator is curious about them. The OL wears a bathing suit in a color that he describes as "belligerently bright,"[45] but it is not really the color that disturbs the narrator so much as a perhaps imagined glimpse of a dark patch on the lower half of the woman's suit:

> Then I had the feeling as if I had seen a kind of vision. Eventually I would grow to think it was not an illusion but rather an after image of

something that the woman's swift movement had hidden at the instant that my absent minded gaze had reached her, but it was somewhat later that I realized this. At first, the vision that I thought I had glimpsed in the faint darkness of the sauna was something like the riddle pictures that the farm children (who were more sexually advanced than we) would draw by the side of the road. This was a gourd shaped diagram thickly shaded in black. Since becoming an adult there have been many times when I have seen a woman's sexual organs, but I had never been concretely able to understand that gourd shaped diagram. Yet now I felt as if I had seen it between the OL's legs.[46]

From the very beginning of the narrative, then, the woman around whom the story revolves is reduced to a sinister and anonymous sexual presence. She is objectified as an OL, and she is morcellized at first into the fragment glimpsed between her legs, and later on, into a pair of breasts. For, the second time when the narrator enters the sauna, he finds the OL with the top half of her suit down and her breasts exposed, and he begins to realize that she is using their sessions alone together in the sauna to sexually provoke the young swimmer Tamari. Up to this point, however, Tamari's only reaction apparently has been a fixed and silent stare.

With the narrator's appearance, the OL changes her tactics and, as the narrator soon realizes, seeks to provoke Tamari further by using the narrator as an intermediary. She engages him in animated and sexually explicit conversation, while the silent Tamari listens absorbedly but betrays no other reaction. Most of the conversation centers on her two rapes, which occurred while she was traveling in Spain and Mexico; she even says meaningfully that one of the men who raped her was "about Tamari's age."[47] This conversation both excites and upsets the narrator. A few weeks after this conversation he is therefore not surprised to learn that the OL (whose name is actually Miss Iguchi) has been tied to a bench in a children's playground (in a manner strikingly reminiscent of a scene from the pornographic comics popular among students and businessmen), raped, and strangled.

He is surprised, however, to learn that her murderer is not Tamari but rather a man of his own age, a schoolteacher who attended the same university as the narrator. To complicate matters further, the presumed murderer, who already has a record of voyeurism and exhibitionism, commits suicide by hanging himself in a pigeon coop before the discoverers of Miss Iguchi's body can reach him.

The remainder of "The Swimming Man" consists of the narrator's growing identification with this anonymous middle-aged man and his increasing suspicion that it is Tamari who is the real murderer. In a series of conversations with Tamari, the narrator does manage to get him to admit that he had gone to the park with Miss Iguchi and left her tied to the park bench with her legs open and her genitals exposed. It appears, in fact, that this was a habitual amusement on the part of Tamari and Miss Iguchi, although she never actually permitted him to have intercourse with her. Indeed, after each such incident, she would revert to her "cold OL manner,"[48] much to Tamari's irritation.

After hearing this partial confession, the narrator, in a highly imaginative feat of detective work, pieces together what he believes to be the true story. He hypothesizes that it was Tamari who actually attempted to rape Miss Iguchi and, when he discovered he was impotent, strangled her in a fit of frustration. It was only afterwards, his hypothesis continues, that the high school teacher, who perhaps had watched the entire incident, actually ejaculated into the body. Then, in a paroxysm of fear and guilt, he committed suicide, "sacrificing himself" for Tamari, a man whom he had never met.

Whether this hypothesis is correct or not is never revealed. The novel ends inconclusively, although with hints of Tamari's guilt. A potentially positive moment occurs towards the end when the narrator suggests to Tamari that, for Miss Iguchi's sake, he should "live so as to uphold decency,"[49] although he uses the English word for "decency" and Tamari seems uncertain as to what it actually means. By rendering "decency" in English, the text underlines the alienness of such behavior; and it is little wonder that Tamari, who is a better swimmer than a thinker, seems confused. The novella's ending suggests that "decency" is unlikely to rule his life; rather, the last page of "The Swimming Man" has the narrator realizing that Tamari may kill again. He even asks himself, "in that case, if help is to come once more, who will take the role of the high school teacher?"[50] His question hints that the next sacrifice will be the narrator himself.

It is finally the narrator's search for identity, be it through the presumably violent Tamari or the unknown high school teacher, that is the real foundation of the narrative, while Tamari's guilt or innocence are simply quibbles, and even Miss Iguchi's bloody murder becomes a textual tool to get the psychological action going. Desire exists in "the Swimming Man," but it is hardly sexual desire. Rather, the woman in all her threatening sexuality is nothing more than the means through which the narrator's true desire to "become" Tamari is fully exposed. Despite the sexual heat of the sauna, the narrator is actually more excited by Tamari's swimming form than by the "riddle picture" shown to him by Miss Iguchi.

That the narrator identifies both with Tamari and the unnamed schoolteacher (who, in turn, identifies with Tamari) is clear in two dreams which the narrator has after Miss Iguchi's murder. In the first dream, he watches a junior high school girl (a major object of erotic attention in the Japanese mass press), with a "strangely extended stomach" taking a shower: "At the edge of her stomach clung about a thumb's worth of pubic hair and from it a view of water trickling down. I had a thought . . . that I would not let that pubic hair climb even a little further up her stomach.[51]

Although the narrator insists that he does not want to kill the girl but only to "destroy [her] sex organs to the point where they cannot be healed,"[52] his desire to keep her "pubic hair [from] climbing any further" suggests a fear of the girl's developing into womanhood, a fear that strongly recalls Kazuo's horrified reaction when Fusako begins to menstruate. Thus, once again the male protagonist's desire to mutilate is also a desire to control nature. The girl's extended stomach suggests pregnancy, another feature of womanhood that is portrayed in a consistently negative manner throughout much of Oe's work, from Yoriko's attempted use of it to entrap Yasuo in *Our Era* to the abnormal "monster" babies produced by the wives in *The Silent Cry* and *A Personal Matter* (*Kojinteki na taiken*).

This threatening aspect of womanhood will be dealt with in the next chapter, but it is important here to note that in the narrator's second dream, the woman is already dead:

> The woman's face was wet with sweat and clumps of her thick tangled hair covered her face, but the bench she was on was the bench of the sauna room and where I was pushing my penis into was a black gourd . . . I was still trying to see that after image while pushing away the screaming pigeons that bumped against me, I tie my belt to the rafters of the shed. The shouting crowd bursts into the playground and there is the sound of my neck breaking with a snap. I feel refreshed as if I had finally accomplished something.[53]

This dream, of course, copies the murder of Miss Iguchi in almost every detail, with the important exception that in waking life it was not the narrator who killed her. That the narrator wishes he could have done so is suggested by the fact that he cannot rid himself of the feeling that his initial dream concerning the junior high school girl had actually happened, with himself in the rapist's role. In fact, at one point in the novel, Tamari accuses the narrator of being Miss Iguchi's murderer. But in the dream at least, the narrator remains only an observer of murder. What, then, has he "accomplished" in his dream? The rape of the corpse is one possibility, but it seems more likely that his relief stems more from his dream suicide, which in turn suggests his fantasy of sacrifice. At the same time, the fact that the narrator even dreams of these events in such explicit detail hints at a basic frustration with his usual inaction.

Even more than in "The Locked Room," however, it is unlikely that the lurking dissatisfaction with dreams will ever cause the narrator to take action because, unlike Kazuo, he has his alter ego Tamari to take action for him. There are hints, however, that the narrator at times feels competitive with Tamari, as illustrated in the scene where they engage in a swimming race, as if the narrator can no longer endure his self-enforced passivity.

In the long run, however, the passive, voyeuristic condition is the only proper role for the narrator as it is for so many of the intellectuals in both writers' works. Although "peeping" (*kaimami*) is an important motif in Japanese erotic literature from the tenth-century *Tales of Ise* to the works of modern writers like Nagai Kafu, it is usually depicted as a means of arousal before engaging in sexual intercourse. The unalloyed voyeurism in Oe's and Mishima's work is of a far more problematic type, having to do with control and power rather than with deriving pleasure from pre-coital excitement. Unlike the scopophilia that is a prelude to an actual erotic encounter, voyeurism in the two writers' work is an end in itself, at best a substitute for the erotic encounter. The narrator of "The Swimming Man" makes no actual move on Miss Iguchi himself, apparently content to serve as a tool to excite Tamari. Kazuo is even more passive since his voyeurism is confined to creations out of his own imagination!

Both authors' textual highlighting of voyeurism is another means of signaling their intellectual protagonists' desire for and inability to control. In all four works, the intellectual protagonist is ultimately powerless. He can ruminate about the world, fantasize about it, and explain it; but all his language and all his intellect cannot change it in the way that a simple violent action can. (An even bleaker twist on voyeurism is Mishima's story "Three Million Yen," where an apparently wholesome young couple performs sex acts for middle-aged women viewers, indicating a society of such aridity that people will pay to watch sex rather than participate in it.)

Oe's work makes that point even more clearly than does Mishima. At least the "locked room" in Mishima's story was a temporary refuge from the outer chaos. In contrast, the sauna room in "The Swimming Man" is itself a wasteland—empty and depraved, where desire is artificially induced through game playing, and where games lead to death in the greater wasteland outside. As the opening page of the novella puts it, "We grow old facing death," which perhaps explains why the narrator is willing to "sacrifice" himself for Tamari; for Tamari, although evil, still seems to have some kind of life force in him, as he grapples with life in both the sauna room and the waters of the swimming pool.

The title of "The Swimming Man" is an ambiguous one since it refers to both the narrator and to Tamari, who are really reflections of each other, meeting finally in the womblike depths of the swimming pool. But the swimming man is also humanity itself in the wasteland of reality, the "destructive element" in which Stein of *Lord Jim* tells Marlow the romantic must immerse himself. Unlike Mishima's character who keeps returning to the locked room of fantasy, Oe's characters know, to their sorrow, that the only escape is down into the world of action rather than in dreams.

3 · Cries in the Wasteland: Sexual Violence

As the works discussed in the previous chapter make clear, Mishima's and Oe's portrayals of sexuality in the real world are far from the romantic evocations of their pastoral novels. *Our Era* and *Confessions* portray sexuality as paralyzing, while in "The Locked Room" and "The Swimming Man" both writers use techniques from mass culture genres—in Mishima's case, the mystery thriller, and in Oe's case, the mystery and the pornographic comic book—to produce works showing sexuality at its most threatening. There is, perhaps, a "romantic" aspect in the contrast between the surreal fantasies in the works and the protagonists's frustrated desire towards these fantasies; certainly it is this tension between fantasy and oppressive reality which animates all four of the narratives.

Obviously, these hallucinatory visions of sex and blood are hardly actions that would be approved of by normal society, but it is significant that even the repressed narrator of "The Swimming Man" feels as if he has "accomplished something" in his dream of murder and suicide. In this chapter we turn from dreams of violence to acts of violence, usually of the sexual sort, actions which do indeed "accomplish something," although for whose benefit is sometimes ambiguous. But it is at least true that, unlike the dreaming intellectuals of the previous works discussed, the protagonists in these novels do indeed immerse themselves within "the destructive element." The works to be discussed in this chapter are among the most confrontational and deliberately provocative of either writers' oeuvre, precisely because they suggest not only that reality is something from which to escape, but that reality should be attacked, and attacked in ways both grotesque and frightening. Only thus, apparently, can one "accomplish something."

SEX BEGETS MURDER: *THIRST FOR LOVE* AND *OUTCRIES*

The first two novels to be considered, Mishima's *Thirst for Love* (*Ai no kawaki*) and Oe's *Outcries* both revolve around sexually inspired murders and contain a number of other important similarities. Both titles, for instance, suggest an intense but unfulfilled desire, not only on the part of their protagonists, but in a general sense. As Mishima himself put it when commenting on his novel, "We live in an age characterized by the search for love".[1] Mishima's title suggests a desire to bring moisture to the barren wasteland, while Oe's title, typically, hints at a more generalized anguish and despair. *Outcries* does involve a definite search, however, the chief protagonist's quest, not for love per se, but to become what he calls "*l'homme authentique.*" Both protagonists are also similar in that their search is a supremely egotistical one and their desires ultimately wreak havoc on those around them.

Takao, the half-Korean, half-Japanese hero of Oe's *Outcries,* is one of the most intensely desiring of Oe's characters, perhaps because he is one of the most quintessential outsiders in Oe's fiction. He is also based on a real person, a Korean youth accused of murder in 1958; and his story has a strongly political element since the Korean minority has been continually discriminated against in modern Japan.

As Matsubara says of him, Takao has been "rejected by the world,"[2] a world which includes his father, his mother, and his fellow countrymen, be they Korean or Japanese. As the ultimate marginal, Takao, not surprisingly, desires to find his own space, which he first tries to do by stealing a small boat and heading out unprotected into the northern seas in an apparent attempt to reach Korea. But Takao is not actually searching for the "real" Korea. Rather, as the novel's sympathetic narrator says about him, "He was looking for a place that was different from this world. Not some abstract world like death or the future, but a place that he could feel was his own, a place that was not on any map, that was somewhere else, some other world."[3]

More than the previous Oe heroes, who are usually hazy in their motivations, Takao is fully aware of his desires; and perhaps for this reason, he is finally able to discover another world through violence.

Unsuccessful in his first search, Takao next joins a band of three other misfits led by an American homosexual named Darius, who plan to build a yacht, to be called *Les Amis,* and sail around the world. The other two members of the group are Tiger, a half-black, half-Japanese teenager, who longs to follow his lost father to Africa, and the unnamed narrator of the story, an orphaned university student with a neurotic fear of syphilis and consequently of sex.

To anyone familiar with Oe's writings, the story of *Les Amis* is a microcosm of some of Oe's most archetypal themes and images. The phantom yacht appears in much later works such as *The Floodwaters Have Come unto My Soul* and *The Women Who Hear the Raintree* (*Reintsuri o kiku onnatachi*), while the yearned-for Africa is a powerful symbol in *A Personal Matter* and *A Silent Cry.* Both images have in common the sense of a private space, beyond the boundaries of the real, worlds of freedom, akin in nature to what the protagonists of *Pluck the Buds, Shoot the Kids* and "Prize Stock" actually found. Like the outcast children of *Pluck the Buds,* all four of the *Outcries* protagonists are "wounded" by society in some way or another, either because of social convention (Japanese society disapproves of mixed race children and does not acknowledge homosexuality), or symbolically, as in the "orphaned," impotent student, another one of Oe's many heroes "abandoned" by his father.

In Oe's use of a group of outcasts, we also see a prefiguring of his more overtly ideological novels, which use a number of heroes to emphasize their political message. Among themselves, the misfits have little in common except that, as Matsubara suggests, they all "share a sense of hatred and hostility toward the world of satisfied normal people."[4] Although I would submit that "despair" is a more appropriate description than "hatred," it is true that the central conflict of *Outcries* is a confrontation between the outcasts' endeavors to create their own worlds or fantasy escapes and what Matsubara calls "the safe real world made up of normal people."[5]

Throughout much of *Outcries,* however, repressive society wins out. *Les Amis* is never built because Darius is expelled from Japan after he is caught soliciting a minor for homosexual activities. (The name of the yacht is itself a poignant reminder of the final uselessness of words: Darius cannot will "friendship" into being on alien soil.) Tiger never makes it to Africa, because, while dressed as an American soldier, an ironic attempt to don the signifiers of one social order to escape the oppressiveness of another, he is caught and killed by some real American MPs. Tiger's death can be read as simply a pathetic effort to return to his American "roots"; but it is also a reminder of the other controlling force in Japan at that period, the American Other, Tiger's imitation of whom only brings about disaster. There is only one character in the novel who ends up more or less accepting reality and that is the narrator, who is finally cured of his impotency by going outside of Japan and having sex with a Greek prostitute. The fact that he has to go outside, however, suggests the oppressiveness of Japanese society in general.

The narrator still regrets "the golden time"[6] when *Les Amis* was being built, and he still keeps in touch with the one member of the group who has tried to impose his alternate vision onto the reality of modern Japan. This is Takao, whose story constitutes the main narrative of *Outcries*, a narrative which once again privileges degraded sexuality and violence. Takao is linked with antisocial sexuality from the start; he is presented to the reader as a chronic masturbator who admits to finding onanism more satisfying than intercourse because women won't "disappear like a puff of smoke."[7] Takao's unwillingness to deal with others is exemplified even further in a bizarre dream that he has his first night with his fellow yacht builders, a dream which he relates in great detail the next morning:

> "First, as to the time and place, it's the middle of a winter night. The rain has stopped and all of Tokyo smells like a wet armpit. Everything around me is dark . . . and in the darkness are four gas tanks that look like monstrous elephant eggs that are expanding and contracting. It seems very real. It's like a place that I've actually seen and actually walked in. And then, out of the dark road comes a girl pushing a bicycle and I, who've been lying in wait having come on a flying saucer from another world, knock her down and perform a ceremony. But at the moment she's knocked down everything gets totally black so we can't even see the whites of each other's eyes. It's as if we were both turned into black caterpillars and it's in that sort of place and in that sort of way that the 'ceremony' takes place."[8]

Naturally, Takao's listeners are confused. "'Did you rape her? Is 'ceremony' some kind of code name for rape?'" one of them asks. But it turns out that Takao does not rape the girl in the dream: "I push down this black girl and the black me takes off my jeans to find that my penis has disappeared and my fingers are touching a live thrush's head." Despite this unexpected turn of events, the dream Takao does not give up:

"I was trying to think, so I raised up my head a little to the black sky and separated my body a little bit from the girl. But when I did that the black girl says to me in a really cold voice, almost as if it were a joke, 'I don't want to see your face. And I won't say anything to the police. Get out of here quickly. Forget all this. This never happened. Nothing ever happened!'

"So I brought my body back to where it had been and I looked for her black throat in this incredible vast darkness, and with the center of my thumbs I crushed it just like that. Then I felt really excited and walked quickly home covered with mud, lifting my nose up to the dark sky inside a black nebula smelling of bubbling blood."[9]

Much of the existentialist symbolism of alienation versus action in this dream is readily understandable; and, in case it is not immediately clear, the text has Takao go on to explain: "In the dream I'm definitely not a being of this world. I'm clearly someone from another, and the instant when I squeezed that girl's throat, I felt as if my personal flying saucer had flashed on its lights."[10]

As Shinohara says, "self-liberation through murder is the novel's overly clear theme,"[11] and it is the overly clear theme of the dream as well. The setting of the dream is the wasteland incarnate where nature, the "monstrous elephant eggs," is degraded into technological products that seem to have a bizarre and uncontrollable life of their own. It is Takao's quest to illuminate this sterile desert through the lights of his flying saucer; but in order to this, he must perform a ritual action. Takao's description of his act as a "ceremony" suggests religious overtones of either initiation rite or sacrifice. If it is initiation, then the dream Takao has crossed the threshold and begun the quest for his identity, his goal of becoming "l'homme authentique."

But it is also an initiation rite into total estrangement from others, as the image of himself and the girls as "black caterpillars" or of himself as a being from a flying saucer both underline. Even more estranging are the words the girl speaks to Takao, words of total denial and annihilation. They are obvious echoes of what the real world has been telling Takao all through his life, and his reaction is thus an entirely logical one. Since he is "clearly someone from another world," he is now allowed to do what he likes, which is to revenge himself on the world that has rejected him.

The notion of revenge links to sacrifice as does the idea of ceremony itself. Of course, the immediate sacrifice is of the murdered girl; but ultimately Takao and his unfortunate comrades are all sacrificed as well, to a society that cannot understand them. They are thus the spiritual descendants of the band of boys in *Pluck the Buds* whose representative runs "into yet deeper darkness" at the end of the novel. The outcast, innocent quality of these protagonists also makes them more sympathetic than the rather self-pitying Yasuo of *Our Era* or the narrator of "The Swimming Man," whose existential despair, although understandable, is less immediately appealing than the plight of the outsider.

Takao's actual murder of a high school girl is, of course, still unforgivable by society's standards. It is also curiously anticlimactic compared to the dream, because most of the textual space is devoted to Takao's intellectual ruminations on why he is committing this deed. Thus, while he stalks the girl on top of a school building he thinks, "If I'm a monster then I want to be a real monster. I'll become a monster and explode."[12] Takao's desire for total fragmentation is actually the same as his desire for his elusive "authenticity," an admission that only an "explosion" of reality, of himself, can paradoxically give him his longed-for unity.

Consequently, as he prepares to murder the girl the words, "THIS KIND OF THING CAN'T REALLY HAPPEN" drum through his head. Up till this point Takao, a would-be intellectual who devours the narrator's collection of Sartre, has not yet crossed the threshold from fantasy into action and is using language as the final barrier against his transformation. As Shinohara says, Oe in this scene is "attempting to create a moment at odds with reality,"[13] a moment when the realistic boundaries waver as the protagonist tries to break through them to become a man of action.

Whether he finally does so is unclear. For example, an uncertainty both within the dream and during the actual crime about whether Takao indeed rapes the girl is suggestive of a sense of impotence on his part so deepseated that only murder can be a satisfactory compensation. There are, however, clues within the text which suggest that at least in his own eyes Takao has fulfilled his quest. Thus, after the murder, he returns to his boarding house and masturbates for the first time in a long while: "The orgasm was the best he had ever experienced, a violent eruption beyond the bounds of anything an onanist could ever have anticipated; he felt for a moment as if everything were in harmony with himself and experienced a sense of liberation."[14]

Though the actual orgasmic moment is, of course, only fleeting, the novel holds out the possibility that Takao's feeling of harmony and liberation may be more permanent. On the one hand, much of the rest of the novel turns to Takao's subsequent encounters with members of the press, whose attempts to analyze his crime disappoint him. He is irritated with the journalists for showing no interest in his existential claims of "monsterhood" and for concentrating instead on the workaday details of the crime, such as whether rape occurred or not and the problem of sentencing. Control and authority, the power to name oneself, are taken out of his hands again. On the other hand, it appears that perhaps his one "moment at odds with reality" has fulfilled him. The reader's last glimpse of him is five years after the crime as he sits in his jail cell, grown fat and apparently placid, waiting patiently for his execution. Rather than embodying an "explosion" into monsterhood, his fatness suggests that he has somehow found autonomy within himself.

Etsuko, the protagonist of Mishima's *Thirst for Love* is also questing for, if not autonomy, then for what one critic calls "self reconstruction."[15] There is some hint that at one point Etsuko, unlike Takao, did have an authentic self. The place where this self existed, however, is not a political or geographical entity (such as the Korea where Takao searches for his) but rather one created by the proximity of death, the hospital room in which she cared for her dying husband. As the novel begins, however, she has been forced out of this place, "rejected by the world" as Matsumoto Tooru puts it.[16] *Thirst for Love* shows Etsuko's attempt to find another place for herself, again through death, but this time the death is murder. Like *Outcries*, *Thirst for Love* is a narrative of vengeance, vengeance on a world that rejects and attempts to destroy her desire.

In this case the world is that of immediate postwar Japan, specifically a country village near Osaka where Etsuko goes to live with her in-laws after her husband's death. Given its time period, the fragmented quality of the household is not surprising. Several generations live and fight within the family over such contemporary problems as money and politics, often in combination. The beautiful country village, then, is not an alternate to urban sterility, as was the pastoral world of *The Sound of Waves*, but in fact has been deeply contaminated by modern society.

Etsuko's house, in particular, is the site of a basic struggle between opposing forces, life and death, nature and artifice, natural desire and degraded desire, with Etsuko as the central pivot around which these contradictions sweep. Etsuko herself embodies both sides of the conflict. On the one hand, she, like Takao, embodies passionate desire, desire far stronger than that felt by such previous characters as Kazuo or the narrator of "The Swimming Man." In this regard she is a more "romantic" character than the fashionably nihilistic antiheroes discussed previously. But Etsuko's desire, although strong, is far from the natural and spontaneous excitement of *The Sound of Waves*. Although she is no intellectual of Takao's rationalizing and abstracting stamp, she is still obsessed with control. Consequently, when she responds to the images of life surrounding her in the village and encapsulated by Saburo, the young farm boy she falls in love with, she is unable to lose herself in them. Instead she must control them and, for her, such control inevitably leads to death.

At first, however, Etsuko appears a strangely passive figure. Orphaned by her father, widowed by her philanderer husband, she buries herself in the country only to passively acquiesce in becoming her father-in-law's mistress. Mishima explains this acquiescence by saying that "[n]ot thinking of things was the basis of her contentment" and that she found "[i]n the emptiness of her hopes, the purest of meanings";[17] but it is also possible to see a pattern of seeking refuge and identity in the nearest male presence, a natural pattern, given the position of most Japanese women. Unlike the typical passive woman, however, Etsuko ultimately does think and does hope, to the point of developing a passionate but futile attachment to Saburo, the farm boy whom she eventually murders.

Etsuko's passionate and fatal love for Saburo makes her seem very much the quintessential romantic hero, the real object of whose desire is death. For, despite her often expressed passion for Saburo, it is obvious that she is deeply uncomfortable with him and his rough innocence, which represents a kind of primitive life force. As textual flashbacks indicate, Etsuko was at her happiest when she was obsessively nursing her typhoid-stricken husband. Taking command of the situation entirely, Etsuko moved into her husband's hospital room, where even his former lovers refuse to visit (for fear of infection), and created an "island for two."[18]

In many ways this "island for two" is the equivalent of Takao's "place that was not on any map," an impossible world not open to anyone else and bounded by death. But Etsuko is luckier than Takao. She actually creates this place within the "real" world. Her feverish ministering to her husband "was almost enough to make an onlooker avert his eyes;"[19] and amid "the incontinence, blood, excrement and horrible odors," "happiness reigned."[20] The text even explicitly calls this grotesque situation "life to the full";[21] but it is a life that is necessarily transient, its intensity close to that of sexual pleasure. In fact an earlier passage compares her husband's dying to their honeymoon: "There was in this trip, as in their wedding journey, the same abuse of body and soul, the same untiring insatiable desire and pain."[22]

This "insatiable desire" is resurrected when Etsuko falls in love with Saburo, whose abundant life presence stirs Etsuko out of her lethargy and seals his fate, as is clear from their first encounter which is studded with images of both flowers and graves. The text shows Etsuko in a cemetery walking down "her favorite path" and gathering herbs when she notices a boy reading a comic book:

> It was Saburo. He felt her shadow as it hovered over him and sat up.
> "Mrs. Sugimoto," he said. At that moment all the starwort and horsetail fell from her sleeve onto his face.[23]

This scene is especially significant in light of a flashback that occurs several pages later in which her husband's funeral is described:

> The sunlight struck the casket and then Etsuko with the force of a cataract.
> In her lap her hands toyed with a bouquet of autumn flowers . . . The front of her mourning dress was sprinkled with yellow pollen.[24]

Once again the imagery is of Etsuko, the grave, and flowers; but here Etsuko's husband is dead, while Saburo in the previous scene is still very much alive. And yet, "He felt her shadow as it hovered over him." For Etsuko to return to life (to self-reconstruct) and regain the sense of control and liberation she had felt at her husband's death, she must find another object of passionate attachment and this object, too, must ultimately die. In many ways a brother of the hero of *The Sound of Waves*, the handsome, simple, and inarticulate Saburo is the doomed reincarnation of Utajima in the gardens of suburban Osaka. It is not surprising that within the reality of postwar Japan he must be sacrificed.

Thus, Saburo's death, like that of the unknown high school girl in *Outcries*, is foreshadowed from the beginning of the novel; and the rest of the story, also like *Outcries*, consists of the stages Etsuko goes through on the way to murder. Although, unlike Takao, she does not have an actual dream of murder, Etsuko does undergo an experience which approaches the dreamlike in its hallucinatory intensity and also foreshadows the actual murder.

This occurs during the village festival, always an important metaphor in Mishima's work for untrammeled intensity and barely concealed masculine sexuality. In this case, the scene is the emotional
and imagistic climax of the novel. Etsuko at first appears merely as
a spectator above the festival scene, which, "viewed from the top of
the stone steps of the sanctuary, seemed like the form of a great
dusky snake, writhing about the flaming poles, throwing off phos-
phorescence in all directions." Significantly, Saburo, who emblemizes
the masculine life force, is down among all the phallic shapes with
their obvious connotations of virile masculinity. Even more significantly, and more ominously for Saburo, Etsuko sees in the light from
the festival "the profusion of November sunshine that fell on her like
an avalanche as they opened the door to carry out her husband's
coffin."[25]

As Etsuko descends into the festival to look for Saburo, the scene
becomes increasingly savage and fantastic. A lion's head goes by, "its
mane streaming ... its golden teeth exposed." Then, "something
dazzling cut across Etsuko's line of vision. It was a band of half naked
young men moving as one in the glare of the flame ... Emitting
animal-like shouts, they churned past Etsuko ..."[26] The excitement
of the festival overwhelms Etsuko and she is caught up in the same
masculine life force symbolized by the procession of young men:
"Something inside her seemed to stand forth out of a vague, mushy
quagmire and to flash forward with almost herculean physical
power." And, at the end, "Etsuko now felt she could do anything."[27]

Having incorporated a variety of masculine signifiers, Etsuko is
suddenly confronted by Saburo's bare back which she "longs to
throw herself into" in a moment fraught with sexual tension and suppressed violence. But, as the text goes on to emphasize, this does not
mean that she wishes death for herself. Rather, her desire is "close to
that of the person who drowns himself, he does not necessarily covet
death so much as what comes after the drowning, something different from what he had before, at the least a different world."

Like Takao, Etsuko longs for a "different world," the equivalent of
her own "personal flying saucer," and she is determined to obtain it.
The festival scene grows even more fantastic as Etsuko stumbles forward and rips her fingernails into Saburo's back. At the same time,
Mishima describes the group of young men jostling each other
around a "brightly blazing bamboo pole," while Etsuko watches
them transfixed, Saburo's blood dripping from her hands. In a final

hallucinatory moment Etsuko sees "a woman with her hair on fire, laughing loudly," and then remembers nothing more.[28]

Although the Freudian implications of this spectacular scene are obvious, they are worth working through, especially in contrast to Takao's dream. In Takao's dream all is black, he is impotent, although surrounded by images of grotesque fertility, and his victim rejects him, casting him out of any potential unity one last time. In contrast, Etsuko's hallucinatory encounter is an obvious metaphor for successful sexual action from the moment "something inside her . . . flashed forward" and she sinks her nails into Saburo's skin. Far from being impotent, the violence of Etsuko's encounter goes along with her sexuality, rather than being an attempt to compensate for it. Furthermore, Etsuko has in some ways been transformed into a male figure; it is she who is in control, symbolically raping Saburo. Very different from the frustrated intellectual hero of *Confessions of a Mask* who wants so desperately to be the other for whom he longs but who is ultimately "torn asunder" between the intellect and the body, the unintellectual Etsuko is able to go seamlessly from desire into action to satisfy that desire.

The festival is clearly the antithesis of the real world in its dreamlike vividness and in the "meaningless shouts" of the young men who, in their drunkenness, have gone beyond the symbolic order back to a world of pure instinctive feeling. Significantly, it is at the end of the festival that the family learns that their maid Miyo is pregnant by Saburo and the couple's ensuing natural and pleasurable sexual relationship stands in implicit contrast to Etsuko's increasingly warped desires.

Compared to the emotional and imagistic intensity of the festival scene, the actual murder of Saburo is as anticlimactic as the murder scene in *Outcries*. Etsuko confronts Saburo at midnight in the grape arbor and bullies him into saying he loves her. Whereupon, dissatisfied at the realization of her longed for dream, she ends up killing him with a mattock. As Takao's dream foreshadowed the manner of his crime so, in many ways, is Saburo's death simply a subdued repeat of the festival scene. The sexual frenzy still exists, but it is now frustrated by the very nearness of the other, so Saburo's back is pierced by a mattock rather than fingernails.

Etsuko initially tries to win Saburo with words, but his inability to understand her and his fumbling lies only make her more angry. This genuine emotion helps reproduce the conditions of the festival and Etsuko enacts a satisfying moment of violence and eroticism without thought. She knows instinctively what Takao learns only after much intellectual trial and error, that action is the one way to achieve a successful vengeance on the world that has rejected one. The unfortunate Saburo is not aware that his hypocritical avowal of love, forced on him by Etsuko herself, is simply a superior form of rejection, showing Etsuko too clearly the impossibility of her desire. But, after the murder, Etsuko sleeps a sleep that comes upon her "like divine favor,"29 reminiscent of Takao's "ultimate" orgasm after his crime.

Etsuko and Takao have a number of other key features in common as well. First and most important, they are both supremely egotistical. Takao, in his single-minded drive to become "l'homme authentique," never shows the slightest guilt or even awareness that in order to accomplish this he has destroyed an innocent life. Rather, he rationalizes to himself that "this can't be happening," refusing to accept the real in his impassioned pursuit of the imaginary.

As for Etsuko, the text makes brutally clear that Saburo is an Other who is simply an object. Thus, when asked why she has killed him, she merely replies,

> "He was making me suffer, that's why."
> "But it wasn't his fault."
> "Not his fault? That's not so. He got what he deserved for hurting me. Nobody has the right to cause me pain. Nobody can get away with that."
> "Who is to say that they can't?"
> "I say so and what I say no one can change."
> "You're a terrifying woman."30

Both Etsuko and Takao are terrifying people in their unrelenting determination to control the world through violence and through self-deluding language, as evidenced by Takao's specious attempts to rationalize his "monsterhood" and Etsuko's final declaration that "I say so and what I say no one can change," like some archetypal romantic artist who declares his solipsistic portrait of the world to be the only correct one. In fact, it is not their language that has changed the world, it is their actions. At heart Etsuko knows this, as is clear in an earlier passage when she listens to her tediously intellectual brother-in-law's spiteful and empty conversation with his wife:

> *Yakichi is chattering, Kensuke is chattering, Chieko is chattering—how useless words are! What petty craft, what futility . . . No one's words can compete*

with this mercilessly powerful rain. The only thing that can compete with the sound of this rain, that can smash this deathlike wall of sound, is the shout of a man who refuses to stoop to this chatter, the sound of a simple spirit that knows no words. Etsuko recalled the mass of rose-color naked figures running before her in the flaming poles, and the sound of their shouting, like the cries of slippery young animals. *Only that shout. That's all that's needed.*[31]

Oe's *Outcries* also highlights the shout, the *sakebigoe* that will cut through the suffocating atmosphere of a reality that rejects and destroys; but the novel's outcries are also shouts of despair, from the cries of Takao as he dreams of rape and murder to the intellectual "shouts" that the narrator begins the novel with: "According to a French philosopher who had lived through an age full of fear, all humans who live in an age of fear waiting for a salvation that comes too late will think, upon hearing far away, the raised voice of someone seeking salvation, that it is their own voice raised in outcry and will doubt their own ears."[32]

Oe's narrator continues on with a description of one such "outcry" he has heard; but in fact the book itself is simply a sustained shout into the darkness where, perhaps, a flying saucer awaits. Etsuko's longed-for "shout" is also into the darkness, searching for the fires that will ignite her life again. Etsuko is both luckier and unluckier than Tadao. She almost obtains the supposed object of her desire, Saburo, only to understand instinctively that her desire is predicated paradoxically on the inaccessibility of the loved object, combined with her ability to control it. In the "island intimacy" of her husband's death she could control all factors and thus "happiness reigned." Unable to control Saburo, whose life force ultimately threatens to overwhelm her, she takes the forceful action of murder with a mattock.

In the case of Takao's murder, the "object" of his desire, the young high school girl, is so obviously a substitution for a whole host of others—his mother, his flying saucer, his mythical Korean homeland leading back to the imaginary—that the text can afford to render the girl herself as totally anonymous. However, the faceless anonymity of the victim makes *Outcries* a far more despairing novel than the infinitely more colorful and romantic *Thirst for Love*. The salvation offered by Takao's flying saucer, moreover, is a sterile one, a surreal light on a world of mud and darkness suggesting no real fecundity, no genuine alternative to the mud of reality, smelling of blood, that

Takao makes his way through as he returns home from the murder. Oe touches on the device of the murder mystery in Takao's stalking of the girl; but even his protagonist knows that "THIS KIND OF THING CAN'T REALLY HAPPEN," and the sacrifice of the girl owes more to French existential preoccupations than to either romance or modern mass culture. In contrast, Saburo may be an artistic cliché but his metaphoric associations with life, growth, and fertility help to suggest that his sacrifice is a way of invigorating the wasteland of the real, even if it is a way that society can not accept.

THE INTELLECTUAL TAKES ACTION:
MADAME DE SADE AND *THE SEXUAL HUMAN*

Oe's ultimate message in *Outcries* may be despairing, but it should be remembered that his protagonist does seem to have obtained a measure of real-world satisfaction through his violent act. This is even more true of Mishima's protagonist. On a personal, temporary level at least, the two have escaped the real world, even revenged themselves on it. In the next two works to be examined, Mishima's play *Madame de Sade* (*Sado kōshaku fujin*) and Oe's novel *The Sexual Human*, the protagonists fulfill themselves through a combination of the intellectual and active forms of sexual violence and perversion. In this regard they are among the most consistently successful of either author's protagonists, at the same time as being the two most likely to be condemned by society. Unlike Etsuko or Takao they have not even been rejected by the world. Rather, they choose to reject the world and create their own, and it is this conscious and unforced choosing on their part which makes them so controversial.

This is especially true of Mishima's play *Madame de Sade*, which highlights an historical figure notorious for his ability to shock the world both through action—his infamous acts of perversion and violence—and through thought—the philosophy which he developed and turned into literature based on his perverse actions.

Written in 1965, it was successfully performed onstage and has been revived several times since. In his introduction to it, Mishima insists that he wrote *Madame de Sade* in order to elucidate the "riddle" of why the Marquise de Sade ultimately rejected her husband after years of devotion to him while he was in prison. In fact, however, the play is more readily understood as an apologia for sadomasochism, perhaps even for the particular aesthetic brand of sadomasochism that Mishima himself seemed to espouse in his works. It is also, like *Confessions of a Mask*, a gauntlet thrown down towards the public, daring them not to be moved or at least impressed by the many flowery passages devoted to de Sade's strange practices.

With the possible exception of the courtesan, Madame de Saint-Fond, the text has no rational or real-world figure to offset the play's lush romanticism; but the text does use the women figures around de Sade as mouthpieces to rationalize his gory world. These women characters with whom de Sade has dallied speak glowingly of the "blood soaked memories"[33] that animated their love making. Whether viewers or readers of the play are likely to be convinced by this probably depends on their predisposition to the Mishima style of aesthetic romanticism; but there can be no denying the lushness of the language nor the sheer shock value involved in making de Sade into a romantic hero, as well as a lauded philosopher of the erotic, about whom his wife can say, "This world we are now living in is now a world created by the Marquis de Sade."[34]

The Marquise portrays her husband as the ultimate romantic, someone who "has always been seeking an impossibility";[35] but he is also an apparently successful romantic for, again according to his wife, he has been able to create an "imperishable cathedral of vice," a back stairway to heaven."[36] Of course, de Sade's "back stairway" cannot be appreciated by conventional people who "know nothing of the nights when holiness and shame imperceptibly switch appearances."[37] Unlike Takao who was simply satisfied to "become a monster and explode," de Sade, a "monster of immorality,"[38] by the very scope and depth of his transgressions fragments all boundaries, exploding the world of socially imposed names and images to offer a glimpse of liberating sexual anarchy. Or is it really anarchy?

Considered as an attempt to *épater la bourgeoisie, Madame de Sade* is certainly successful in its no-holds-barred celebration of degraded sexuality. It is also perhaps the fullest exposition of Mishima's own erotic philosophy in fictional form, although it should also be emphasized that the play is quite faithful to de Sade's philosophy as put forth in his writings, in themselves an attempt to create "a sexual world." As Tanner following Barthes makes clear in discussing the historical de Sade, this world is the ultimate non-place that mocks the real by the very formality and complexity of its debauched codes.[39] Both de Sade's own writings and *Madame de Sade* are carefully worked out assaults on the bourgeois system itself, presenting a brilliantly constructed alternative vision. As it follows de Sade, it is clear that Mishima's "message" is that, for a particular elite, a sexual world made of intellect and action in combination can be possible. The play's end, however, indicates that such a world is possible mainly in fiction.

Thus, the last words on de Sade's world are spoken by his wife and these last words tend to undercut all the encomiums she has given previously. For Madame de Sade does indeed reject her husband and everything that he has stood for, everything she has defended; and the audience is left with the riddle of why she chooses to do so. There are many possible explanations for this rejection, the simplest being that de Sade has become, for his wife, her own version of the impossible romantic quest. Consequently, his approaching liberation from prison causes him to lose his appeal. But the play makes clear that Madame de Sade is particularly incensed that the Marquis has written a book in which his exploits with and without her are described.

Discovering that she has been "locked up in the pages of novel," she finds that "our whole lives and all our suffering have ended in wasted effort."[40] The Marquis, the quintessential man of action who yet has a probing intellect, has performed the ultimate treason: he has turned his back on action, which, Mishima makes clear, is the one true road of escape, and has instead sold out to the symbolic order, the world of language. The "back stairway to heaven" has been inscribed into a book, into the world of language where the intellectual Marquis is the only one in control.

Up to this point, his wife had believed that by indulging in his perversions she had helped to manipulate him and together they had shattered the conventional world. Now, faced with the fact that her husband has been in the last analysis a manipulative voyeur all along (as she herself once admits, "Alphonse is obsessed with seeing"),[41] she can no longer face the real world. It is hardly surprising that she turns to the church at the end of the play in search of her own "back stairway."

Mishima's play is thus a nihilistic one on many fronts. On the one hand, it sets up a realm of the imaginary, romanticizing a sadomasochistic hero in eighteenth-century French finery, as an implicit contrast to the "real world" of Japan in 1965. It also privileges an elite and abnormal sexuality that only aristocrats are apparently privy to. But as Madame de Sade's final rejection of her husband makes clear, even in the doubly artificial world of a stage set purporting to be France, true satisfaction is possible only through inscribing the self into language.

Only Etsuko, of Mishima's protagonists thus far, has actually managed to break out of the real world, and then only for a moment. J, the hero of Oe's *The Sexual Human*, seems to stand between de Sade and Etsuko in his intellectual attempts to create a sexual world and his final realization that action is the only way to achieve true escape.

Very different in tone and style from *Madame de Sade*, *The Sexual Human* still features a protagonist who combines intellect and action into a particularly bizarre form of sexuality that, like de Sade's, is a brutal assault on the conventional sensibilities of society. Unlike *Madame de Sade*, however, with its elite escapist world of echoing French chateaus, J's frontal assault takes place firmly within the wasteland of postwar Japan itself.

Indeed, more than in most of Oe's novels, the wasteland of *The Sexual Human* is a particularly far-reaching one, extending from the urban depths even out to the country, a region traditionally associated in Oe's novels with liberation and life. The narrative beings with a memorable portrait of a seaside village that is a classic wasteland in the *Golden Bough* tradition, as Yamanouchi points out,[42] a fishing village where no fish are being caught. Into this infertile place drive J and his friends, wealthy dissolute young people complete with Jaguar sports car, who hole up in a seaside villa to make a pornographic movie set in Hell. Like de Sade, then, J is setting himself to be a master of degraded sexuality, hoping to construct what he himself calls a "sexual world,"[43] through his filmmaking and other activities.

The film is never made, however. A village child spies on a couple's lovemaking and rushes away, screaming "I've seen devils," bursting through a glass door as he does so. The incident incenses the villagers, who, blaming their lack of fish catch on the decadent film makers, force them out of town. The film project collapses and J must look for a new way to create a sexual world.

In the novel's second half, J begins an initially solitary career of perversion. Like de Sade, he has been accused of infernal practices; and like de Sade, he proceeds to prove his accusers correct. Unlike Mishima's remote and romantic hero, however, J wreaks his sexual desires in a quintessentially modern, even quintessentially modern Japanese form: he becomes a *chikan*, a word that simply means "pervert" but in this context refers to men who ride the crowded commuter trains in search of women with whom they engage in anonymous and usually unwanted sexual practices in the relative security of the crowded cars.

The "train pervert" is a brilliant encapsulation of the anomie of modern Japanese life. It is a perversion that could not exist without modern technology and an industrial system that crowds workers onto the trains at rush hours, while the utter sterility of the sexual practices described is in its own way almost as disturbing as anything hinted at in de Sade's sexual world. But the novels' most brilliant stroke is that even within this circular ride to nowhere the quest for love still exists.

Thus, the text describes J's first sexual encounter on a train in a way that suggests both its emptiness and the need which precipitates the encounter. The tension of the moment, the fear/hope that the woman he is touching might cry out, gives J an intense feeling of excitement. This feeling is only momentary, however, for he finds to his dismay that the woman not only permits his caresses but actually appears to want them. "Then J was freed from his fears but at the same time *desire left him* [my italics] . . . he thought coldly, 'It's always this way. They'll let you do anything.'"[44]

In an atmosphere where "they'll let you do anything" echoes the "infernal" (actually banal) sexual coupling that went on with his film group, J can find no real satisfaction. The ultimate horror of the postwar world is that even perversion is no longer shocking. Unlike de Sade, safe in a world where Catholicism can condemn his practices as evil, J cannot find enough obstacles to make sexual desire meaningful. But another desire takes its place, the desire for emotional connection. Perhaps because J finally "felt on the fingertips of his two hands the unknown woman's lonely orgasm," a new form of connection has been made; and "[a]lthough it might seem odd, J spent several weeks thereafter, keeping watch at the same time at dusk feeling that, if he could ever see the woman again, he would entreat her to marry him and spend the rest of her life with him."[45]

This perhaps most naked evocation of desire in any Oe novel, is never fulfilled, for J never meets the woman again. He does, however, achieve a bizarre form of connection by becoming friends with two fellow train perverts. It is in this grotesque little community which they style a "perverts' club" (*chikan kurabu*) that J feels accepted and secure in a way which he never achieves in the outside world. The notion of a club recalls the "Club of the Covenant" of Mishima's

"Locked Room" but with the difference that these perverts are more than simply figments of the protagonist's imagination. Indeed, the youngest member of the club wants to give it legitimacy within society by writing an epic poem about the club; and although this is partly a sign of Oe's black humor, it is also similar to de Sade's inscribing his activities into the symbolic order. But J understands that the club must forever exist outside society. This is made clear when his father persuades him to come back to normality by accepting a job in the corporate world and he agrees, only to break his word and go back to the haven of the trains one last time.

This time J is caught and led away, but the reader's last glimpse of him suggests that he is somehow fulfilled as he walks out of the station handcuffed to two policeman, weeping "tears of joy." Although J is less unambiguously "innocent" than the young men of *Pluck the Buds,* the final "message" of *The Sexual Human* is not so different from that more overtly ideological novel. J, like the hero of *Pluck the Buds,* has lost his comrades and is no longer a member of society; but in this case, as the last pages make very clear, it is his choice to reject the world and the word of his father. Even more than Takao, he has for a brief time achieved his place not on any map but, most subversively, within the heart of modern society itself. Incidentally, this final scene impressed Mishima greatly. It is perhaps significant that Mishima's quintessential antihero de Sade was also captured and imprisoned by the authorities and remained happily unrepentant throughout.

Whether Mishima's de Sade makes any kind of emotional connection through his perverse practices is more open to question since at the end even his devoted wife rejects him. Of course, it can be argued that de Sade is questing for an absolute rather than for love as J seems to be, but there can be no denying that both protagonists are extremely conscious of others and of justifying themselves in the eyes of others. These are not simply outsiders but outsiders determined to trumpet the fact, to glory in their "devilhood."

Both also attempt to create an outsider's alternative within the real world, a non-place where a little community of like-minded deviants can exist, although J is in some ways more subversive than Mishima's hero. J's non-place, the constantly moving trains, strikes at the heart of modern Japan by appropriating one of its symbols of industrial success as its own. In contrast, Mishima's non-world is safely removed from Japanese reality. Oe's narrative, although never conventionally romantic, certainly has its surreally intense moments but they achieve that intensity precisely because they are grounded so firmly in the bleak reality of contemporary Japan.

AFFIRMATIVE VISIONS: *A PERSONAL MATTER* AND "PATRIOTISM"

Up to this point, I have dealt more with sexual issues than emotional ones because Mishima's and Oe's works depict more sex than feeling. This is due to two major factors. First, although there are, in fact, certain very strong emotions described, they are usually the negative and solitary ones of fear, longing, and despair. The texts implicitly claim that the real world is not a place where positive emotions and normal desires thrive. Thus, although all the protagonists discussed have shown a strong awareness of others, the authors seldom portray those others (especially the women) in three dimensions.[46] Indeed, the relative objectification of women is the second major factor behind the lack of emotions in these works. The only exception in the above examples, besides Etsuko, obviously is Mishima's Sonoko in *Confessions of a Mask;* and her very three dimensionality becomes a torment to the mask who cannot love her. As for Oe's works, the protagonists' typical attitude is summed up in Takao's preference for onanism because a real woman won't "disappear like a puff of smoke" when one is finished.

I should like to end my discussion of sexual violence by examining two works in which, despite their violent subtext, an emotional connection between sexual partners is achieved; I shall then discuss more generally the role of women in both writers' works. The two works are among the most brilliant and well known by either writer, Oe's *A Personal Matter* (*Kojinteki na taiken*) and Mishima's "Patriotism." Although very different from each other, both works are notable in describing basically positive heterosexual relationships occurring within violent contexts. As such, they shed light both on each author's depictions of violence and on what sort of woman the authors tend to present as an ideal.

The marriage of Lieutenant Takeyama and his wife Reiko in "Patriotism," depicted within a claustrophobic setting of death, duty, and intense sexuality, seems to be a portrayal of what Mishima would consider a perfect heterosexual relationship. The story, a love suicide for ostensibly "patriotic reasons," might be called an erotic ideological narrative since it puts forth both its erotic "message" and its political "message" in its strongest and clearest terms. The political message will be examined more closely in Chapter Five but in the context of this chapter it is useful to see what Mishima posits as the ideal erotic encounter.

As is typical in Mishima's ouevre (*Spring Snow* and *The Sailor Who Fell from Grace with the Sea* being other prime examples), three elements can be seen to be key here: beauty, youth, and death. In "Patriotism" there is the added element of politically sanctioned death, signified in the couple's samurai-style ritual suicide. Lieutenant Takeyama is the classic Mishima romantic hero: strapping, handsome, unintellectual but keenly aware of his duty to the "Imperial Forces" which he feels can be fulfilled only through suicide. It is he, even more than de Sade who "deserves" sexual fulfillment, in Mishima's elitist erotic vision. Thus, before their death, he and his wife make love one last time; and this scene, lasting almost half the narrative's length, is one of the most powerful ever written by Mishima. The intensity, of course, is related to the couple's awareness of the imminence of death, the ultimate fulfillment, of which the couple's erotic encounter is only a foreshadowing.

Reiko, the perfect traditional wife, makes no effort to argue with her husband's plans for suicide. Beautiful, calm, and totally subservient to her husband's wishes, she yet possesses a strong will of her own which carries her through the terrible process of watching her husband disembowel himself. Even in lovemaking, Reiko is perfectly obedient, desisting immediately when her husband decides that "it is time." But she is also willing to enjoy herself, even requesting permission to look at the husband's body in a scene of exquisite erotic detail, although, as is typical of Mishima's death-centered vision, her gaze lingers on her husband's "youthful firm stomach . . . soon to be cruelly cut by the sword."[47]

Reiko's pleasure is, of course, under her husband's control but it is clear that she is fulfilled. The text cuts short the actual erotic encounter, preferring to suggest that "what ecstasies they explored after these tender exchanges may well be imagined."[48] But even with its emphasis on preliminaries, this scene is the most erotic one Mishima ever wrote, managing to demonstrate the lovers' passion without descending into either overripeness or pornography.

"Patriotism" succeeds beautifully in getting across its implicit "message" on what constitutes erotic satisfaction: the combination of immediate sensory pleasure and the sweet presentiment of death.

These, set within the ideologically fulfilling framework of serving the emperor, make a virtually complete expression of Mishima's ideal erotic vision. Although "Patriotism" tries for realism by grounding the double suicide in the famous incident of February 26, 1936, when a group of young officers attempted the "Showa Restoration," the story is in many ways as romantic as Mishima's later, more overtly romantic *Spring Snow.*

Isolated from the real world in their little house, the couple locks out reality as effectively as Kiriko's key helped to protect the "crystal chaos" of the locked room in Mishima's earlier story. Indeed the characters themselves are classic exemplars of Frye's classification of the hero of romance or even myth, as superior in degree to a mere mortal.[49] This is not only elitist sexuality, it is also a highly unreal sexuality, as is apparent from the fact that not only the woman, but even the hero Takeyama is morcellized into a series of physical parts centering on his "youthful firm stomach." Obviously there is a touch of the homoerotic in that description, but it is also clear that the degree of these characters' sensual satisfaction is almost directly related to their two-dimensionality. Reiko and Takeyama are types, exemplars of an aesthetic and sensual realm unreachable by more fully realized characters. As should now be clear, intellectual characters in Mishima are very unlikely to find sexual fulfillment.

This is also usually the case in Oe's work, where intellectuals are typically doomed to perverse sexuality at best or impotence at worst. An important exception to this despairing pattern, however, is his 1964 novel *A Personal Matter,* in which a passive young intellectual becomes, if not a man of action, at least a responsible human being, largely through the medium of sex. *A Personal Matter* is an extraordinarily powerful work, at once brutally realistic, while at the same time revealing an archetypal mythic underpinning, framing a young man's initiation into manhood and into acceptance of the social order. In some respects the work is highly autobiographical, functioning as a sort of "coming of age" for Oe; but knowledge of the author's life is unnecessary to appreciate this powerful and often grotesquely funny portrait of a young man's journey through his own personal wasteland.

Bird, the young man in question, is very much the symbolic heir of Yasuo in *Our Era,* suffocating within a loveless relationship and afflicted with the usual lack of sexual desire. Like Yasuo, Bird desires escape to Africa, but he does not even allow himself the luxury of dreaming of "heroic battles" there. His plan is to write a book. Perhaps Bird's dreams are less grandiose because they have even less chance of coming true. He is already trapped in a loveless marriage with a child just about to be born. *A Personal Matter* is the narrative of Bird's flight from the reality represented by his wife, his dreary job, and the new baby who turns out to be abnormal, through an alternative to that reality made up of sex and violence, and back to reality again, not as a committed criminal but rather as one who has accepted his place within the social order.

His partner in his road to self-discovery is a former girl friend named Himiko, not only one of Oe's most memorable female creations but also one of the most three-dimensional and interesting female characters in all of postwar Japanese fiction. The relationship between Bird and Himiko is the closest thing to a love story in Oe's fiction. Bird turns to Himiko when his child is born with severe brain damage and he must decide whether to operate on it, let it die gradually, or have it killed. After a series of surrealistically horrific encounters with doctors who, as in Abe Kobo's novels, are crudely unsympathetic, if not actually murderous themselves, Bird leaves his wife in the hospital and calls Himiko. Taking refuge in her small dark apartment (ironically evocative of the womb), Bird and Himiko engage in a graphically described sexual marathon involving an apparently painful act of sodomy which Himiko herself suggests.

The sexual marathon occurs at the psychologically and symbolically lowest point of Bird's quest. Hiding in the dark room, engaging in what he himself calls "malefic sex," a "fuck rife with ignominy,"[50] he has symbolically descended into Hell where he must grapple his worst fears, "the vagina and the womb,"[51] as Himiko succinctly points out when suggesting sodomy instead of normal intercourse. Up till this point Bird had been impotent, destroyed by the knowledge of what sex with his wife had produced. But Bird is not really afraid of only the vagina and womb. Like so many of the protagonists discussed in this chapter, he is afraid of the life and nature they represent. The act of sodomy enables him to enact these fears in a violent, cathartic manner, symbolically murdering the woman without actually admitting the desire to "rip" her that Kazuo entertained.

Sodomy is also a form of control, indeed dominance, and in this case the object of dominance is clearly woman in all her forms. It is women in their socially sanctioned form of wife and mother-in-law who have oppressed Bird, forcing him to give up his dream of Africa and take a job that he loathes, so that he can prepare himself for the dreary responsibilities of parenthood. But it is woman in her sexually submissive role who offers the potential for refuge and even cure.

Sex with Himiko, then, becomes far more than an escape or even a compensation. Rather it is a full-fledged attack on Woman who in turn represents the suffocations of society. As Bird thinks during the act, "I'm trampling a woman now in the most ignominious way."[52] There may also be an element of self-loathing in this form of intercourse but, unlike autoeroticism, the act is fundamentally other-directed. Unlike the lonely, anonymous sex of J and his accomplices or the suffocating tedium of Yasuo's conventional sexual relationship with Yoriko, Bird's violent domination of Himiko paradoxically brings them closer together. The fact that afterwards Himiko is totally and calmly accepting of what Bird has done to her is perhaps even more helpful in giving him a sense of freedom and "peace"[53] than the sodomy itself.

From deviant sex, Bird and Himiko progress to normal sex; and, after Himiko reaches orgasm, they lie together in total contentment:

> Bird felt like a rooster watching over a chick. Smelling the healthy odor of sweat that rose from the head half hidden beneath his chest, he lay perfectly still, supporting his weight on his elbows lest he oppress the girl beneath him. He was still terrifically aroused, but he didn't want to interrupt Himiko's natural sleep. Bird had banished the curse on anything feminine that had occupied his brain a few hours ago, and though she was more womanly than ever, he was able to accept Himiko completely.[54]

This passage is remarkable in Oe's fiction for its humanity and normality. In contrast to the despair-ridden copulations of *Our Era* from which, after they are over, Yasuo shrinks with horrified self-loathing, the notion of Bird's enjoying the "healthy smell of sweat" shows how far he has progressed away from his original spiritual brotherhood. Even more unusual is the consideration Bird shows for Himiko, not wishing to awaken her even though he is still "terrifically aroused." Through the very intensity of their sexual experience, Bird and Himiko have gone beyond the purely sexual to a state which, if not love, is at least one of the most positive sexual relationships in any of Oe's writing.

From a Western feminist perspective, however, the role of Himiko remains problematic. Compared to Reiko's total subservience to her husband, the relationship between Bird and Himiko appears at first glance to be quite liberated. Himiko's freewheeling lifestyle (she has many lovers besides Bird), the openness of the language which the two use together, and the actual sex act they perform all seem to have a definite postwar tinge to them. Yet is Himiko herself really so liberated? True, she drives an MG sports car through the night in search of the perfect orgasm, and it is she who suggests to Bird that they try sodomy. Indeed her spontaneity about sex and life in general are what eventually galvanize the passive, impotent Bird into taking action. But in the final analysis, Himiko's role is a submissive one. She is, for much of the narrative, an all-accepting "earth mother" figure, sacrificing herself for the man's good. While Mishima's character proved his identity through the sexual domination of his wife and then his subsequent violence towards himself, Oe's character forges a new identity through the sacrifice of Himiko.

In the literatures of modernizing countries, including the West, women characters have frequently been the vessels through which male characters work out their fears and desires.[55] Thus, Reiko's utter subservience, although possibly accurate for 1936, is particularly emphasized in "Patriotism" precisely because the world in which Mishima was writing had come a long way from 1936. Reiko's beauty, highlighted by her traditional garb, her obedience, and above all her traditionally submissive character, signify a world of lost calm and security where relationships were defined and control was firmly in the hands of a virile male. On a more diffuse level, Himiko's caretaking attitude and her womblike little apartment offer refuge for a male adrift in the atomizing sea of modernity.

Unlike Mishima's work, however, *A Personal Matter* does allow Himiko a non-refuge role as well. In fact, after he abandons her to return to his wife and baby, she ends up taking from Bird the mantle of romantic hero with impossible but burning desire. It is Himiko who refuses to give in to reality and who will make the longed-for voyage to Africa, thus becoming the genuinely active hero of the novel.[56] Her action allows the text to have it both ways, to offer a "realistic" ending in terms of Bird's acceptance of responsibilities, but also to allow for the power of romanticism by having Bird's escapist vision infect Himiko.

This vision is not only escapist, however, as is clear from later Oe novels in which leaving Japan is seen as a critique as much as an escape. In later novels, in fact, it is women who will come increasingly to figure as the harshest critics of modern society, refusing to make peace with a reality that includes nuclear war and the destruction of the environment. Indeed, even in *A Personal Matter* it is Himiko's role to make the larger connections with the increasingly threatening world outside. It is she, for example, who brings up nuclear testing as a possible cause for Bird's abnormal baby, a possibility which he ignores, preferring to wallow in self-pity.

In *A Personal Matter* Oe appears to be moving to a new vision of woman and of sexuality, but it is still a sexuality that is bounded by violence and humiliation. The erotic scenes in the narrative are extraordinarily well written; indeed, Mishima described them as "the best in postwar fiction";[57] but their subtext is both violent and anti-female, even if we agree that "female" here represents in the main the oppressiveness of society. Sexual fulfillment is still the prerogative of the male, although after her "sacrifice," Himiko is "rewarded" by normal intercourse which she, too, finds pleasurable.

Mishima's view of eroticism is also a bipolar one, but his poles are the elite versus the majority, the mythic figures who experience ecstasy versus the rest of humanity who find only disappointment. Reiko is allowed sexual gratification by being the perfect traditional wife, but she is at least allowed it. From that point of view, Mishima's sexuality is based on mutual fulfillment, as is obvious from the glowing accounts by de Sade's women as well. The erotic scene in "Patriotism" is almost as extraordinary as in *A Personal Matter*, but it describes an encounter that is obviously not available to the average mortal. Even these young lovers can reach that pleasure only once, and its price is death. Thus, violence is also a necessity in Mishima's sexual ideal as well.

SEXUALITY AND THE ROLE OF WOMEN

Women characters in their sexual roles are very important in the works of both writers, but Mishima's and Oe's fiction contain other kinds of female characters as well, which are worth discussing as they illuminate the role of women in general in both authors' works. Turning first to Mishima, it is interesting to see that, on the whole, women are depicted both positively and sometimes with more depth than the male characters. This is particularly interesting in light of the admittedly homoerotic atmosphere of a number of his works. Perhaps because of his many beautiful male characters, Mishima has been accused of misogynist impulses by both Japanese and American critics.[58] Indeed one Japanese critic has gone so far as to accept the sadistic acts against women in Mishima's fiction as simply expressions of Mishima's homosexual and therefore anti-female tendencies![59] Certainly there are moments in his writings, such as when Shunsuke in *Forbidden Colors* describes the "piglike smell" of "Woman,"[60] that might make one suspect an anti-female bias, or at least a bias against female sexuality. The detailed descriptions of imaginary violence against women in "The Locked Room" might also be given as additional proof.

This would be oversimplifying the issue, however. It may well be that woman in a purely sexual role as a coital partner or in giving birth can be anathema to some of Mishima's heroes. As Petersen points out, the birth scene in *Forbidden Colors* is described extremely negatively.[61] Even more obviously, Kazuo in "The Locked Room" flees at the first indication of Fusako's menstruation. In these works, however, women's natural functions have as much to do with the oppressiveness of reality as with womanhood per se, hinting at a world that the male characters can no longer control. Thus, Reiko's sexuality is limned in a totally positive light because she is completely under her husband's control. Furthermore, unlike many writers, Mishima is also willing to describe women in non-sexual, even non-maternal roles.

One might better argue that Mishima's work shows strong traces of misanthropy rather than misogyny. It must be remembered that *Confessions of a Mask* contains many examples of young men being gorily dismembered while the female characters such as the mask's grandmother, mother, or Sonoko are rendered in largely sympathetic terms. It is true that his works sometimes identify women with animals (Etsuko, for instance is described as having "dumb bitch's eyes")[62] but this animal identification is also extended to both sexes. Thus, Kazuo in "The Locked Room" surveys couples at a dance hall and finds that they resemble nothing so much as "a lot of dogs dancing on their hind legs."[63] It is not gender per se that makes a character unappealing but usually lack of aesthetic attractiveness.

How, then, are women distinguished in Mishima's fiction? First, as I have suggested, by their specifically feminine reproductive functions. In an essay on Mishima's women, Tanaka argues that the hero in "The Locked room" is both threatened and attracted by women because they represent "life" or the "chaos of nature" in contrast to the masculine artificiality of Kazuo's bureaucratic job or even the ornately imagined sadist's club.[64] (It is interesting to remember that in his first dream Kazuo goes down a long "female" roadway only to find the club empty. It is in the next dream, when the female symbols are totally expunged, that the club really takes shape. Women are then allowed back in but only as objects of the males' sadistic imaginations.)

The locked room, needless to say, is also a female symbol that is controlled by Kiriko, who locks the door with the masculine symbol of the key. The text explicitly states that it is "important" that the woman lock the door, perhaps to suggest that the man becomes emasculated or powerless once he is inside the mysterious female realm. And when Kiriko dies, she is replaced by another "woman" in the locked room, Fusako, exactly like the series of images on the label of the bottle. This time, however, the occupant of the room is not yet a mature woman and Kazuo's desire to rape her before she reaches puberty indicates that he is seeking to assert control over the "chaos of nature" that the women represent. It is the story's ironic point that nature itself does the "ripping" rather than the masculine artificial world represented by Kazuo.

Tanaka goes on to submit that Kazuo, in fleeing the locked room, is fleeing nature's and women's attempts to dominate over art, citing Mishima's frequent complaint about the lack of "masculine abstraction" in Japanese literature.[65] Thus, the masculine world outside the locked room is really the world of art and the artist must free himself from the feminine chaotic world in order to achieve greatness. Without denying the artistic and artificial elements in the presentation of Kazuo's personality, it is still possible to question exactly how women represent a threat to art in Mishima's works. Certainly there is a threatening element to many of Mishima's women. The old woman in "Sotoba Komachi" is responsible for the death of a poet by her imaginative powers. The heroine of After the Banquet (Utage no ato) intrudes on and upsets her husband's pleasantly intellectual life to the point where it never recovers. An even more obvious conflict between femininity and the masculine intellect occurs in "The Priest of Shiga Temple and His Love," when an old priest is deflected from his preparations for the afterlife by his passion for a beautiful courtesan. Even Sonoko, one of the most appealing of Mishima's female creations, is perhaps the greatest threat of all to art, because her very existence threatens to rip off the mask that the protagonist has worked so patiently to create.

Yet, one may argue that it is not so much that women threaten artistic pretensions, but rather that they threaten the pretentious artist, the passive intellectual protagonist. For example, in "the Locked Room" Kazuo's dreams may be considered masculine but they are also artificial, to the point where the dreamer himself seems dissatisfied with their ornateness and seems about to turn to genuine violence. The fact that he is frightened by the "natural violence" implicit in the onset of Fusako's menstrual period only underlines his distance from raw reality and life. The scenes of torturing women in "The Locked Room" may consequently be interpreted as attempts by the artist to control nature.

Not only are women associated with life, they are also associated with action, from the small symbolic gesture of control when Kiriko turns the key in the lock, to the grand passion of Etsuko's murder of Saburo. In general, then, Mishima's women share many characteristics with Mishima's heroes of action. They are usually physically attractive, spontaneous, narcissistic, and extremely unintellectual (one thinks of the refreshing charm of Kazu in *After the Banquet* compared to the effete stuffiness of her bookish husband). Like the male heroes of action they are "natural."

If women are threatening, they are threatening in the way that the active hero both threatens and attracts his intellectual alter ego, by making him aware of the sterility and emptiness of his life and his artistic vision. This is not to say that Mishima's women are absolutely identical with his active heroes. At best they are lesser heroes of action, sometimes silly and almost never noble. Mishima can even make fun of women's silliness, as in his satire on middle-aged hypocrisy, "The Pearl"; but by satirizing them he makes them even less threatening.

In fact, women can play positive roles as well, in somewhat different ways from the direct stimulation provided by the men of action, and this is in their links to life and nurturing. Although Petersen correctly points out the grotesque descriptions of pregnancy in *Forbidden Colors*, motherhood, or at least the ability to care for and nurture is not always shown in a negative light. The memorable scene in *The Temple of The Golden Pavilion*, where the priests watch a woman offer milk from her breast to a soldier on his way to war is a good example of both a positive and aesthetically pleasing description of the nurturing function.

It is true that this scene is essentially a voyeuristic one, with the young priests "spying" from afar on the mysterious couple, and later on in the narrative the woman herself is shown in a pathetic and unattractive light; but this does not negate the beauty of the scene. Instead it only serves to emphasize the impossibility of such beauty in the real world. An even clearer example of a mother figure is Mrs. Kaburagi in *Forbidden Colors* who virtually sacrifices herself for the handsome but empty Yuichi. It is surely no coincidence that Mishima, in describing his favorite types of women, mentions Mrs. Kaburagi as an ideal example.[66]

Where Mishima's men of action are associated both with life and violent death, his women characters are associated with life and the violence of birth, the mystery of renewal. As a character in "The Lady Aoi" puts it, "A woman sheds blood, dies, and comes back to life time and time again."[67] Women are mysterious then, but not necessarily threatening. In fact, through their beauty they are associated with the aesthetic, one of the few consistently positive values in Mishima's writing.

Overall, Mishima's women play both an active and a positive role in his fiction, often even setting the narrative into action through the intensity of their desires (Etsuko or Kazu in *After the Banquet* being the prime examples). It would be far more difficult to make such a blanket statement about the women in Oe's fiction.

Although, as in Mishima's works, they are consistently associated with life and eroticism, in Oe' literary world this association has a generally sinister quality to it. Furthermore, they are identified far more explicitly, and in a far more limiting manner, with sexuality. Yoriko, Yasuo's prostitute girlfriend in *Our Era*, for example, is basically nothing more than a "vagina" as one Japanese critic puts it,[68] simply an organ of entrapment and suffocation for the male. This constant sexual association helps to underline the overall negative depiction of women in Oe since, as we have seen, sexuality is almost always linked to the despair of the wasteland in his works.

In Mishima's fiction, women do occasionally betray and humiliate the male; but it is usually a desiccated intellectual, such as the lecherous old writer Shunsuke in *Forbidden Colors,* whom they traduce. In Oe's work, however, women are simply one more snare that the real world has devised to entrap and disillusion his heroes. Thus, in an early short story, "Dark River, Heavy Oars" ("Kurai Kawa, Omoi Kai"), a young boy's dreams of running off with a prostitute are dissolved and made fun of by the very woman who had engendered the dreams in the first place.

One should also note that the women in Oe's early works are often prostitutes; and, although his insistent depiction of the prostitute with Japanese pimp and American lover is largely for reasons of political symbolism, one cannot help but find a sort of prostitute, or at least highly submissive, mentality on the part of women in many of his later novels as well. Of course, part of this is related to Japanese society with its traditional emphasis on the submissive female; but, even compared to those of many modern writers, Oe's female characters are notable for playing secondary roles alongside the more strongly highlighted scenes of male bonding.

In general, the female characters in Oe's novels when they are described in positive terms are "good" largely because they are totally accepting, both sexually and emotionally. Even Himiko, despite her intellectual vibrancy and liberated lifestyle, is helpful to Bird and thus a "good" character, because she is willing to sacrifice herself for him, not only on the sexual level but also in her willingness to let him use her house and her car; she even offers to finance his dream of going to Africa. In a later work, *The Game of Contemporaneity*, the sister of the narrator, although presented as having some power as a quasi shamaness, has as one of her primary functions the role of nurturer of the so-called "destroyer" (*kowasu hito*) who is the savior of their race.

The Game of Contemporaneity, by the way, marks a transition in Oe's novels to portraying pregnancy in a beneficial light. While in *Our Era* pregnancy was simply another means of entrapping the desperate Yasuo, in *A Personal Matter* it comes to have a specifically threatening quality all its own when Bird's wife gives birth to a "monster" baby. This threatening quality is underlined even more explicitly when Bird explains to Himiko his fear of "the vagina and the womb." The negative linkings among women, sex, and pregnancy are made still clearer in *The Silent Cry* when, after the birth of their deformed baby, Mitsusaburo's wife refuses to sleep with him, becomes an alcoholic, and eventually has an affair with his younger brother. Women may be associated with life, but it is usually a destructive or even monstrous form of life. (It should be noted however, that the *product* of pregnancy, the abnormal baby, is depicted very positively throughout Oe's work. As will be discussed more thoroughly in the following chapter, the abnormal baby is the ultimate outsider and is thus the one being who is entirely unconstrained by reality).

Mothering (as opposed to simply childbearing), is also not presented particularly positively in Oe's works. In *A Personal Matter*, Bird's wife and mother of their baby is virtually ignored while he abandons himself in sexual dissipation with Himiko; and, when the text does allow a few glimpses of the wife, she is usually cold and critical. Even her mother is depicted as something of a shrew who abets her in spotlighting Bird's faults. Even more memorable is the cantankerous mother in "The Day He Himself Shall Wipe My Tears Away" ("Waganamida o nuguitamau hi"), who is depicted as being harshly critical, almost castrating, since she consistently forces her version of "the truth" onto her son's narrative.

On the other hand, women in their role as critics do play an important role in Oe's novels as tellers of truths that the weaker male characters hide from. Even Himiko, who is one of the most genuinely nurturing female characters in Oe's oeuvre, has some accurate, if unkind, observations about Bird's character and destiny. In that regard, they resemble Mishima's women characters in their role of stripping away male artifice. But Mishima's women also have positive values of their own, in terms of their liveliness and beauty, whereas Oe's women seldom have any notably attractive attributes.

Perhaps the most memorably unattractive woman character in Oe's canon is the unfortunate Miss Iguchi in "The Swimming Man." Like a Mishima female character, Miss Iguchi is linked to life. She reminds the narrator of a German figurine of summer. She is given to wearing bright clothes, most inappropriate for a woman in her thirties according to Japanese custom. Her face, perspiring from the heat of the sauna, is red and glowing, suggesting a direct sensuality uncomplicated by makeup or other artifices. Yet she encapsulates the darkest side of femininity, and her fate comes right out of the popular pornographic comic books.

Miss Iguchi's sexuality is perhaps the most calculating and genuinely "obscene" of anything in Oe's work. Not only is she far from being a nurturing provider of life, she lacks even the uninhibited enjoyment that Yoriko and Himiko possess. Even more than Yoriko, she is morcellized into being simply a female sex organ and a sinister one at that. From the glimpse of the "black gourd shape" in the sauna, to her grotesque death tied to a bench with her genitals exposed to the headlights of passing cars, she seems to have been created for only one purpose: to humiliate and torment men until they wreak their revenge on her.

For this reason, one cannot help but be reminded of the extraordinarily violent and genuinely misogynistic depictions of women in the extremely popular *manga* (comic books), read by so many Japanese men. Compared to a full-blown character such as Himiko, Miss Iguchi is quite one-dimensional and that dimension is the threatening sexual one. Although the narrator describes her as sexually "vulnerable" (using the English terms, which only emphasizes her alienness), this description seems both accurate and disingenuous. Her aberrant hungers and her grotesque fate are pathetic; but, on the whole, rather than being vulnerable, she is extraordinarily threatening to the men in the story. She is rather like Mishima's Etsuko but even more thinly realized as a character; her desires embody the dark side of sexuality, provoking, tantalizing and finally terrorizing the male until he must kill her. Her story is not a unique one, however, as we can see from Ian Buruma's summary of a similar woman character in a comic book:

> A fair haired foreign woman living in a suburban apartment block seduces every healthy Japanese boy she can find: . . . nobody, but nobody is safe from this man eating tigress. Finally they decide something must be done and they ambush the woman, tie her to a tree and then torture her. "Oh!" she cries . . . "in my country it is usual to do what I did." The boys are naturally horrified and torture her even more."[69]

Of course Miss Iguchi is not a fair-haired foreigner, but simply as a woman she is "foreign" to the men. (And she has traveled abroad!) The suggestion here is not that Oe is slavishly following the strictures of misogynistic Japanese pornography but that, in telling a story which is really about male identification and the problems of getting old, he hit, perhaps unconsciously, on an important stereotype of Japanese mass culture, the woman who by her aberrant behavior "asks" to be tortured.[70]

But the death of Miss Iguchi also seems to be related to the previously noted point about the absence of control in the postwar world. The obsession with inflicting sadistic torments on women shown in the more extreme of the many popular *manga* suggests a deep-seated dissatisfaction on the part of Japanese salaried men, unable to control their lives, their jobs, or their world in general. What begins in "The

Locked Room" with a vision of ripping and fragmentation turns into full-blown reality in "The Swimming Man," with a vision of a woman impaled on a park bench, unable to move, or threaten, simply existing as a pure sexual icon to be tormented and displayed.

Of course, Oe's intention in "The Swimming Man" is far from pornographic. If anything, Miss Iguchi is simply a narrative tool to get the real story, that between the narrator and Tamari, under way. Nor would it be fair to suggest that Miss Iguchi's portrait is typical of Oe's recent fiction. Ironically, the very book in which "The Swimming Man" constitutes the final story is largely a collection of pieces highlighting women characters in very positive, even independent, roles.

This 1982 work entitled *The Women Who Hear the Raintree* is actually a series of novellas centering on a variety of unusual women. In the first story, "The Clever Raintree" ("Atama no ii reintsuri"), the narrator attends a party at a mental home in Hawaii, where he meets Agatee, one of the patients, who tells him about a mysterious "raintree" that curls up its leaves at night in order to retain the fallen moisture and thus sustains itself during the day. "A clever tree, don't you think?" she asks, and the narrator agrees.[71] This lyrical scene is undercut, however, by the story's climax where the narrator, Agatee, and some other guests happen upon another woman patient who has covered herself with menstrual blood, at which point the party collapses into pandemonium. The madhouse where a phantom raintree contrasts with an all-too-realistically described scene of blood and madness is, of course, an appropriate symbol for the modern world itself, but it is interesting to note that in this case women are the key to both the imaginary and the real.

The association of women with life and nature is given a somewhat more conventional treatment in two more stories from *Raintree* involving a woman named Penny, "The Upside Down Raintree" ("Sakasama no reintsuri") and "The Women Who Hear the Raintree" ("Reintsuri o kiku onnatachi"). Still in Hawaii, the narrator encounters an old classmate of his, an alcoholic writer named Koyasu Kachan (who, in many ways, is a dark doppleganger of the narrator himself) and his Chinese mistress Penny. Penny resembles an older Himiko, an intelligent and articulate critic (of the narrator, not of Koyasu) and also a patient nurturer to male fantasies. She is endlessly indulgent to Koyasu's demands and is even willing to engage in a bizarre, if grotesquely humourous, sexual congress with him while the narrator watches in both horror and fascination, a voyeuristic rite that is reminiscent of the triangular relationship in "The Swimming Man." Like Himiko, Penny is also aware of the degraded society around her and, at the novel's end, makes a decisive attempt to escape. She rescues Agatee from the ruins of the mental institution, which has recently burned down, and sets off for the South Seas to begin a new life, far from the polluted and nuclear skies of the industrialized countries.

This view of women as decisive and redemptive and also as firmly opposed to the political order of society is not new in Oe's works. It is presaged in his earlier apocalyptic novel *The Floodwaters Have Come unto My Soul* when the protagonist's girlfriend Inago is left with his child as the only survivors of the band of Freedom Voyagers who have died in battle with the Self-Defense Forces. No longer purely sexual, these women point to a new and better life, away from industrialized society.

Even in these relatively optimistic works, however, relations between the sexes are often depicted negatively. At best, women may point the way out of the oppressiveness of modern culture, but the men do not seem to want to follow in that particular direction. Rather, they want to escape the real world on their own terms and often this means an escape from women as well.

4·In Search of the Garden

The previous two chapters concentrated on works that highlighted both the postwar world in its worst aspects and relations between men and women in that world. If the protagonists considered escape, it was through either dreams or acts of sexual violence. The texts to be discussed here are also written within a realistic framework, but their romantic alternative worlds are described in much more detail and are all virtually free of female influence. The narrative structures tend to be much more confrontational—not quite the "good" imaginary versus the "bad" real of the early, pastoral novels but still giving the alternatives far more textual space than was offered in the brief flickers of revolt that flared in the works discussed in Chapters Two and Three. In those works, realistically bleak descriptions of society tended to dominate with overwhelming force, although "The Swimming Man" and "The Locked Room" also played with the genres of suspense fiction and pornography.

The novels in this chapter are encompassed by a highly specific historical reality, from the corruption of the postwar Buddhist priesthood depicted in Mishima's *Temple of the Golden Pavilion* to the self-absorbed materialism of his later *Sailor Who Fell from Grace with the Sea*, or, in Oe's case, from the anomie of early 'sixties self-satisfied economic development in *Our Era*, to the horrors wrought by modernization that are profiled in *The Floodwaters Have Come unto My Soul*. Despite the "historicity" of these works, however, they are closer to romance than to realism in terms of actual plot structure, imagery, and most importantly characterization: their supremely romantic protagonists war actively against historical reality.

In a sense, these characters stand between the struggling protagonists lost in the wasteland of sexuality and the youthful heroes of the
pastoral novels. While the young characters in the earlier pastoral
works existed largely within the world of romance, the protagonists
of these novels are exiled from the worlds of utopian plentitude. The
hero of *Pluck the Buds, Shoot the Kids* accepted exile but these protagonists desperately seek either to return or to recreate the lost worlds
through attempting to bend reality to their own visions. They are
thus active mediators, questing between the real and the imaginary.
As Nathan says of Oe's early heroes, they "have been expelled from
the certainty of childhood";[1] and it is clear that part of them, at least,
craves a return.

It is this quest/ desire for return that animates all the texts to be
considered in this chapter. Desire, in fact, is the major motivating
force behind all the narrative structures to be considered. It is suit-
able, therefore, that this chapter concentrates both on the heroes and
their desires and on the objects of their longings. These objects can
still include the Edenic images familiar from the texts of the pastoral
novels but, in these more urban stories, the objects of desire are usually more concrete. They range on the ethereal side from the nostalgic beauty of a five-hundred-year-old temple in *The Temple of the
Golden Pavilion* to that most romantic icon of all, the sea, in *The
Sailor Who Fell from Grace with the Sea*, or its metonymic substitute,
the schooner in Oe's *The Floodwaters Have Come unto My Soul*. On
the more vulgar side, they include the marvelously banal "large-size
truck" that propels the dreams of the youthful protagonists in Oe's
Our Era.

Despite the variation in type of objects desired, the narratives do
contain other important common elements. Not only are the actual
characters more three-dimensional than in the pastoral novels, but
they all fit superbly into Girard's definition of the romantic hero:
"the hero is always he who desires most intently."[2] These characters
are truly consumed with desire, and the usually frustrating interaction between them and the objects or worlds of their desire provides
the narrative tension of each novel.

These imaginary worlds and objects also share some important
characteristics. They are virtually all masculine worlds in which
women play largely negative roles, serving on the most basic level as
sexual threats, such as the impotence-causing women in Mishima's

Golden Pavilion or Oe's *Our Era*, and, in a wider sense, as threats to romanticism in general, as repressors of masculine dreams of adventure and beauty, such as the obdurately ambitious mother in *Golden Pavilion*. Women are not the only representatives of the real, however. Authority figures of all kinds run a close second, from the mysterious Superior of the Golden Temple to the entire military-industrial establishment that assembles for an apocalyptic shootout in Oe's *Floodwaters*.

Beyond its human representatives, the wasteland of the postwar world is also well represented in terms of setting. In opposition to the pastoral character of the earlier works, reality in its most bleak and brutal form envelops all the characters in these novels: the Second World War and its immediate aftermath in *Golden Pavilion*, 'sixties anomie in *Our Era*, material emptiness in *Sailor*, and the final horror of imminent nuclear holocaust in Oe's *Floodwaters*. At the same time, the attractions of the imaginary are also carefully delineated and are shown as having an even stronger hold on the protagonists than in the pastoral novels; but the fantasy becomes an alternative that must be actively sought, celebrated and defended.

Another important aspect shared by these works is their detailed depictions of violence, including murder (*Sailor*, *Our Era* and *Floodwaters*), terrorism (*Our Era* and *Floodwaters*), and arson (*Golden Pavilion*). These violent acts might all be termed retaliatory or even compensatory actions, moves aimed at a society that does not appreciate the protagonists' special qualities nor offer them any hope of a fulfilling life. In keeping with their violent nature, the actions are consciously antisocial, providing undoubted ideological resonance as well. Mishima's hero does not burn down just any temple, he sets ablaze one of the most famous places in Japan, while Oe's protagonists in *Our Era* do not simply plot a murder, they plan to assassinate the emperor. Furthermore, a strongly apocalyptic cast colors these novels, suggested even in the titles of the Oe works (*Our Era*, *Floodwaters*) and by the megalomaniac sentiments of the characters created by Mishima.

The third important element in these novels is one they share with Oe's pastoral stories: their overt, if problematic, ideologization. Particularly clear in Oe's novels, but evident in Mishima's works as well, is a consistent and highly self-conscious cutting back and forth between the disappointing nature of the world and the protagonists' need, or right, to rearrange the world to their individual likings (this need made all the clearer through dialogue that often seems quite unnatural), all of which suggests that a message is being put across. This message, common to all the novels thus far examined, states that the world is disappointing and oppressive and must be changed through art, action, or both. The actual alternatives to this disappointing reality may be more romantic than realizable, but they are still vividly depicted, as are the characters' deep dissatisfactions and their attempts to deal with these frustrations.

What kinds of characters are these dissatisfied protagonists? They are quintessential romantics, among the most romantic of either writer's oeuvre; but they are also romantics with a difference—their activism. Where the young people in *Pluck the Buds* and *The Sound of Waves* were impelled by unconscious and unseen forces (benevolent ones in the case of Mishima's story, malevolent ones in Oe's), these heroes attempt to control the forces around them and are motivated by intense desires. As befits the romantic hero of Girard's definition, these protagonists desire with extraordinary intensity and they are willing to undertake extraordinary action to satisfy their desires.

Besides being romantics, these heroes are also thoroughly egotistical, reminiscent of such characters as Etsuko in *Thirst for Love* and Takao in *Outcries*. They are also all young, as is appropriate for romantic visionaries; but these are not the innocent children of *The Sound of Waves* or "Prize Stock." These are embittered children, expelled from their yearned-for gardens, and attempting to return, through acts that are immature and destructive, what Noguchi Takehiko has called the "violent infantilism" of the romantic who will not, or perhaps cannot, accept reality.[3]

This egotistical character who is unwilling to accept reality is also allied to a more positive figure, the artist, for the visions of these violent youthful protagonists have a creative function equivalent to that of the artist. Mishima, in fact, described the hero of his *Golden Pavilion* as an artist with an "idée fixe,"[4] an image that could fit other protagonists as well. Indeed, it is arguable that the very strong, even infantile, feelings of disappointment and longing combine with the sophisticated vision of the artist to give these works their special appeal.

This combination of artistic vision and raw desire to escape reality is certainly the essential dynamic of *Golden Pavilion,* which many critics have seen as Mishima's masterpiece.

WHEN YOU MEET THE BUDDHA, KILL THE BUDDHA:
THE TEMPLE OF THE GOLDEN PAVILION

The Temple of the Golden Pavilion offers one of modern Japanese literature's most brilliant meditations on desire, the Other, and the imaginary. Mishima uses a real-life incident, the burning of a famous temple, to develop one of his strangest love stories. In the protagonist's obsessive descriptions of the temple, beauty, love, and need are richly evoked, while the protagonist's desire is presented as both thoroughly abject and overwhelmingly powerful. Yet *Golden Pavilion* is not simply a meditation on aestheticism and the impossibility of attaining the desired ideal. It is also an extraordinary rendering of postwar Japanese society, inspiring a gamut of readings, from attempts to interpret the work as a "Zen novel" to one suggestion that Mishima had tried to create in the image of the temple a substitute for either the Christian god or for the emperor in the wake of the defeat.[5] Indeed, emptiness and loss pervade the novel, surround the temple, and are fully encapsulated in the all-needing, all-desiring character of its pathetic protagonist, Mizoguchi.

The narrative itself is extremely simple since it centers on a single action, the burning of a five-hundred-year-old national treasure in Kyoto (an incident that had occurred five years before Mishima wrote his novel); but the fire itself occupies only the last three pages of the text. As in Takao's murderous act in Oe's *Outcries,* also based on a real incident, the act itself is less important than the narrative that leads to it. The novel is not, however, simply an attempt to explore the psychology of a psychopath, as the author of its English introduction suggests.[6] The character of Mizoguchi, although arguably superficially drawn as Miyoshi indicates,[7] is not totally one-dimensional. The fictional Mizoguchi is dissimilar to the real perpetrator and, in fact, strongly resembles certain aspects of Mishima himself; but, rather than condemning Mishima for this, one might instead read both *Golden Pavilion* and Mizoguchi himself for their ideological message.

Golden Pavilion is not an attempt to create a realistic approximation of a news event along the lines of *In Cold Blood.* Rather, it puts forth Mishima's complex vision of postwar Japanese society. Mizoguchi's story is a superb example of a romantic's failure to come to grips with the reality of that society: a society which, in the postwar "chaos" of the 1950s is a place of loss and absence, where beauty apparently has no right to exist, making Mizoguchi and his love and hatred for the temple the perfect symbol of postwar Japan.

Mizoguchi's tragedy is that he is all too perfectly a representative member of the real world, and the unlikeliness that he will ever be a romantic hero of Lieutenant Takeyama's type is what makes his desire for the Other so traumatic. The son of an ineffectual country priest, Mizoguchi is ugly, awkward and thoroughly isolated from those around him. Even more significantly, he has a bad stutter. He cannot affect the world through words, only through action. At the same time, he desires inordinately to be everything he is not. As Girard says, "The Other is fascinating the less accessible he is";[8] and as Mizoguchi himself admits, "It is no exaggeration that the first real problem I faced in my life was that of beauty."[9]

An early scene in the novel shows Mizoguchi sitting a little apart from but listening avidly to a handsome young naval officer who is surrounded by a group of listeners who are in turn surrounded by "May flowers." Only Mizoguchi is isolated. As he says, "Such was my manner. Such was my manner toward the May flowers and toward that pride filled uniform and toward those bright peals of laughter."[10] Mizoguchi may strive for distance; but, like the mask in *Confessions,* he both despises and yearns for all that he is not.

Throughout *Golden Pavilion* these antinomies occur again and again: brightness and darkness, beauty and ugliness, desire and repression. The narrative structure itself is based on these contradictions, because most of the action occurs as attempts either to control or transcend them. One means of overcoming them is through death, with which, both as a priest and the son of a priest, Mizoguchi is well acquainted. At times he consoles himself with the thought of his special priestly role, the "knowledge that I was to stand waiting in a dark world with both hands stretched out" to receive the souls of those haughty beautiful young men who die on the battlefield.[11] Death thus becomes both a kind of compensation and a means of control. At other times, Mizoguchi forgets death and simply dreams of power, fantasizing a world in which he will wield authority as a stuttering tyrant over helpless minions. More than death or power, however, Mizoguchi desires beauty, the beauty of the Other, a being of absolute perfection symbolized to him by the Golden Temple.

Mizoguchi's relationship with the Golden Temple is consequently an ambivalent one, mixing both love and hatred as is appropriate in a relationship with the other. As Girard says "The romantic state of mind is pervaded by *ressentiment.*"[12] Desire to destroy and desire to possess are the two extensions of this ambivalence, and here is where Mishima's characterization of Mizoguchi as an artist carries weight. Not only does Mizoguchi possess the requisite egotistical and obsessive personality, combined with his sense of alienation and inferiority towards "others," he possesses a powerful and creative imagination which transforms the temple into an Other of almost divine proportions, perhaps comparable to Ahab's vision of Moby Dick.

It is his artist's desire to create and control that ultimately drives Mizoguchi to destroy the temple. For Mizoguchi wants the temple all to himself and on his own terms. The text makes this conflation of temple with personal possession right from the opening lines, "Ever since my childhood, father had often spoken to me about the Golden Temple."[13] The temple is a special place reserved specifically for priests. As Mizoguchi admits, "In more ways than one it was a great relief for me to be there. No longer was I stared at for being the son of a priest. For here everyone was in the same position."[14] It is also a world without women, a fact of peculiar, although unconscious, importance to Mizoguchi, who has despised and resented his mother since the night he and his father were forced to be passive observers of her adultery.

The temple is a place with no one to mock Mizoguchi for his strangeness. For the first time in his life, Mizoguchi is in a world that, at least initially, does not threaten or humiliate him. Conditions are particularly unusual the first summer of his apprenticeship because the Second World War is still raging, causing the temple to be deserted by both priests and sightseers. This heightens the perfect alterity of the situation; Mizoguchi is in as magical a world in its own way as was the island in *The Sound of Waves.*

He is even able to accept without jealousy the wholesomeness and charm of his fellow acolyte Tsurukawa, one of the few genuinely agreeable characters to be found in a Mishima novel. Tolerant, relaxed, and apparently satisfied with life, Tsurukawa is, as Mizoguchi himself states, the "positive picture" of the negative Mizoguchi.[15] This is clear from the first scene in which Mizoguchi encounters him, on a morning "noisy with the twittering of birds":

Next to [the fence] lay a young boy in a white shirt. A bamboo rake leaned nearby against a low maple. . . .
   The boy raised his body with such energy that he seemed to gouge a

hole in the soft summer air which hovered about us; but when he saw me, he simply said, "Oh, it's you, is it?"[16]

This scene exemplifies Mishima's use of nature to suggest an alternative world. Although its style is somewhat artificial, there is a certain low-key perfection to it, as in the effective touch of having a bamboo rake leaning against a low maple. (As in Oe's *Pluck the Buds*, the beauty of the natural scene is also heightened by the reader's knowledge of the war raging along its borders.) Tsurukawa, of course, is completely at ease in this scene; and by calmly accepting Mizoguchi with a simple "Oh, it's you, is it?", he enables Mizoguchi, if only temporarily, to become part of this alternative world as well.

This scene is also similar to Etsuko's first meeting with Saburo in *Thirst for Love*. Once again, the text shows us a youth lying among lush vegetation, seemingly indolent but actually full of suppressed life. And once again a dark, potentially menacing force hovers over him.

No hint of a sexual relationship exists between Tsurukawa and Mizoguchi, however. Rather, as was basically the case with Etsuko and Saburo, too, the contrast lies between the hero who desires and the Other who is everything that he or she desires, the alter ego. Like Saburo, Tsurukawa offers the longing-filled outsider an entry into an alternate world of light and life, a world which Etsuko and Mizoguchi both see and fear. Whereas Etsuko must kill Saburo to stop her dreams from becoming disappointing realities, Mizoguchi must reject the beauty implied in Tsurukawa's life affirmation so that he may seek to possess a darker, even more impossible form of beauty, that of the temple, which ultimately he must also destroy.

At this point in the novel the final rejection is still far away and the scene ends on a poignant note: "His [Tsurukawa's] white shirted stomach rippled with laughter. The rays of the sun that poured through the tree made me feel happy. Like the young man's wrinkled shirt, my life was wrinkled. But wrinkled as it was, how white his shirt shone in the sunlight! Perhaps I too?"[17]

In this scene Mizoguchi comes closest to finding a human alternative to his own isolated world, a world of friendship and community. But this alternative is ultimately not enough for him, just as alternatives are insufficient for most of Mishima's later heroes.

Nor are sexual relationships adequate to satisfy the intensity of his desire. The book details unsatisfying encounters between Mizoguchi and various women. In the first and most memorable one, his adolescent attempt to meet the village beauty Uiko, Mizoguchi is verbally impotent. Although he has summoned up the courage to confront her, he can only stand stuttering and humiliated in front of her. His later sexual encounters are similar fiascos on account of a physical impotence which Mizoguchi, true to his egotistical artist persona, blames on the temple itself, because it somehow inserts itself into his mind at the crucial moment.

Regarding this, Watanabe Hiroshi has suggested that the temple represents "art" while women represent "life,"[18] and this view might be expanded even further: Women also represent the Other, and their presence is a reminder of the life that Mizoguchi cannot have, that of virility and masculinity. This inability to leave the imaginary and take part in the world of the Word of the Father is underlined by his verbal impotence as well. It is significant that the most satisfying "encounter" that Mizoguchi has with a woman is a voyeuristic one, the famous scene in which he and Tsurukawa watch silently as the beautiful woman offers her breast milk to a soldier on his way to battle. Both men are deeply impressed by the classical beauty of the moment. Later on, however, when Mizoguchi actually meets the woman and she offers herself to him, he again becomes physically impotent.

Watanabe also notes that Mizoguchi's later decision to destroy the temple represents his attraction to life over art. The motivation behind Mizoguchi's action is more complex than that, however. In order to live in the "real world," the disappointing reality where he must accept that he is ugly and stutters, Mizoguchi must first internalize the object of his desire. And the only way for him to do so is to destroy the "reality" of the temple so that only he can possess it.

Mizoguchi's turning away from the "real" in the form of woman to the imaginary in the form of the beautiful is prefigured from the very beginning of the novel in the scene where he and his father are forced to lie passively awake while his mother has intercourse with her lover. As previously noted, voyeurism plays a major role in the works of both Mishima and Oe in terms of highlighting the extreme differences between the intellectual, passive protagonists who can only watch and the romantic, active heroes who are the watched. In *Golden Pavilion*, this emphasis on passivity and frustrated desire is given a new twist when the young Mizoguchi's father actually covers his son's eyes from the reality of his mother's adultery and the son acquiesces and focuses inward to contemplate the image of the golden temple.

Mizoguchi's obsession with the temple is thus a form of compensation at its most obvious, but what makes this compensation so dangerous is that Mizoguchi first envisions the temple in his mind. He thus creates his own image of perfection, with which the real temple cannot compete, as is apparent in the scene where Mizoguchi actually views the temple for the first time. Instead of the glorious vision of his childhood, he sees "merely a small, dark, old, three storied building."[19]

Typically, in keeping with Mizoguchi's character of an artist manqué and an egotist, he refuses to accept the possibility that his disappointment may stem from any possible "deficiency in aesthetic appreciation"[20] on his own part. He feels "deceived" by the temple, preferring instead the temple's shadow in the pond.

Mizoguchi's misfortune, or rather the temple's misfortune, is that Mizoguchi actually does deal with the temple in its reality; indeed there is even a chance that he will be made the successor to the abbot of the temple. For a "normal" person (that is, not a romantic), this promotion would be highly appealing; but for Mizoguchi, the greater the possibility of his taking over the temple in reality, the more dissatisfied he becomes, until he reaches the point where he decides that the temple must be destroyed, to keep its inaccessible Otherness inviolate.

At first, Mizoguchi hopes that the temple's destruction can be achieved through bombings by American pilots in the last stage of the war, which would preclude any actions on his part. In this passive hoping for apocalypse, Mizoguchi allies himself with his spiritual counterpart in *Confessions of a Mask* who had hoped that American forces would invade Japan and thereby solve his personal problems. Mizoguchi longs for an apocalyptic moment when he and the temple will be consumed by the flames, thus simultaneously accomplishing his revenge against society and achieving his glorious romantic fate. As he says in his usual egotistical manner, "I was encouraged by the fact that the golden temple and I shared a common danger in this world."[21] Mizoguchi's desire for a fiery demise is not granted, however. When the temple is not destroyed by bombers, nor later on by a hoped-for typhoon, Mizoguchi is forced either to live with the disappointing reality of the temple's existence or take action against it himself.

Reluctantly, Mizoguchi decides to take action, but it is important to note the slowness of the buildup of what he portentously describes as his "evil" deeds. His first act is essentially a defilement of the temple, his trampling of a pregnant prostitute in front of the temple gate at the behest of an American soldier. Significantly, this action occurs shortly after the abbot has recommended him to continue at the university, a recommendation that would ultimately put him in line for successorship to the head of the temple. Thus, just at the moment when it appears that Mizoguchi might triumph in the "real world" and thereby lose his raison d'être as a romantic hero, he begins to take the forcible action that will prevent his real-world success. The action of trampling on the prostitute possesses extraliterary significance as well, since it is performed at the command of an American soldier. The symbol of old Japan is thus contaminated by two Japanese humiliating themselves at the instigation of the American conqueror.

Mizoguchi lies about the incident to the abbot and is allowed to continue at the university; but, once there, he immediately seeks out the one person sure to have the most objectionable influence possible on him. This is his fellow student Kashiwagi, and it is his relationship with Kashiwagi that precipitates Mizoguchi toward his final destructive act. Kashiwagi is clearly the dark angel to Tsurukawa's "positive picture"; but, with all his didactic pedantry, he is also the voice of the real world at its ugliest and most insistent. If Tsurukawa is the alternative to reality which Mizoguchi can never possess, then Kashiwagi is the reality which destroys all alternates and which Mizoguchi must ultimately transcend.

The difference between these two opposing "angels" is highlighted in the scene of Mizoguchi's first encounter with Kashiwagi. As in the scene with Tsurukawa, Mizoguchi stands looking down at the young man sitting among flowers: "He was self-sufficient as he sat there in the light. . . . He was a shadow that asserted itself, or rather he was the existent shadow itself." And when Mizoguchi approaches him, "My shadow fell on his food and he looked up."[22]

Whereas Tsurukawa's brightness "gouged a hole in the summer sky," Kashiwagi is an "assertive shadow" into which Mizoguchi's own shadow blends itself. While Tsurukawa's "alchemy" makes Mizoguchi's most negative notions seem pleasant, even humorous trifles, Kashiwagi turns everything he associates with into the grotesque. Kashiwagi's role has been much debated by critics; but the pattern of his actions–his humiliation of beautiful women, his manipulation of Mizoguchi into stealing irises from the temple garden, and his goading of a former mistress into smashing a perfect flower arrangement–make clear that at least one of his roles is to be the annihilator of beauty. He is specially the annihilator of any loveliness associated with the traditional arts of Japan, including the tea ceremony, flower arrangement, and the temple itself. Most disillusioning of all, Kashiwagi destroys Tsurukawa's memory, whose accidental death he reveals to have been in reality a suicide.

Golden Pavilion is full of shattered illusions and shattered beauties, as Gwenn Boardman Petersen points out.[23] In Petersen's view, this penchant for destruction is simply typical Mishima perversity; but, although authorial intentions no doubt play a part, it appears that the constant interplay of beauty and destruction throughout the novel has a larger sociological resonance as well. Although Mishima's "message" is not as simplistically ideological as that of a genuine *roman à thèse*, the consistent pattern of broken traditional beauty is still significant. This is not to suggest that the figure of Kashiwagi "represents" something as obvious as the war or modernity, but a Kashiwagi figure, a destroyer, is an integral element in preparing the reader for the final destruction of the temple.

Even more important is the contrast between Kashiwagi and Mizoguchi who is both a destroyer and (in his own eyes at least) a preserver. Mizoguchi feels compelled to make his romantic fantasies concrete in order to preserve some fragment against the ruins. Kashiwagi takes no action; he is content to manipulate others to act out the dance of the death of tradition that he nihilistically delights in.

In this regard, Kashiwagi's interpretation of the crucial Zen parable "Nansen kills a cat" makes sense. The interpretation arises out of an argument between Kashiwagi and Mizoguchi over action versus knowledge. Kashiwagi, the typical modern antihero who desires nothing and glories in that autonomy, naturally believes in knowledge, while Mizoguchi, the romantic, inevitably chooses the opposite tack. As he recalls, "'Knowledge can never transform the world,' I blurted out, skirting along the very edge of confession. 'What transforms the world is action. There's nothing else.'"[24] Kashiwagi disagrees, citing as support for his point the parable which the abbot quotes on the day of Japan's surrender, concerning the killing of a kitten whose beauty aroused the greed of rival monks. Kashiwagi interprets the parable and the monk Choshu's response as saying that "'beauty . . . must be protected by knowledge because beauty is an illusion.'" Thus, we understand that Kashiwagi needs constantly to undercut and defile beauty in order to prove that it in itself is illusory, without knowledge. Illustrating the emptiness of illusions is a basic practice of Zen; but it is important to emphasize that Kashiwagi, by expounding on a parable first quoted in the novel by the Temple's Superior on the day of Japan's surrender, implicitly links this practice to contemporary events and suggests that knowledge rather than action is the more appropriate response to the ruined world of postwar Japan.

Whether Kashiwagi is "right," however, is a different matter. By this point in the text, he has made a point of cynically shattering the illusions of love, the tea ceremony, and beauty itself, offering in their place the nihilism of knowledge. It is Mizoguchi, however, who turns the interpretation upside-down through action. It is Mizoguchi's aim to prove by force that one does not shatter illusions to preserve reality, rather, one shatters reality to protect the illusion. And it is action, not knowledge, that will accomplish this task.

Initially, Mizoguchi is not interested in actively preserving his illusion. It is only after uncontrollable circumstances, such as the possibility of becoming head of the temple or the increased number of tourists arriving with the end of the war, force reality onto him that his relationship with the comfortable inaccessibility of the temple is affected. It is during this period that he hopes for a deus ex machina such as American bombs to come and save him. When his hoped-for salvation does not come. Mizoguchi still hesitates until finally he more or less backs into action.

By maintaining a lackadaisical attitude towards his studies and initiating a campaign of bizarre but petty tormenting of the temple's corrupt abbot, Mizoguchi forces the temple superiors to treat him as an outcast. Even after making the decision to burn down the temple, he continues his roundabout manipulations by spending his school fees on a prostitute, thereby providing the abbot "a perfectly reasonable excuse for expelling me from the temple,"[25] and also giving himself a deadline by which time he must destroy the temple. In a sense, then, both Mizoguchi and his dark mentor Kashiwagi are the archetypal intellectual heroes of a realistic novel who play with ideas and attempt to manipulate others. The key difference between them is that Mizoguchi goes beyond the intellectual wasteland of passive observation and manipulative indirect action into the world of romantic action.

It is significant that even at the very last moment Mizoguchi hesitates in true self-analytical intellectual fashion: "Does not the reason for all my careful preparations lie in the final knowledge that I would not have to act in earnest?" But at this penultimate moment he remembers another parable that Kashiwagi has quoted to him, "When you meet the Buddha, kill the Buddha!", which propels him to eradicate the disappointment of reality.[26]

In order to retain the Buddha/Temple within his own mind and thus restore it to its original illusory beauty, Mizoguchi must destroy it in actuality. In the world of shattered dreams and traditions that mark postwar Japan, the Otherness of beauty can live only in the mind. Tsurukawa's world of sunlight and flowers, everything that Mizoguchi desires so avidly, cannot exist for him; and he is egotistical enough to believe that only his feelings are important. Perhaps the novel's most telling line is Mizoguchi's first impression of the temple: "the shadow was more beautiful than the building itself."[27]

Mizoguchi has been expelled from the garden at birth; but, by taking possession of the temple, he can reenter the garden. At the same time, he can work out his rage against the circumstances of his own reality, which had denied him the garden. As Nakamura Mitsu points out, it just never occurs to Mizoguchi to think of the ethical dimensions of his act.[28] He is simply and totally self-obsessed.

Golden Pavilion can shed light on an aspect of Mishima's own life. In his own violent ritual suicide, Mishima had decided to kill the Buddha: to reject endurance, knowledge, and even art. It is ironic that the novel's last lines are "I wanted to live." Mizoguchi at least was able to project his desire onto the Other in such a way that by destroying/preserving it, he could finally get on with his own life. Mishima, however, tried to make himself into the Other and ultimately had to pay the final price.

THE BITTER TASTE OF GLORY:
THE SAILOR WHO FELL FROM GRACE WITH THE SEA

The Temple of the Golden Pavilion has obvious affiliations with an ideological novel, with its repeated scenes of traditional beauty being destroyed against a background of wartime Japan and the increasingly ugly world of postwar Japan where even the abbot of the temple keeps a mistress and deals on the black market. But what *Golden Pavilion* posited as an alternative to the postwar wasteland is a more

than usually abstract vision of alterity, not easily grasped, at least judging from the myriad of interpretations surrounding the novel. I have
suggested that the alternative here is a romanticized view of beauty
as an absolute. But a priest's longing for an abstract realm of beauty
symbolized by a temple, although it may intrigue the average reader,
is still unlikely to move him emotionally. Readers may sympathize
with the unlovely psychopathic character of Mizoguchi, but they are
most unlikely to identify with him, and thus the book's message
remains a strongly elitist one.

The basic message comes to be inscribed on a more popular level
in Mishima's 1963 novel *The Sailor Who Fell from Grace with the Sea*.
This novel, written seven years after *Golden Pavilion*, has been
viewed by at least one critic as another retelling of both that novel
and *Confessions of a Mask;*[29] and in terms of basic narrative structure,
he is certainly correct. Once again the text highlights an egotistical
romantic, in fact two egotistical romantics, who may also be called
artists manqué, each obsessed by a vision of alterity not to be found
in the disappointing real world. And once again the artists are willing to commit violence in order to protect that vision. But *Sailor* also
has a peculiar fascination of its own, and this is in its unabashed
romanticism, of a type that is far more accessible than the bloody
inverted dreams of the mask or the arcane aesthetic vision of Mizoguchi. The novel also presents a more tension-filled narrative in that
this time the object which is desired and must ultimately be sacrificed is a human being rather than a temple.

In many ways, the novel that *Sailor* most resembles is not one of
Mishima's but Conrad's *Lord Jim*, both in terms of its use of such
basic romantic archetypes as sea and sailor and in its brilliant interweaving of boys' adventure story at its most stereotypically romantic
with a realistic (in Mishima's novel nihilistic) vision of extreme irony.
Of course, *Sailor* lacks a Marlowe figure who, as a sympathetic but
detached narrator, gives *Lord Jim* its special tension, since Marlow is
both attracted and repelled by Jim's romantic vision. It does, however, present an initially sympathetic observer figure who, if not the
actual narrator of events, plays a crucial role of chronicler, commentator, and judge. Furthermore, as in *Lord Jim*, it is this interaction
between the observer and the active character that creates the story's
powerful dynamism.

In terms of essential narrative structure, *Lord Jim* and *Sailor* also
appear similar, with both based on a young romantic dreaming of

finding glory on the sea. Because of one mistake, he almost loses that chance for glory but eventually finds it again by redeeming himself through death. In both stories the question of whether the romantic himself is "satisfied" is a highly problematic one, which touches on the nature of romanticism in general.

Ryuji, the "active" hero of *Sailor*, is formed from a quintessentially romantic mold. Young, handsome and utterly unintellectual—although, like Conrad's hero, given to indulging in sentimental discourses about the sea—he ships out to sea at an early age and has adventures that any young romantic would envy. Unlike Jim, however, he never experiences the opportunity of becoming disillusioned with himself; instead, Ryuji becomes disillusioned with the process and the discovery that "a ship was another kind of prison."[30] In this respect, he resembles the other-directedness of a Mizoguchi, who blames all disappointments on the outside world rather than on his own shortcomings. Finding that the object of his desire cannot exist in reality, Ryuji proceeds to create another kind of dream world which is so romantic and so fanciful that it is unlikely ever to be spoiled by reality.

Ryuji's dreamworld, like that of Mizoguchi, is an apocalyptic one; Ryuji believes that "the world would have to topple if he was to gain the glory that was rightfully his." He begins to passively anticipate a "special destiny," a combination of three elements—the sea, a beautiful woman, and death.[31] Unlike Mizoguchi, Ryuji attains his desires; but he accomplishes his goals through a grotesquely ironic twist which plays on the reader's and the characters' expectations concerning romanticism.

The first step and first irony is that, in order to achieve this, Ryuji must be transformed into a totally passive hero, less a human being than a romantic icon. This is in obvious distinction to *Golden Pavilion* where Mizoguchi finally chooses action over passivity in the form of knowledge.

In *Sailor*, it is the second leading character, the apparent observer hero, who ultimately takes action and "helps" Ryuji attain his destiny. As it happens, this helper role contains echoes of the archetypal monomyth in which the hero is aided in his quest by magical outside forces usually crystallized into a helper character. But, of course, with Mishima's perversely ironic twist, the "aid" that this helper figure renders is of a questionable sort.

Twelve-year-old Noboru is the son of the beautiful woman with whom Ryuji falls in love just at the point when the sailor is beginning to despair of ever reaching his "destiny." Noboru is a precociously intelligent boy who is also activated by intense desire. In this case, his desire is for something "terrific," as he puts it; and he finds it when he spies on Ryuji and his mother making love: "It was like being part of a miracle ... Assembled there were the moon and a feverish wind, the incited, naked flesh of a man and a woman ... a cramped breathless peephole, a young boy's iron heart ... He was choked, wet, ecstatic."³²

This scene is almost the quintessence of romantic Otherness, with its highly colored imagery and intensity. In its depiction of a young boy looking in awe at a romantic alien figure, it also contains echoes of Oe's "Prize Stock" and the boys' fascination with the black soldier. The imagery here, however, emphasizes the gulf between the boy and the Other, because Noboru watches all this romantic intensity through a peephole. While "Prize Stock" allows the children to partake actively in the black soldier's exotic radiance, most notably in the scene where he bathes with them at the spring, Noboru is only permitted a totally passive voyeurism onto a world of magic. Noboru attempts to enter the magic world; but his own intellectual intelligence prevents him from actually joining with his idol, the sailor, and instead leads him to attempt to control the magic.

The problematic relationship between Noboru and his idol is what paradoxically forces him into an active role, despite his initial textual appearance as a voyeur and the apparent highlighting of the sailor as the genuine man of action. Whereas "Prize Stock" depicts the black soldier as a cross between a god and a beast, the narrative of *Sailor* dehumanizes Ryuji into a flat icon almost from the beginning. Ryuji is first described in terms of religious architecture: His flesh is "gold" and "his broad shoulders were as square as the beams in a temple roof." Even more explicitly, as Noboru watches the sailor prepare to have intercourse with his mother, "Noboru gazed in wonder as, rippling up through the thick hair below his belly, the lustrous temple tower soared triumphantly erect."³³

Just as Mizoguchi has a proprietary attitude toward the Temple of the Golden Pavilion, or as the boys in "Prize Stock" had to "their" soldier, so Noboru feels that he has created both the sailor and the erotic scene he has just witnessed. In true romantic egoist fashion, he feels that "[i]f this is destroyed it'll mean the end of the world" and vows that his will never happen: "I guess I'd do anything to stop that, no matter how awful!"[34] While the boys in "Prize Stock" have their fantasy worlds extinguished without even knowing what they had and Mizoguchi only reluctantly backs into action, the passive voyeur, Noboru, is placed into a potentially active role from the beginning. As it turns out, however, action does not come easily to him; it must be precipitated by an involved series of events much the same way that Mizoguchi was reluctantly forced into action.

Even more than most Mishima characters, Noboru is inordinately conscious of the limiting real world around him. In fact, he and his little group of similarly precocious friends tend to wax eloquent on the many disappointments of society, especially the problem of fathers. As the group's leader asserts, "'There is no such thing as a good father because the role itself is bad . . . They stand in the way of our progress while they try to burden us with their inferiority complexes, and their unrealized aspirations, and their resentments, and their ideals, and the weaknesses they've never told anyone about, and their sins, and their sweeter-than-honey dreams, and the maxims they've never had the courage to live by—they'd like to unload all that silly crap on us, all of it!'"[35]

As noted previously, the inadequate or absent father is of crucial importance in both writers' works. In the case of *Sailor* (again in an echo of "Prize Stock"), fathers are the jailers of the wasteland, playing on youthful dreams only to suppress them. Oe's "Prize Stock" and *Pluck the Buds* emphasized the complicity of the fathers with the war, with entrapment and finally with murder. In Mishima's novel, the fathers are also connected with evil; but it is the evil of conformity and sterile dreams, of tedious bourgeois existence. The Word of the Father in Mishima is the discourse of what he called in his interview with Oe "ordinary life," and it must be rejected at all costs.

Fathers, then, are in opposition to everything that Ryuji the sailor stands for—an untrammeled autonomous existence, complete with brightly colored tropical ports and, always in the background, the sea. But, for a brief moment in *Sailor,* Ryuji is threatened with the possibility of being turned into a father, the embodiment of the mundane world; and it is from this fate, far worse than death for any true romantic hero, that Noboru and his friends must save him.

Noboru's mother, Fusako, becomes the enemy in this battle for Ryuji's destiny. Although women in Mishima do not always play a negative role, in conflicts between the real and the imaginary, mother figures tend to side with grey reality. *The Golden Pavilion,* for example, posits the greedy and adulterous mother as the emblem of everything that Mizoguchi must run away from. In *Sailor*, however, Fusako plays a slightly more complex role because, in her beauty and sexual passion, she figures as the second element in Ryuji's romantic dream of the sea, the beautiful woman, and death. At the same time, however, she is also the owner of a luxury goods shop, thus becoming metonymically associated with materialism at its most obvious. Furthermore, she is a mother, concerned about security and a proper home life; thus inevitably she becomes a shackle on Ryuji's adventurous spirit.

At least this is how Noboru sees it, since he has already transformed Ryuji into the epitome of romantic Otherness. Noboru watches with horror as Ryuji, happily trading in his romantic dreams for marriage with Fusako, starts wearing "smart" English clothes and reading "silly novels and art books."[36] Expecting him to go off to sea again in an appropriately adventurous fashion, Noboru instead is forced to watch passively as Ryuji is molded into a father figure, alternately full of hypocritical ingratiation and blustering bullying. In a final pivotal scene, Fusako catches her son spying on them and persuades Ryuji to play his new role of father and lecture the boy, to the embarrassment of them both. Thus, even the last magic of the peephole is shattered and Ryuji is revealed as disappointingly, embarrassingly, human. Where Noboru had earlier boasted to his friends that the sailor would "do something terrific,"[37] he is now reduced to apologizing for the sailor's fall from the romantic to the real.

It is Noboru and his friends who decide to remedy the situation, forcing the real to give way one last time to the romantic or, as the leader of the group puts it, " 'giv[ing] that sailor a chance to be a hero again.' "[38] Their method of deliverance differs sharply from the Kiplingesque adventures of Jim on Patusan, however, or even the cathartic excitement of the firing of the temple in Mizoguchi's saga. The sailor does meet his death through a combination of the sea and a beautiful woman; but the fateful scene, as Sato has pointed out, is the antithesis of the romantic ideal that Ryuji supposedly represents.[39]

In contrast with the glorious summer day on which Ryuji first appeared, the sailor's death takes place on a dismal winter afternoon. Moreover, instead of being on the sea, it occurs in "dry dock," a cave in the mountains, with the ocean only a dull glint on the horizon. Yet Ryuji's death is the direct result of his love for the sea and a woman, because it is due to his decision to marry Fusako and renounce his sailorhood. Ryuji is murdered by the six thirteen-year-old boys who have literally "towed" him to his execution, in order to restore him by death to his original romantic persona. Thus, the "glory" which was a homonym for the "towing" in the afternoon of the novel's original title in Japanese (*Gogo no eikō*)[40] is ultimately reduced to a grotesque form of murder, a cup of poisoned tea followed by the dissection of his body, a dissection which has been prefigured in a previous passage recounting the boys' killing and dissection of a kitten.

Is Ryuji's death, then, simply to be equated with that of a cat? And is the book's "message" that all dreams of glory end in dry dock? The answer is not a simple yes or no, but is dependent upon the reader's reaction to this interweaving of romance and realism. On a "realistic" level, the sailor's dream of a romantic destiny is a farce, a melodramatic boys' fantasy that cannot exist in the real world of ordinary fathers and sons. From this perspective, the boys' cold-blooded murder of Ryuji is simply the last act of the farce, proof that dreams of romantic destiny can only be twisted into petty horror.

From the opposite point of view, however, it is possible to make a case for the success of the romantic alternative, and this depends on the success or failure of the characterization of Ryuji and Noboru and of the attractiveness of the romantic imagery around the sailor. Ryuji is reduced to a romantic icon in Noboru's eyes through his association with the clichéd elements of ship, sea, and tropical port and the text's own architectural imagery. Indeed, Mishima exposes one seafaring cliché after another to the merciless light of modern realism, as Conrad does in *Lord Jim*. But, as in *Lord Jim*, these adventure-story stereotypes begin to assume a power of their own when seen through the eyes of the matched protagonists, the romantic Jim and Ryuji and the intellectual but still romantic Marlowe and Noboru. It is not the clichés of Patusan or the tropical parrots that ultimately strengthen the credibility of romanticism but rather the two kinds of protagonists' intense attraction to them.

On a realistic level, the boys are evil, cold-blooded, over-intellectual brutes, capable of killing a man for having disappointed them and justifying their actions through the pretense of objectivity. Yet the boys and the sailor are joined by desire; and it is the effectively rendered intensity of this desire, perhaps even more than its rather misty objects (heroism, death, glory), which makes the novel something other than a nihilistic explication of the perils of romanticism. Thus, the novel's last scene with its evocation of desire abandoned is a peculiarly poignant one.

Having shed his smart foreign togs, the sailor meets the boys in his old shipping outfit and they proceed to the boys' hideout ("dry dock"), where Ryuji proceeds to tell them stories. He is unaware that he is about to be murdered, and the occasion opens his memories to the times when he dreamed of glory. As the stories continue, his young listeners become enraptured and, through the double prism of man and children's excitement, the reader, too, is stirred. When Noboru's "chief" hands Ryuji the poisoned tea and he drinks it down, one can almost empathize with the young boys for rescuing the sailor from the fate of ordinariness. The novel's last line, "Glory, as anyone knows, is bitter stuff,"[41] referring to the bitter taste of poisoned tea, can thus be read both as an ironic blast at the sailor's sentimentality and as a straightforward, perhaps even autobiographical, expression of Mishima's own longing and despair. In the real world, glory must always be bitter stuff, achievable only through dreams and the magical language of the storyteller.

SUMMER HAD PASSED THEM BY: *OUR ERA*

The environments that Mishima's fiction offers as alternatives to the real world are notable for their lyrical beauty and use of such traditional romantic clichés as the sea, the garden, and beautiful women. The two Oe works to be discussed here and in the next section depict heroes either searching for or defending worlds which, although certainly romantic in the sense that they, too, are vivid alternatives to reality, are less obviously products of an aesthetic sensibility. In fact, one of the charms of the alternative world in *Our Era* is that it crystallizes around a "large-size truck," an object of utter homeliness but one desperately coveted by the novel's young protagonists. The works also differ in that the level of explicit political commentary is even higher than in Oe's "Prize Stock" or *Pluck the Buds*. Although Mishima's *Golden Pavilion* may arguably be read as a nihilistic allegory of postwar Japan, with the implicit suggestion that only the illusion remains of traditional Japanese culture, Oe's novels go much further in dissecting the ills of postwar society.

As with Mishima's works, Oe's solution to the overall "problem" of postwar Japan is usually a violent one. Indeed, both writers' novels, different through they are in style and imagery, share a common apocalyptic sensibility, whether it be manifested in the bombers that Mizoguchi hopefully awaits in *Golden Pavilion* or in the "floodwaters" which Oe's protagonists confidently expect to rise in *The Floodwaters Have Come unto My Soul*. The protagonists examined in this chapter are united by a sense that the escape from or the alteration of the real world is achievable only through destruction.

The fact that Oe's heroes are doomed to remain forever in search of a lost garden may account for these stories' pessimistic atmosphere. At least his heroes in "Prize Stock" and *Pluck the Buds* were allowed, if only temporarily, to escape into a vibrant summer or adventurous winter. Mishima's heroes too, have a chance to experience an approximation of the romantic in the real world, even if only through the voyeuristic peeping in which both Mizoguchi and Noboru engage.

In the case of Mishima's protagonists, the very experience of romance in reality impels them deeper into the world of illusion and the destruction necessary to sustain that world. Mishima's heroes, then, have understood that the alternate to the real can only be an illusion and they destroy reality in order to sustain the illusion. But the characters in Oe's *Our Era* and *Floodwaters* never even come close to fulfilling their dreams. Consequently their fates are darker and their reactions even more violent than those of Mishima's protagonists.

As discussed in Chapter Two, *Our Era* traces Yasuo's self-pitying fall into despair, a story worthy of the grimmest Naturalist fiction. The story of Yasuo's younger brother Shigeru is so generically different as to be almost a separate novel within a novel. In contrast to Yasuo's claustrophobic intellectual world, Shigeru's story comes as close to being a romantic, if grotesque, adventure as is possible within the limits of a realistic novel. Shigeru is a jazz pianist and in his own way a romantic hero who desires. His dreams are simpler than those of the sailor or Mizoguchi, however, centering on the desire for what he and his friends call "EXCITEMENT" and his craving for a "large-size truck." In this truck he and the fellow members of his jazz trio "The Unlucky Young Men" can wander throughout Japan wherever and whenever they please, like Japanese Huck Finns, but on a highway rather than a river.

Indeed, like Huckleberry and Tom, the "Unlucky Young Men" have no desire to be "sivilized" and seem pleased to contemplate a world without women who, inevitably, do not understand their dreams. Thus, an early scene shows Shigeru boasting loudly to a girl that "'I'd do anything to get that truck, even kill someone!'"[42] and being angry when she does not understand his desire for the freedom of the road.

In a sense, the "freedom" of a romantic non-place is a major goal for all the protagonists discussed in this chapter, but the question remains: freedom from what? In the case of Shigeru and his friends, one could suspect that what they really search for is simply freedom from boredom since they themselves admit that what they want in their lives is EXCITEMENT. That this rather pathetic search ends in blood and death, with no concern for other people, only serves to remind us once again of the previously quoted comment by Noguchi concerning "the violent infantilism of the romantic."

The relative childishness (Shigeru is actually only sixteen) of the protagonists can be disturbing, but their naiveté has a touching side as well. The very artlessness of the object of desire, the truck, is far more realistic and accessible than the abstract dreams of beauty and glory that Mishima's suspiciously precocious young protagonists share in *Sailor.* As it turns out, however, the truck is ultimately even more unattainable than the visions of Noboru and his friends, although Shigeru's previously mentioned vow to the girl sounds similar to Noboru's vow to "do anything" to protect the sailor's romantic quality.

Of course, the truck is only a symbol for Shigeru's dissatisfaction with the world around him and his intense desire for romanticized alternatives. Another object of his desire (in the sense of wanting to be like the Other) is Taka, the third member of his jazz trio. A twenty-three-year-old Korean, Taka is the oldest member of the group and, with his experience in the Korean war, is idolized by Shigeru as a "man's man."[45] This idealization turns out to be one of the novel's many ironies; for Taka is actually a homosexual and a former prostitute for American soldiers, who lives in terror of having his sexual preferences discovered.

The ironies continue as the group advances fortuitously into a bizarre act of violence, their decision to throw a bomb under the emperor's car. Instead of the long, steady buildup to action that occurred in the two Mishima works, the three youths almost fall into violence as result of their whimsical search for EXCITEMENT. Their hunt first leads them to participation in a right-wing rally welcoming the emperor's visit to a department store (another irony, of course, since the emperor, as a former god, should be above material goods), during which they fantasize gleefully about being "real fascists" like the Nazis and raping and torturing Jewish women. Their excitement soon changes to disappointment when they catch a glimpse of the emperor through his limousine window. "'He doesn't seem Imperial,'" laments Kenzo, the youngest member of their group, while Shigeru says sourly, "'He was just sitting there and taking it easy.'"[44]

Incensed by the emperor's boring behavior, the trio decides to "give that quiet guy a shock" that will cause a "scandal throughout Japan"[45] and finally provide them with their sought-after EXCITEMENT. Both their decision to bomb the imperial car, and their motivation behind the decision are reminiscent of Noboru and his group in *Sailor*. For both groups of young romantics an idol, an emblem of the world of romance, has fallen from his pedestal and must be forced back in place through destructive behavior. The heroes of *Our Era* create a scheme that is quite simple: They will throw a leftover hand grenade belonging to Taka in front of the emperor's car. Presumably, they do not wish particularly to kill the emperor, or any innocent bystanders for that matter; but like Mishima's Mizoguchi, they are so obsessed by the nature of the deed itself that such mundane ethical considerations never trouble them. All they can concentrate on is the EXCITEMENT they will feel when the bomb is actually thrown, a feeling perhaps comparable to the wonderful moment when they finally get their truck.

In fact, the car bombing becomes strangely intertwined with the possible attainment of the truck. While Taka waits as lookout for the limousine's arrival, he thinks: "Just as long as the bombing went okay, they were sure of getting their hands on the truck. This was the gamble. If the bombing failed they would have lost the truck forever and their lives would be like rotting apples . . . Their fates were gambled on a small hand grenade the size of a musk melon."[46] Such a childish conflation of action and wish fulfillment obviously has no place in reality but, like Mishima's heroes before them, Oe's protagonists are determined to create their own realities.

The story itself becomes increasingly unreal as the scheme's grotesque denouement unfolds. Suspense and bizarre humor combine as two of the boys wait, sweating with apprehension, in the bathroom of a building above where the emperor's car is expected, the hand grenade concealed in an empty sanitary napkin receptacle. There are some funny moments as the boys wait in agony while various office workers come in to use the coed facilities. Their tortured wait turns out to be for nothing, however, because a woman office worker unknowingly foils the plan by using the napkin disposal for its proper function, presumably not noticing the hand grenade inside. The boys are subsequently overcome with reluctance to deal with the bomb; and a memorable scene follows, showing Shigeru opening the receptacle and being so repulsed by its contents that he "crumbles" to the floor and "with both knees on the wet tiles he began to vomit. The vomitus flowed out in a ceaseless stream, dirtying the head of the grenade which poked up through the bloodstained cotton." And, as he watches the emperor's limousine come into view, "sitting on the toilet, he groaned above his sobs."[47]

Such a bloody, tawdry fiasco is totally alien to romantic dreams of glory or even EXCITEMENT. By comparison, Ryuji's death appears almost dignified, while the successful burning of the temple comes across as a romantic triumph. And yet, the boys' romanticism is just as keen as that of Noboru or Mizoguchi. The following passage poignantly sums up their disappointment: "The 'Unlucky Young Men' had abandoned the gamble and chosen humiliation. No large-size truck would ever be theirs. Their pride and their friendship would now be smeared with dirt . . . the summer had passed them by, so had the sea, so had sweat, so had desire. From now on the lives of the 'Unlucky Young Men' would be dark. They would never feel EXCITEMENT. It was 3:30. They left the building with their heads down."[48]

Unlike the fantasies of the various other romantic heroes thus far profiled, the boys' scheme of violence is so obviously a disaster that, even in their imaginations, they cannot turn it into something honorable. It is in keeping with the theme of woman as a hindrance that it is a female, attending to one of the most obvious of her reproductive functions, who foils their plot. The young men's reaction to their failure hardly fits a stalwart masculine stereotype: They return to their jazz club and dissolve into sobs, lamenting their failure and, above all, mourning the loss of their truck. Ironically, it is their still potent desire for the truck that brings on another bout of violence, but this time the violence is unplanned and even more disastrous.

The descent into disaster occurs almost immediately after the grenade incident and is initiated by Taka's meeting with a former American lover with whom he goes to bed. Buoyed by an excess of good feeling and trust, he asks the man for money to buy the truck; and, on being refused, he strangles the American in a disappointed rage. He then flees to the jazz bar and tries to persuade Shigeru to escape with him to Korea. Shigeru, who "had been waiting for something crazy like this,"[49] agrees with alacrity; and, for a moment, it seems as if the two might realize their dream of becoming unshackled wanderers.

The pessimistic dynamics of *Our Era* make such an agreeable outcome impossible. Kenzo, on hearing that he is to be left behind because he is weak and a "troublemaker," insists on proving his masculinity by challenging Taka to a game of "chicken" with the hand grenade. Not surprisingly, the game results in their both being blown up. Only Shigeru remains, and he ends up dying in an hysterical and totally unnecessary shootout with the police.

The message in *Our Era* is a bleakly clear one. Attempts to change the real world through action will end only in death, destruction and ignominy. Oe's use of the mixed genres of boy's adventure with the angst-ridden realism of Yasuo's fate is as successful as Mishima's similarly ironic use of mixed genres in *Sailor* to drive the discouraging point home. As Toshizawa Yukio says of Oe's purpose in placing the passive hero Yasuo together with the active but unsuccessful Shigeru, "[This shows that] those who have lost the chance to act become impotent and elderly or, if they reject that fate, they can only become terrorists or murderers."[50] In fact, *Our Era*'s message is even bleaker, since the heroes do not even become very *good* terrorists and murderers. As Mishima does in *Golden Pavilion*, Oe creates a redundant pattern of shattered illusions: Taka is not a masculine symbol. The boys are not brave terrorists. Assassination attempts can be foiled by a sanitary napkin. And, finally, desiring something enough will not necessarily obtain the longed-for object.

In the scene with the sanitary napkin, Oe unquestionably aims at farce; but the farce is hardly lighthearted. While Michiko Wilson correctly identifies Oe's belief in the crucial importance of humor,[51] it must be emphasized that this comedy is of the most despairing kind. In the face of the wretchedness of reality, it may well be that laughter is the only recourse possible; but it can only be laughter of the most mordant kind.

In their naiveté, Oe's protagonists are at least more sympathetic than the precocious youths of *Sailor;* and in terms of an ideological novel, one could argue that they triumph in the end because their hearts remain "pure." But by any realistic standards, they are fundamentally pathetic. Their romanticism cannot bring about effective change, and their political concerns are notable for their confusion. Even the role of the emperor, which becomes a potent symbol in later stories by Oe, is curiously low-key here, as if the enormous potential symbolism must be repressed.

Unlike Ryuji, whose romantic qualities are described in purple prose, the better to make the reader appreciate Noboru's disappointment, the emperor seems a relatively unimportant figure, taking second place as an object of desire behind the large truck. It is as if the era that has produced the "Unlucky Young Men" is too drab even to give them bright visions. It is perhaps significant that Oe makes his trio musicians, for it is only in the scenes where they play jazz together that a feeling of transcendence is communicated. Like the story-telling moments of Ryuji with the boys, music touches a realm that reality cannot destroy.

APOCALYPSE NOW: *THE FLOODWATERS HAVE COME UNTO MY SOUL*

Defense and destruction form the two poles around which the narrative discussed in this chapter have revolved. All the protagonists are attempting to escape or change the world through defending the romantic while destroying the real; and, in the case of Mishima's characters at least, the text seems to allow the heroes some measure of triumph. In the stories of both Shigeru and Yasuo, Oe's *Our Era* allows no such ambiguity: Shigeru is dead; and Yasuo is contemplating suicide when the novel ends, such being the nature, as the last page reminds us, of "Our Era."

In a sense, the fourth novel to be considered in this chapter, *The Floodwaters Have Come Unto My Soul,* is an intensified and extended form of the same cry of despair that animated *Our Era.* This time, the message, although still apparently despairing, is also an implicit call to arms against modern Japanese society and simultaneously a vision of an alternative world that is far more comprehensive than anything in Oe's previous work. In *Floodwaters,* the horrors of the real world are not simply boredom or ugliness or even the Second World War, but the threat of nuclear and ecological catastrophe, while the alternative is essentially a grown up and radicalized vision of the pastoral utopia of *Pluck the Buds.* The overt politicizing is important not only in marking a major development in Oe's fictional growth, but also in the way it affects the narrative itself. For in *Floodwaters,* a complex but genuine example of one type of the *roman à thèse* exists, what Suleiman calls the novel of confrontation, a novel that pits a highly explicit "good" against an equally explicit "evil."[52]

In terms of ideological framework, *Golden Pavilion* and *Sailor* may be called ideological "apprenticeship novels" since the protagonist serves an apprenticeship of learning under various mentors and, through observing the apprenticeship, the reader learns something too.[53] But, the "something" learned from these novels is highly problematic. In Mishima's works, the ultimate message is that reality must be destroyed, while *Our Era*'s "message" is that our "era" is so unspeakable, and at the same time so oppressive, that the only means of escape is death. Appropriate for novels of apprenticeship, the three works focus on only a few individuals, since the narrative's function is to trace their development. The novel of confrontation, however, takes over a much wider canvas, both in terms of the broad brush strokes it uses to limn its actors, who are usually depicted in group rather than individual terms, as well as the wide stretches of society and the social issues it treats. In fact, these issues are really mega-issues, what Suleiman calls, quoting from one such book, "a struggle between heaven and hell."[54]

Oe's novel, as the explicitly biblical title taken from *Psalms* 69:1 underscores, occupies a firm place within such apocalyptic confrontational works. The "good," who style themselves self-consciously as "Freedom Voyagers," although depicted with more complexity than might be expected, are basically virtuous, sure of their collective dream of a world far superior to contemporary Japanese society, which is represented throughout the novel at its most loathsome, in the form of politicians, police, and the Japanese Self-Defense Forces, the last of which engage in a final apocalyptic shootout with the Freedom Voyagers. This final struggle is a "moral" war as Suleiman asserts the novel of confrontation must involve. As she says, "The antagonistic hero does not fight in order to achieve 'glory' either for himself or for the group to which he belongs, he fights for truth, justice, freedom, or his fatherland—in a word for transcendental and absolute values."[55] Where the novels previously discussed in this chapter also privileged absolute values in the form of aesthetics or romanticism, they still focalized these values through the perceptions of individual protagonists. *Floodwaters,* however, heads this study in the direction of the collective and the overtly political.

By highlighting the collective, *Floodwaters* inevitably slights such typical novelistic issues as character development. Unlike characters in the novel of apprenticeship, the characters in *Floodwaters* do not particularly change or develop. They always know what is "right" and the narrative's concern is in showing the struggle between those in the right and those in the wrong.

There is one exception in *Floodwaters*, however; and through it an interesting extension occurs, an attempt to graft a story of apprenticeship onto a confrontational structure. Ironically, in this case the apprenticeship is not served by a young man but by the novel's passive intellectual protagonist, Oki Isana. In some ways, Isana is the moral center of the novel and, in ideology at least, is clearly similar to Oe himself. Although Isana is not actually the narrator of the novel, the story is seen through his eyes; and thus, if the reader is sympathetic to him, his or her sympathies are gradually extended toward the group of Freedom Voyagers as Isana becomes friendly with them. In contrast, if there is not sympathy with the narrator, then the work ultimately both disturbs and disappoints; and the more overt the narrator's ideology, the more likely the reader is to lose sympathy.

Indeed, the very strength of the ideological message is one of *Floodwater*'s weaknesses, beginning with the opening itself, which immediately sets the stage for an us-versus-them confrontation. The novel opens with a rejection of contemporary urban society as a man who calls himself Oki Isana (Big Tree Brave Fish) moves into a nuclear fallout shelter on a hill outside of the city. The son-in-law of a corrupt and powerful politician, Isana has decided to renounce the world for the sake of his idiot son, Jin. He is also waiting to carry out his self-assigned role of "representative" of "the best things on earth," the whales and the trees.[56] Because a vision of the "last day" when all the bombs have fallen and the floodwaters have risen dominates Isana, he lives quietly with his son preparing for it. On that day he and Jin will emerge from the shelter to greet the "things that come after" and transmit the messages of the trees and the whales.[57]

Isana is already committed to a definite vision of what is wrong with the world, most notably ecological and nuclear disaster; but at this point in the story, he seems content to be a passive observer. He simply rejects the modern technological world of hovering disaster, putting his trust into the nonhuman creatures with whom he believes he can communicate, seeing them as "close to gods"[58] and, in moments of stress, apologizing to them for the damage mankind has done. Thus, although Isana's vision of an alternative world is a richly detailed, almost Shintoesque, one of floods and godlike creatures, it is essentially a passive one, a world which he is content to wait for.

The group of young people he falls in with, however, are not so patient. The Freedom Voyagers are a group of youthful outcasts, who have all been involved in some form of criminal or at least antisocial activity and are united in their opposition to the authorities, whom they sarcastically call "the strong and righteous people." They are united by one more thing as well, and in this they trace their lineage to earlier Oe heroes—their shared dream of a ship that will carry them out to sea. On the sea they will become, as Inago, the lone female member of the band tells Isana excitedly, "citizens of the country of the Freedom Voyagers. We'll live without being bothered by anyone and we won't have anything to do with the strong and righteous people. We'll just live on the ship."[59]

The dream of the ship obviously resembles the many other worlds of desire of Oe's heroes, such as Africa, the yacht *Les Amis* in *Outcries,* or Shigeru's truck; but in this case, the vessel almost exists. Takagi, the leader of the Freedom Voyagers proudly shows Isana the double-masted schooner they have stolen and reconstructed in their hideout, an abandoned movie studio. The image of the movie studio reinforces the romantic unreality of the ship, which, as it rises out of the floodlit studio floor, is an eerily beautiful tribute to the romantic imagination. Indeed, there can be no doubt that these young outcasts are romantics, although their romantic vision is a far darker and more carefully thought out one than that of Shigeru and his comrades, and an even more apocalyptically destructive one than that of the romantics in Mishima's *Golden Pavilion* or *Sailor*. Their plan even has a certain insane logic to it, in some ways resembling the cold-blooded calculations of Noboru and his comrades.

The Freedom Voyagers' plan is based on their expectation of a major Tokyo earthquake. On that day, for which they are steadily preparing, they plan to block traffic so that the "powerful people" cannot escape first; then, they themselves will make their way to the sea and board their ship. Thus, like Mizoguchi in *Golden Pavilion*, they initially await a deus ex machina that will lead them to a union of death and destruction, but on a far greater level than even Mizoguchi imagines. Isana, in fact, is initially quite shocked after a revealing conversation with the girl Inago. He asks her, "'What if you get attacked by the strong and righteous ones?'" only to have her calmly reply, "'It's in preparation for that, that Tamakichi has collected all those weapons, don't you see? And didn't I tell you that we've all had experience with violence?'"

Even more apocalyptically, she goes on to explain in concrete detail what will happen if they are attacked: "'But in the end it's certain that we'll be crushed, so the plan is to stockpile enough dynamite so that the cruiser can blow itself up, Takagi says. And then, if we broadcast to the people on the shore that we've been pressed to the point that we have no choice but to blow ourselves up, then we might be able to create sympathizers among the people on the shore, who'll supply us food and water and resist the interference by the police or the coast guard.'"[60]

Although initially shocked by the cold-bloodedness with which the group plans its destructive actions, Isana becomes increasingly drawn to them. He is, however, slightly repulsed by the ease with which they float into violent acts, from stealing cars and hijacking meat trucks, to a more mysterious event that may or may not be a fantasy. This is the dream that Takagi, one of their leaders, recounts to Isana, in which he claims to have seen a village stoning take place underneath what he calls a "whale tree." The image of the whale tree creates a common bond between Takagi and Isana because Isana sees trees as godlike objects which "render meaningless the boundary between life and death,"[61] although Takagi's image of the tree has a much more brutal cast to it. In the dream he recounts to Isana, a family dressed in white is led by a "black" group of people to a point beneath the tree:

> "The clothes and the people who are wearing them aren't clear. It's like when you see a naked woman in a dream before you've ever done it with a woman. But I'm sure they were all wearing white square paper clothes and they were all one family. And then those silent black people surrounding them all threw stones at them. That went on for a while until the family that had been hit by the stones all fell over and dropped into a hole that had already been dug . . . Everyone was quiet and the only sound was the rustling of the whale tree's leaves."[62]

Considered as a dream or "vision" (*buijion*), to use the Freedom Voyagers' favorite English word, the fantasy has an eerie, stylized beauty. But is also suggests a union of the pastoral fantasy of "Prize Stock" and *Pluck the Buds* with youthful collective violence, an ideological and narrative development of great significance. Whereas in these two earlier works, the violence was entirely the work of faceless adults and the children were innocent victims of the outside world, in the 1970s Oe's work highlights violence by the "innocent side" as the best means of escaping/destroying the world.

The union of violence, ideology, and youth is most evident when Takagi and his friends stage a grotesque reenactment of his "whale tree" dream in front of Isana. This time, however, the object of violence is not a mysterious family in white, but a bizarre character with a "shrinking disease," whom the text calls The Shrinking Man. Originally a close comrade, he is discovered by the group to have sold photographs of their paramilitary activities to a weekly magazine; and they subject him to a brutal self-criticism session in which his disease, his betrayal, and his homosexuality are all held up to ridicule.

Although he maintains his self-control throughout, the Shrinking Man eventually goads one of his former sex partners into kicking him and from then on, he and the reader are plunged into a maelstrom of bloody violence culminating in a graphic scene where the Shrinking Man is "spitted" onto a pointed wooden stick. The actual stoning, which takes place soon after, is also graphically described; but, compared to the bloodiness of the previous events, it is almost anticlimactic. In an ironically appropriate gesture, the group then buries the Shrinking Man's body under a giant zelkova tree, the same kind that Takagi had previously identified as the whale tree of his dream.

The Shrinking Man's death is obviously a sacrifice, a scapegoating; and it is significant that this time it is an adult who is sacrificed by "children," as Isana affectionately calls the group of young people. Thus, *Floodwaters* offers a twisted version of the world of "Prize Stock" and *Pluck the Buds,* where the children were sacrificed and scapegoated by the adults. This time, the children are no longer running away into the darkness but are fighting back, attempting to revitalize the wasteland on their own terms, through conscious and deliberate bloodshed.

Takagi justifies the murder to the still shocked Isana in similar terms. According to Takagi, the Shrinking Man actually wanted to be murdered. Since he was already dying of his strange disease, he was apparently willing to martyr himself to the group so that, through their collective murder of him, the group would be bound together in a way no other circumstance could create. Depending on the degree of the reader's sympathy with the group, the explanation may seem a trifle self-serving; but Isana willingly accepts it to the point that he offers himself as the next martyr. This willingness on the part of a middle-aged man to sacrifice himself for a youth is reminiscent of the older man's death in "The Swimming Man," but Isana is not simply doing this for the "children" but for the all-important trees and whales.

In the novel's last scenes, Isana hands over his inarticulate son Jin to the motherly Inago, who has become his lover, and proceeds to join the last two members of the Freedom Voyagers in a massive shootout with the Japanese Self-Defense Forces, a shootout that will inevitably lead to their deaths. In the novel's final lines appears Isana's last vision of the trees and whales: "He fired a third shot. A strong blast hit the inner wall of the underground shelter and the repercussions overwhelmed him. Falling again into the already deep water he fired a fourth time . . . In the distance nothingness was beginning to appear. Turning to the spirits of the trees and the spirits of the whales, he gives them his final salutations. 'All is well.'"[63]

The apocalyptic ending of *Floodwaters* is curiously moving, perhaps because of its invocation of the trees and whales, the innocent outsiders forced to suffer through human agency. Another outsider who deserves mention is Isana's idiot son, Jin. Ever since *A Personal Matter*, the abnormal child in Oe's fiction has symbolized both the monstrous aspects of the modern wasteland and the way out of it. The idiot child who cannot understand reality is the ultimate victim and the ultimate outsider. He is also, in his innocence, the ultimate savior. Thus, the fact that Isana hands Jin over to one of the Freedom Voyagers is significant, emphasizing once again that these terrorists are also, in reality, "children."

Even if the Freedom Voyagers themselves are violent, the implication is that their violence is just, given the horrors perpetrated by man. Although in realistic terms, the Freedom Voyagers may be nothing more than a gang of depraved young thugs playing at politics, in the romanticizing ideological substructure that Oe creates, they are just as much victims as the trees and the whales. True to protagonists of an ideological novel who triumph even in disaster because they are "right," the Freedom Voyagers know that their deaths will not immediately change the world; but at the same time they still insist that they are proud to go down fighting for their "vision of the ship," their romanticized imaginary, far from the constraints of civilization. Isana too, is determined to sacrifice himself for his own vision of alterity, the trees and the whales. As he explains it to himself, "If I'm surrounded by hundreds of soldiers and shot, that will clearly show human beings killing the representative of the trees and whales and also, since the TV, radio, and newspapers will be reporting it, it's the best possible chance to get the message across."[64]

And the message is very important in this novel of confrontation, although whether the reader agrees with it is another question, one that is to some extent dependent on how effectively Isana's conversion to violence is rendered, since it is Isana who guides the reader through the maze of violence. In the case of *Pluck the Buds* and "Prize Stock," the identification with the children is almost automatic because they were obviously innocent victims; but in Isana's case, especially given the cruelty of the youths towards the Shrinking Man, the identification becomes a more complex one. The problem of reader identification, however, is an inevitable aspect of the ideological novel which, at its most strongly ideological, almost requires a basically sympathetic reader. As Suleiman notes, ". . . the role of the reader in the *roman à thèse* . . . is strongly programmed."[65] Oe can be a satirical and humorous writer on the subject of terrorism (witness the brilliant sanitary napkin disposal scene in *Our Era*), but it is less easy to discern such distancing humor in *Floodwaters*. *Floodwaters* instead leaves the reader with a disturbing and powerful fantasy of regenerative violence and bloody sacrifice. The sides are clearly drawn. In the ranks of the "evil" are the authorities, symbolized by the politicians and the Self-Defense Forces, and characterized by their reliance on a technology that will destroy not only the Freedom Voyagers but the entire world. On the alternate side are the Freedom Voyagers, who are characterized by their affinity with nature, a delineation supported by their explicitly naturalist names (Inago means "locust," Takagi "tall tree") and by their overtly antitechnological stance. Although willing to use the mechanical weapons of the modern world, their long-term plan is to allow the technology of that world to destroy itself, at which time they will escape on their resolutely antitechnological schooner. Isana starts out the novel as the mediator between the two sides (in a voyeuristic echo of *Sailor*, he spies on the Freedom Voyagers for several days before actually confronting them), but at the novel's close he totally rejects modern society for an heroic sacrificial death.

Floodwaters may be the most explicit, but it is certainly not the only novel discussed here that privileges violence and sacrifice as the only way to protect the alternatives to the modern world. In their perverse way, both *Golden Pavilion* and *Sailor* are also works of desire and sacrifice. Mizoguchi sacrifices the real temple to preserve his illusion of beauty, while Noboru sacrifices the sailor for the same reason.

Violence becomes the last frontier of opposition to the wasteland of the real.

In *Violence and the Sacred*, Rene Girard explains that the idea of sacrifice comes originally from the community's desire to ritually cleanse and purge itself,[66] and certainly an element of purgation exists in all three books. But the crucial difference is that the "community" that is purging itself in these works is an outcast one. In Mishima's works, it is a community of elitist romantics who understand the need for violence which the common people cannot, while in the case of *Floodwaters*, the purgative function is even more obvious, since the murder of the Shrinking Man is clearly the instrument that unites the group through its shared intense and illegal experience.

Significantly, in Mishima's novels, neither hero actually sacrifices himself. Although Mizoguchi will be punished, he still asserts at the end of the novel, "I wanted to live," while Noboru and his group are highly conscious of the fact that, if they commit murder before the age of thirteen, they will not be arraigned for it. Thus, Mishima's heroes are doubly triumphant; they can transform their romanticism into real-world action but ultimately can escape from paying a major price for their decision to act. In a sense, then, his two novels may be considered as having happy endings, especially *Sailor*, which contains aspects of the perfect romantic's wish-fulfillment fantasy.

Oe's heroes, of course, suffer very different fates: the pathetic and basically unconscious Shigeru dies for no real reason beyond a desire for excitement, while Isana when last seen is preparing to lay down his life for the trees and the whales. Isana's fate can, however, be considered a triumph when read in both ideological and romantic terms. Unlike the fundamentally voyeuristic Noboru, who can transform only the sailor into a hero, Isana makes himself into a hero.

In all these works the protagonists are fighting back, whether successfully or not, in an attempt to protect their alternative worlds. As will be apparent in the next chapter, violence is also important in the two writers' treatment of the emperor; but for the moment it is worth considering why violence should be increasingly highlighted, especially in Oe's case, from the random, despairing violence of *Our Era* to the carefully thought out, if ultimately unsuccessful, violence of the Freedom Voyagers.

Indeed, increasingly in Oe's fiction of the 1970s and 1980s, characters who may once have served simply as passive sacrifices are being converted to active defiance, as is apparent in *Floodwaters* (1973), *The Pinchrunner Memorandum* (1976), and *The Game of Contemporaneity* (1980). In the last work, for example, Oe creates his most comprehensive vision of rural collective violence when an entire village holds out for fifty days in a war against the "Greater Japanese Empire."

The reasons for this narrative development are both literary and extraliterary, but undoubtedly one of the most important causes must be found outside the literary sphere in the violent cauldron of youth, ideology, and mass movements that boiled over in the 1960s. The changes actually started as early as 1960 with the massive demonstrations against the security treaty between the United States and Japan. The demonstrations then subsided until the late 1960s and the explosion of violence that culminated in the mass demonstrations of 1968 when Tokyo University was closed for three months and students took to the streets to war against the police.

For both Oe and Mishima the days of the 1960s were vital ideological signals, flashpoints signaling an increasingly apocalyptic world where no one could escape the violence. Oe's sympathies were strongly with the students, not only in Japan but across the waters in China, where the tremendous reverberations of the Cultural Revolution were being felt. It is undoubtedly the echoes of the Red Guards' torture and self-criticism sessions (reinterpreted by the Japanese Red Army) which helped to form the narrative events of *Floodwaters*. Until recently, twentieth-century visionary literature has tended to model itself either on the Soviet Union or on the United States; but Oe bases his fantasy on a third, the Chinese model, where youth must overthrow and crush the oppressive traditions of the elders. Closer to home, the apocalyptic ending of *Floodwaters* has echoes of the devastating 1972 shootout between the Japanese Red Army and the Self-Defense Forces.

The importance of youth also helps to explain the story's visible ties to the boyish dreams of romantic action that played a significant role in *Our Era*. Even Isana is essentially recovering his youth, living out a fantasy of heroism and martyrdom against the military-industrial establishment. The fact that the extreme violence of the establishment's reaction is never logically explained is beside the point in this fantasy. As Isoda comments, the Self-Defense Forces can be seen as simply a narrative necessity to provide a properly apocalyptic us-versus-them kind of ending.[67]

In terms of narrative structure as well, the need for collective and overpowering violence can be understood as a response to the ever more extreme events going on outside the pages of literature. Even Mishima moves from individual to collective violence in the years between *Golden Pavilion* and *Sailor* (and from arson to murder), as if acts of individual rage no longer provide enough shock value. A sense of the magic of violence pervades all four of these stories as well, as if the world will be saved only by the magic of destruction. Ultimately, although these works contrast greatly with the childlike innocence of *The Sound of Waves* or *Pluck the Buds*, they still impart the flavor of a child's world, of a child's desires to make everything simple again just through the wish to make it so, and, if that does not work, through destruction.

For Mishima, beauty must be destroyed so that beauty can live. An alternative exists to the disappointing real world, but it is in the mind. The illusion is not only more satisfying than the real, it must take precedence over the real. Oe's argument is more overtly political and more nihilistic. Readers must be shocked and disgusted by scenes of violence to force them into an awareness of the need for apocalyptic cleansing violence. This need is generally presented in grotesque and parodic form, but in *Floodwaters* he seems to be reaching a state of ideological closure: The alternative to the modern world is death and destruction although, in its bizarre way, it is noble death and destruction.

Like Mishima, Oe emphasizes the powers of the imagination in *Floodwaters,* not only in the group's favored word, "vision," but in Isana's insane but comforting belief that the trees and whales will overcome once the floodwaters of the soul have subsided. For this reason, *Floodwaters* maintains the image of the schooner even though the text of *Our Era* explicitly shatters any hopes for the truck. The schooner, half built, half unfinished, rising out of the floodlights of the studio, is a perfect symbol for a fantasy of escape, the one beautiful image that is permitted to the reader among the floodwaters of destruction.

"I'll ask you something. Suppose . . . suppose his Imperial Majesty had occasion to
be displeased with either your spirit or your behavior. What would you do then?"
"Like the men of the League I would cut open my stomach."
"Indeed? Well then, if he was pleased what would you do?"
Isao answered without the least hesitation: "In that case, too, I would
cut open my stomach at once."
Mishima Yukio, Runaway Horses[1]

"There was nothing more frightening than not being a Japanese, not being the
child of the emperor. It was more frightening than dying. The reason that I'm
not afraid of death is that even if I die his Imperial Highness will live. As long
as his Imperial Highness continues to live, there's no possibility that I will ever
vanish into nothingness . . . as long as I am a Japanese I have nothing to fear,
as long as I am the emperor's child I have nothing to fear."
Oe Kenzaburo, The Youth Who Came Late[2]

5 · Death and the Emperor:
The Politics of Betrayal

The works discussed in Chapter Four contained signs of an explicit
ideological concern on the part of both writers, especially Oe. This
chapter examines works in which ideology is foregrounded and
revolves around one particular cultural icon, the Showa Emperor. For
both writers the imperial house became an object of political and personal obsession; but, importantly, it was an obsession that went
beyond the personal to strike chords in Japanese society as a whole.

In the Japan of the early 1990s, the problem of the emperor system initially seems almost irrelevant for a society that is one of the
most modern, pragmatic, and materialist in the world. Yet the imperial house continues to excite controversy and concern, as is clear in
the full-scale media coverage given to an imperial visit or an imperial
illness, not to mention the massive media coverage of the succession;
and this controversy is on a far deeper and more divisive level than
would be the case for such ostensible equivalents as the British royal
family. The reasons behind this are in some ways obvious, but important for understanding modern Japan: The Showa Emperor was, of
course, tied to the Second World War and the whole complex of emotions that middle-aged Japanese feel towards it. But, on a broader
level, he was also tied to modern Japanese history overall and, thus,
inevitably to the whole problem of the Japanese conception of themselves in the postwar period.

Harootunian has described the emperor in Mishima's thought as essentially a free-floating signifier,[3] and it is indeed in the very amorphousness of its function that the imperial system remains so powerful. Not only does it have a clear-cut and important ideological and historical referent, but it has less obvious but even more important emotional associations as well, connoting a lost world of tradition, communality, and beauty. More than any other single signifier, the emperor is the ultimate Other, an object of desire which may vary depending on who desires it, but which is always distinctly and utterly different from the reality of modern Japan.

Nowhere is this problematic function of the emperor more apparent than in the fiction and essays of Mishima and Oe, who have both written extensively, even perhaps obsessively, on the Showa Emperor and his relation to Japanese society and history. As should be clear from the two quotations above, in the two writers' fiction, the emperor's role ranges widely but importantly. Although the two writers treat the imperial system very differently, however, the fundamental role of the emperor remains fascinatingly similar in both authors' works and that is as the ultimate refuge from postwar history.

Thus, in his relatively early novel *Kyoko's House* (*Kyōko no ie*), Mishima describes an unthinking young boxer named Shunkichi who lives for nothing except the violence of the ring. In Shunkichi's world there is only one other admirable way of living; and that is exemplified by his dead older brother, a kamikaze pilot who died for the emperor. In one early scene the boxer ponders while standing over his brother's grave: "Had he lived, he would have been thirty-four, but in place of that pathetic older brother stinking of business like prudence, and stained with the grime of the world, he had a radiant brother, eternally young and eternally soaring in a world of battle. This realization filled Shunkichi with happiness. His brother was a paragon of action . . . Shunkichi, who never envied anyone, envied his older brother."[4]

Shunkichi is obviously thinking more of the happiness of glorious young death than of serving the emperor. Significantly though, after his boxing career ends through an accident, he ends up joining a right-wing group. In Mishima's still cynical world of the 1950s, however, the boxer's conversion to politics is seen in ironic terms. At the end of the novel, when asked by his friends what the group's purpose is, Shunkichi simply answers, "'It doesn't matter.'"[5]

Yet *Kyoko's House* with its implicit equation of right-wing fanaticism with youth, glory, and happiness is one that many Japanese would also understand. In the book *Long Engagements,* David Plath chronicles the life of a former fighter pilot, for example, who lost his entire raison d'être after the defeat, finding only a pervasive emptiness in the postwar world. But it is not only fighter pilots who feel this sense of loss, as is clear in Oe's 1959 novel *The Youth Who Came Late,* in which the protagonist spends his entire life regretting the fact that he had "missed out" on the war. For both writers, then, the imperial system functions as a signifier tied to a variety of lost and yearned-for ideals, emotions, and experiences. Thus, the fact that a writer of the left and one of the right should come up with such a fundamentally similar function is important, not only in its implications for Oe's and Mishima's fiction but also for what it suggests about Japanese society in general.

This chapter, then, takes us into the ideological heart of Mishima's and Oe's work. At the same time it takes us into the ideological heart of Japan's present political leaders, most of whom were either children or adolescents at the time of the war. Finally, even though under the Showa Emperor the average young Japanese of recent years was not particularly conscious of the imperial house, it takes us into the spiritual territory of contemporary Japan in general as it struggles to define itself in the postwar era.[6]

THE EMPEROR AND POSTWAR JAPAN

This struggle is of course most clear among the older generation, emblematized by Mishima and Oe, who grew up with what I have called a schizophrenic world view, as a result of one hot August day in 1945 when the emperor announced Japan's defeat. Consequently, on one side of the older generation's spiritual divide lies prewar orthodoxy, an emperor-centered communalist philosophy of obedience to certain absolute values that were presented as being uniquely Japanese. On the other side lies an American-enforced, supposedly internationalist perspective, based on a belief in individual rights and democracy. It is this division, between what Kataoka in describing Oe calls being a "patriotic youth" (*aikoku seinen*) and being a "democratic youth" (*minshushugi seinen*), which still exists within many postwar Japanese. Obviously, when it comes to real human beings, this divide is not so clear and easy to measure; but there can be no question that even in the 1990s among most people born before

1945, the war still casts a long shadow. For that generation the emperor was a living god for whom one had to be ready to sacrifice one's life, as the above question from Mishima makes clear, and as Oe echoes as well in "The Day He Himself Shall Wipe My Tears Away" when the young protagonist is asked if he is prepared to "slit open his belly and die for the emperor."[7]

Part of the problem for any intellectual Japanese is the contradiction of the continued existence of the imperial house within the postwar democratic system. Despite the fact that the issue was apparently solved at the end of the war by making the emperor into a "figurehead" without actual power in the postwar constitution, the shelves of space in any bookstore devoted to the problem of *tennosei*, the emperor system, attest that the problem is still very much alive in Japanese politics. As Wakamori Taro in his book on the psychology of the imperial system points out, the problem of the continued existence of a symbol of prewar militarism as the head of a democratic state is one with which all modern Japanese have had to grapple.[8]

The problematic synchronic existence of an imperialist symbol within a democratic society frames the political writings of many postwar writers. The left-wing intellectual would suggest that the continued existence of the emperor system symbolizes the continuance of such negative prewar values as the suppression of the individual to authoritarian rule, while for the right wing, the emperor system is used to represent the best of traditional Japanese culture, now degraded owing to the American Occupation and modernization in general.

In their broadest terms, these two attitudes may be seen as representing Oe and Mishima's differing views of the emperor, as seen in their nonfictional works. But if we examine their fiction more closely, we find a far more complex and ambivalent vision of the emperor. Although the works to be looked at in this chapter are all overtly ideological ones with strong political messages, they are far more than simple tract variations of *romans à thèse*. The intersection of ideological literature and society is a complex one, if the writers have any sophistication at all. Thus, Oe's work may seem to oppose the emperor system; but, on closer inspection, we find a far more ambivalent attitude expressed through the actions and attitudes of his tormented and driven characters. Conversely, while Mishima's work may seem to glorify the imperial house, his fundamental fascination with aesthetics and equally deep-rooted inability to believe in his own romanticism can actually undermine his apparent textual message.

Furthermore, as the characterizations of Shunkichi in *Kyoko's House* or of the protagonist in *The Youth Who Came Late* suggest, the role of the emperor as free-floating signifier is one that can manifest itself in personal as well as ideological terms. Thus, on the political level, Oe may wish to excoriate the imperial system as evil; but on the personal level, the emperor is caught up with memories of childhood, innocence, *kyodotai*, and what one of his characters calls "concentrated life," and even with the excitement of a war that his too youthful characters have "missed out" on. Similarly, Mishima's high-flown intellectual abstractions concerning the emperor and beauty carry less emotional weight than his conscious association of the imperial house with death, honor, and a transcendent experience, the other side of Oe's "concentrated life".

It is little wonder that the four works in this chapter—Mishima's "Patriotism" and *Runaway Horses* and Oe's "Seventeen" and "The Day He Himself Shall Wipe My Tears Away"—often revolve around issues of betrayal and abandonment, or rather the desire not be abandoned, not to lose one's best chance for union with a transcendent Other. It is also little wonder that the works, especially "Patriotism" and "Seventeen," had such strong impact on many Japanese readers. Oe's and Mishima's concern with the emperor and the lost world that the emperor signifies, are of course extreme and highly personal ones. But at the same time these personal concerns are deeply embedded in the supra-personal realities of postwar Japanese history.

The works in this chapter are both "confrontations with history," to borrow Hashikawa Bunzo's description of Mishima,[9] and also attempts to escape it. In Mishima's case they are a conscious attempt to recover and transcend history through rewriting it, whereas Oe's works are an attempt to minimalize, even change history through parodying it. In these attempts to escape, we see the major link between the two writers' emperor-centered fiction and the fiction discussed in previous chapters, and also why the emperor is the ultimate refuge. In the narratives discussed in earlier chapters, this escape is accomplished through sexuality and violence that contain no overt ideological function, although, as I have tried to show, they do function implicitly on an ideological level. In this chapter, too, we see some of both writers' most explicitly sexual prose and grotesque depictions of violence; but here both eros and violence are bounded by the ideological framework of the imperial house. It is this bizarre amalgam of private and public, of the sexual domain with the political, that makes the works, especially the first two to be considered, so memorable, and ultimately so disturbing.

OH, MY EMPEROR!: "PATRIOTISM" AND "SEVENTEEN"

Mishima's "Patriotism" and Oe's "Seventeen" are among the most shocking and memorable stories either man ever wrote, and their overt political messages make clear that they were meant to be. The stories make a kind of matched but obverse pair, from the timing of their publication (both in 1961) through the similarity of their subjects, to their strikingly different treatments of sexuality, death, and the emperor—or rather death for the emperor, since both protagonists end up giving their lives for him. "Patriotism" seems to glorify right-wing emperor worship and the beauties of self-sacrifice for the imperial house; "Seventeen" seems to attack the right wing, since its protagonist's suicide is depicted grotesquely. Taken at face value then, the two stories are close to being classic *histoires à thèse*, containing forceful but simple ideological messages. Yet their political messages are undercut by certain ironies, ironies that seem unlikely to have been intended. These subversive ironies result from the authors' artistry in treating complexities of character and incident; and they ultimately create more powerful and more interesting, if more problematic, works than simple doctrine could ever do.

In style, "Patriotism" and "Seventeen" differ greatly. Indeed, in literary terms they belong to two different worlds. As will be recalled from Chapter Three, "Patriotism," the story of a young couple's ritual suicide arising out of the rebellion of February 26, 1936, is a modern version of romance (or even myth, since the characters are more than once associated with gods) and is written in a florid, ornate style. In contrast, the style of "Seventeen," the account of a young man's conversion to right-wing assassin and his final suicide, might be called grotesque realism with its pathetic, all-too-realistic protagonist and its grim, quotidian imagery. The works do share one important imagistic similarity, however, and that is in the intensity and ornateness of their imagery surrounding their depictions of sexuality and violence.

In extratextual matters, another important similarity is their almost simultaneous publication in January of 1961. Although the timing initially seems amazingly coincidental, the events of 1960 make their shared publication date very natural. These events can all be

subsumed under the heading of the U.S.-Japan Security Treaty Distur-
bances. Relatively unnoticed in the United States, the renewal of the
security treaty between the United States and Japan was a time of
great political conflict in Japan between the left, which saw nonre-
newal as an opportunity to expel the humiliating presence of the
American military, and the right, which believed that for reasons of
security the treaty must be renewed, and the even further right,
which saw it as a chance to reopen discussion about Japan's own possible militarization. In other words, the security treaty became an
opportunity for national self-examination of what it was to be Japanese in the postwar world.

This self-examination took the form of enormous popular demonstrations, including a riot in which a girl student was killed, and on
a literary level led to a number of reexaminations of the emperor system. Besides "Patriotism" and "Seventeen," the most notable piece of
writing was a sharply satiric work by Fukazawa Shichiro which envisioned a popular revolution in which the Crown Prince and Princess
end up being decapitated. Although recounted in a poetic, almost
precious style as a "dream," the brutality of the imagery outraged the
right wing to the point of inspiring the attempted murder of the publisher of the magazine in which the story had appeared.[10]

The emperor and the system he symbolized had suddenly become
an important focal point, both for literature and for action. Indeed,
the attempted murder of the publisher was not the only murder associated with that period. In October of that year, a young right-wing
youth had assassinated the chairman of the socialist party with a Japanese sword, and it was this so-called Asanuma Incident that was the
obvious inspiration for "Seventeen." The immediate inspiration for
"Patriotism" is less clear since until "Patriotism" Mishima's fiction
had, with the exception of Kyoko's House, steered entirely clear of
overt political references. What seems most likely is that the general,
inflamed atmosphere of the treaty demonstrations, plus the unusual
terrorist act of assassination, finally turned Mishima's interests away
from pure aesthetics and eroticism toward the bizarre union of aesthetics, politics, and eroticism which is the world of "Patriotism."

"Seventeen," loosely based on the Asanuma Incident, chronicles
the development of a shy seventeen-year-old into a right-wing terrorist and, with its many explicit descriptions of emperor-focused autoeroticism, was considered by many members of the right wing to be
a strident attack on the emperor system. Indeed, the story itself was

so viciously attacked by them that its second half was withdrawn from publication. To this day, in fact, that part, "The Death of a Political Youth" ("Seiji shonen shisu"), has never been included in any set of Oe's collected works.

In many ways, the rightists had reason to be angry, because the characterization in "Seventeen" of the young right winger as a pathetic loser and a chronic masturbator was hardly likely to increase their converts. In fact, on a superficial level "Seventeen" is an excellent example of a *roman à thèse* designed to warn off the reader from the very ideology it is describing. Emperor worship is an alternative to the wasteland of modern Japan, but it is shown as a false alternative. By portraying the development of an exceptionally unattractive young man into a right-wing terrorist, "Seventeen"'s obvious message to its readers is an admonitory one: "Do not become like this!"

Certain aspects of "Seventeen" are almost parodies of the *Bildungsroman* or novel of apprenticeship.[11] In the classic *Bildungsroman* a young person (usually male) in the course of the narrative changes from callow innocent to seasoned adult through a variety of learning experiences involving both helpers and enemies. We have seen this process in the previous chapter's examination of *Floodwaters*, where Isana was converted to the "good" cause.

"Seventeen" and its second half show the opposite process: A youth who, although hardly prepossessing, is initially not actually harmful to anyone, becomes a murderer who ends up hanging himself in his jail cell, apparently because of the ideological promptings of the right-wing organization he had joined. The boy is a total loser who only gets worse as the narrative continues; his mentors are knaves and fools; and his end is pathetic.

Unquestionably, this is a dark and bitter attack on the ideological process which "Patriotism" extols to narrate the same end, a death for the emperor. And yet, "Seventeen" is not quite the perfect anti–right-wing work that it at first appears to be. Although it is unlikely that the reader, upon finishing the story, will want to go out and join a right-wing organization, at the same time he or she may actually experience a certain sympathy for the protagonist and even with the protagonist's bizarre form of emperor worship. Furthermore, the supposed "good side," that is the left-wing intellectual who appears in the novel, is shown in a less than a consistently positive light.

Part of the problem in consistency lies paradoxically in the literary quality of the story. Although brutally satiric in parts, the narrative is not quite capable of creating the one-dimensional, black-and-white characters needed to get the message across most effectively. Even more important, the reality that the hero of "Seventeen" flees from is so grim that even his bizarre emperor-centered visions become almost appealing in comparison. Finally, the characterizations of the protagonist and of his doppelganger, a left-wing intellectual, are too complex to be thoroughly satisfying from an ideological viewpoint.

Such is not the problem with Mishima's "Patriotism," the two characters of which, it will be recalled, step straight out of heroic myth. The handsome and pure-hearted Lieutenant Takeyama, indignant about his lack of inclusion in the aborted February 26 rebellion of 1936 but unwilling to attack the rebels who were his former comrades, chooses to commit suicide at home. When he returns to his house, his beautiful and equally pure-hearted wife Reiko asks permission to accompany him; and, after making passionate love one last time, they kill themselves. Their suicide note concludes with the sentence, "Long live the Imperial Forces."[12]

With its simple plot, its obvious pro-imperial ideology, and its larger-than-life characters, "Patriotism" seems to be an excellent example of an intensely realized *histoire à thèse*, praising the virtues of death for the emperor. The text does not give readers any chance to distance themselves from the narrative. Instead, they are plunged almost immediately into the claustrophobic world of the protagonists' last passionate moments inside their little house in Yotsuya. Redundancies, particularly concerning the superiority of the protagonists, are everywhere. They are of course consistently described in terms of their remarkable beauty and nobility. Even more obvious, "Patriotism" starts with a paragraph-long summary of the story, ending with the pointed words, "The last moments of this heroic and dedicated couple were such as to make the gods themselves weep."[13] From the very beginning, the reader is given one and only one way to interpret the events described in the text, and that is to see the characters and the events as privileged glimpses of a romantic world totally at odds with the real.

The actual narrative begins by showing this couple's superiority to reality in their mutual willingness to leave it through suicide. On their wedding night the lieutenant's first action is to give Reiko a lecture on the duties of the soldier's wife, most particularly the need for her to "know and accept that her husband's death may come at any moment."[14] His wife's reaction to the announcement is, of course, exemplary: "Reiko rose to her feet and took out what was the most prized of her new possessions, the dagger her mother had given her," silently showing her own resolve in this matter.[15] Death and love are thus linked from the first.

Consequently, it is not surprising that such deeply patriotic devotion to duty is rewarded by an equally passionate physical relationship between them. But, of course, these "soaring pleasures of the flesh" are never "mere pleasure." As the text is careful to inform us, "Even in bed these two were frighteningly and awesomely serious."[16]

At first glance, no greater contrast could be imagined between two such godlike creatures and the pathetic specimen of humanity who is the narrator and central protagonist of "Seventeen." Hereinafter referred to as "Ore," the vulgar first-person pronoun with which he refers to himself, that protagonist makes such previous Oe characters as *Our Era*'s self-pitying Yasuo or the perverted J of *The Sexual Human* seem almost admirable. He is even further away from the heroes of "Patriotism." While Takeyama is handsome, a good soldier, and seemingly of high social status—the go-between for his marriage was an important general—the weak, unpopular hero of "Seventeen" considers himself ugly: "My face was like a pig's," he says at one point.[17] But both Ore and Takeyama die for the sake of the emperor; and, although their motivations are different, they both may be characterized as desiring to be a romantic hero.

At first, however, what Ore desires most is escape, escape to anywhere as long as it is away from everyday life. This normal life is a particularly unappealing one, realized in far more dreary detail than the quick sketches of everyday existence that frame "Patriotism." The first half of the story does an effective job of skating between unpleasant reality and black-humoured parody as the text delineates the misery of being an awkward adolescent in an apathetic family at an unfriendly school. Even the narrator's most extreme humiliations, such as losing control of his bladder after a bad showing in a gym class race, are entirely believably described, almost as if they were lifted from a school story or a novel of growing up. Indeed, viewed from this grimly realistic light, Ore's decision to join the right wing may be seen as a natural attempt to gain, if not popularity, at least the respect of his fellow students.

The text grows increasingly more extreme as Ore first attempts to murder a left-wing writer and then, after a "revelation" from the emperor, actually does assassinate a left-wing politician. Like "Patriotism," however, the story is still framed by ordinary life; and it is this contrast between the everyday normality of school and family and Ore's increasing obsessiveness that gives the work much of its alarming power.

Ore is moved to assassination and suicide by a highly realistic combination of motives—humiliation, hatred, and loneliness. It is significant that when he first hears a right-wing speech, it is soon after his embarrassing experience in gym class. Hearing the speaker's hate-filled invocation, "'We'll kill them all!'" in reference to any who might oppose the development of the true Japanese spirit, Ore's first reaction is pleasurable empathy.[18] Even more significant is his intense and initially unexpected pleasure in being taken for a rightist by a trio of female office workers. He thinks:

"That's right. I'm a rightist."
I trembled, struck by a sudden fierce joy. I had come in contact with my true self. I was a rightist!
I turned toward the girls and made one step forward. Holding onto each other, they raised small, frightened voices in protest. Standing in front of the girls and the men nearby, I looked at them, my eyes filled with hostility and hatred toward them all. They all stared back at me. I was a rightist! I felt a new person inside of me, one who was not embarrassed when strangers stared at him. I felt as if I had wrapped my weak, petty self inside strong armor and had isolated myself from other people forever. Rightist armor![19]

By donning his "rightist armor," Ore is suddenly transported out of the world of adolescent angst and into a world of power and intimidation and even, poignantly, of belonging. Soon he is taken up by his fellow rightists as a model youth representative and begins to speak at rallies, much to the admiration and congratulations of his new friends.

All of this contrasts with Mishima's hero who, one can assume, has never worried about belonging. Indeed, Takeyama joyfully anticipates being reunited with his fallen comrades after his death. Despite this difference, however, both Oe's social misfit and Mishima's sterling young warrior are motivated in their efforts to serve the emperor by a desire to be "special" and to participate in a transcendent, ecstatic experience.

Viewed from this angle, the textual redundancies of "Patriotism" begin to give off a more ironic air as Mishima's hero is revealed to have both selfish and narcissistic characteristics. Indeed, Takeyama is given a good deal of textual space to ruminate over his exceptional destiny: "There was some special favor here. He did not understand precisely what it was, but it was a domain unknown to others: a dispensation granted to no one else had been permitted to himself."[20]

Ostensibly, Takeyama is motivated by duty; but, in fact, his actual motives could be read as largely egotistical. The lieutenant is constantly aware of the dashing figure he cuts as when he lectures his wife on their wedding night, sitting "erect on the floor with his sword laid beside him,"[21] or, as he shaves himself prior to seppuku, thinking, "There must be no unsightly blemishes. There was a certain elegance, he even felt, in the association of death with his radiantly healthy face."[22] Even more obviously, the lieutenant is shown experiencing a "bizarre excitement" at the idea of performing seppuku in front of his wife: "What he was about to perform was an act in his public capacity as a soldier ... a lonely death on the battlefield, a death beneath the eyes of his beautiful wife ... in the sensation that he was about to die in those two dimensions realizing an impossible union of them both, there was sweetness beyond words."[23]

Despite the overt textual message that Takeyama is laying down his life for "The Imperial Household, the Nation, the Army, the Flag,"[24] the text's subliminal message suggests less noble motivations. Through his death, he is able to gratify three desires: the narcissistic; the erotic; and his unarticulated yearning for an intense transcendent experience, an intensity that he has already approached sexually a few moments before. Although the text never explicitly makes the connection, it is clear that the heroes' sexual gratification is enormously intensified by its association with the imperial house and with the presentiment of dying for that house.

On a less exalted level, the "hero" of "Seventeen" experiences the same duo of satisfactions, sexuality and death, within the framework of his worship of the emperor. Thus, Ore's ultimate escape from reality is initially foreshadowed at the end of the novella's first half when his rightist friends take him to a tawdry Turkish bathhouse, where a prostitute masturbates him to orgasm while he sees a golden vision: "My organ was the sun's radiance. My organ was a flower. I was overwhelmed by the pleasure of an intense orgasm and in the darkness of the sky I saw floating a golden being. Aah! Ooh! Your imperial majesty, my radiant sun. Aah, aah, ooh. After a little while, my eyes, recovered from their hysterical vision, saw on the girl's cheeks my spent and scattered semen, glistening like tears . . ."[25]

Obviously this is exaggerated and satirical prose. It could almost be a parody of "Patriotism" in its coincidence of sexuality, patriotic fervor, and intensity. Indeed, on reading "Seventeen," one is irresistibly reminded of such flamboyant lines in "Patriotism" as the description of the couple's lovemaking: "From the heights they plunged into the abyss, and from the abyss they took wing and soared once more to dizzying heights. The lieutenant panted like the regimental standard bearer on a route march."[26] In Oe's novella the satirical aspects of this combination of sexuality, death, and patriotism are intensified at the story's ending, when the hero masturbates one last time, calling on the emperor to come and take care of his "beloved Seventeen."[27] The last line of "The Death of a Political Youth" reads simply, "The officer who dragged down the hanging body said that he smelled semen."[28]

Despite the tawdriness of setting and the exaggerated quality of the prose, however, it is possible that this lonely yet ecstatic death is not totally satire. Just as "Patriotism" occasionally undermines through irony its apparent attempt to celebrate death for the emperor, so "Seventeen" undermines its supposed excoriation of such patriotism through its occasional lack of irony at certain crucial narrative moments and through the complexity of Oe's characterization of his protagonist.

One might expect the "democratic youth" persona which animates the mature Oe's writings and politics to feel condescension, at best, towards such a proto-fascist hero. Indeed, the second half of "Seventeen" was banned partly owing to pressure from right-wing extremists who felt that his portrait of Ore, based as it was on a real person, was too insulting. Yet, if we examine the story closely, we can find little evidence of insult or condescension. Oe himself has stated, "I have never for even the slightest moment had any desire to ridicule the hero of this novel,"[29] a statement which can be supported by a closer examination of the text itself.

Although the first half of the story, ending as it does with the protagonist's passionate orgasmic vision of the emperor, betrays a heavily satirical hand, Ore is still portrayed throughout as an understandable, if not sympathetic human being. The use of first-person narration (until the final paragraph), the rapid pace of events, and above all, the painfully vivid descriptions of Ore's loneliness and various humiliations do not allow readers much room to stand back and smile ironically. Rather they are drawn inexorably into Ore's savage and pain-filled world to the point where his primary reaction, "I'll kill them all,"[30] seems readily understandable, if not approvable within the story's context.

But the first half of "Seventeen" still keeps its basic parodic framework intact by the very exagerratedness of Ore's emperor-centered visions. Although readers may occasionally sympathize with Ore, his very abjectness combined with the absurd grandiosity of his visions reminds us that we are watching the development of a fanatic who is ultimately not one of us. However, the novella's second half, "The Death of a Political Youth," is less tightly conceived and even occasionally loses its satiric bite altogether. For example, the narrative, with no apparent satirical purpose whatever, has Ore go off to a farm where he communes with nature, animals, and a beautiful, saintly farm girl whom he comes to love and admire from a distance. It is probable that Oe's point was to offer a contrasting pastoral vision to Ore's daily life, one which would also contrast to the youth's pathetic imperial fantasies; but, in doing so, he makes his character a more sympathetic and complex character, thus softening the story's satirical thrust.

Even more puzzling, if we wish to view "Seventeen" as antirightist *roman à thèse,* is Oe's portrait of the only left-wing character in the story, a leftist writer named Minamihara who is Ore's first intended assassination victim. In an important scene, Ore confronts Minamihara in an empty coffee shop, wielding a knife and threatening to kill the writer if he does not retract an insulting statement he has made about right-wing violence. The scene is a significant one in that it underlines the complexities and ambivalences in Oe's political outlook, at the same time as providing an interesting glimpse of another of Oe's passive intellectual heroes.

A liberal intellectual, Minamihara is reminiscent of Yasuo in *Our Era* as a typical antihero. Confronted by the frenzied Ore, Minamihara takes no action to defend himself, but instead breaks into a terrified sweat. Yet, despite his terror, the writer refuses to retract his statement and even induces Ore into a theoretical argument, thereby blunting the youth's will to kill him. Eventually, Ore is moved to reluctant admiration. He reflects,

That bastard's a coward. But for thirty minutes now, with sweat pouring down him and tears blurring his eyes, he's been crawling steadily forward through a dark tunnel of fear and gradually, through his own perseverance, he's recovered himself. So there are actually men who live like that ... without turning his eyes away from the horror of reality, without turning away from the humiliation of reality, just crawling forward like a pig, dragging his belly covered with the ugly stinking mud of reality. But me, I've been running away from the horror of the real world with all possible speed and I've jumped into the glittering, rose colored ravine of emperor worship. Could it be that that guy is the one with the right idea?[31]

This passage encapsulates both a vision of modern society in all its "stinking mud of reality" and the role of emperor worship as a false "rose colored" alternative in Oe's writings. Indeed, some Japanese critics believe that Minamihara's willingness to "crawl like a pig" through the mud of reality is Oe's basic manifesto on the sort of behavior that can, at most, be expected of any decent, thinking individual in today's world.[32] This may be true but, if so, its impact as a manifesto is blunted by a coda to this first meeting, a second encounter between Ore and the writer.

This occurs in a bar where Ore's rightist friends are partying, the very evening of the youth's aborted attempt on Minamihara's life. Happening into a back room, Ore again confronts the writer, but this time the man is stinking of alcohol rather than sweat. It turns out that Minamihara is also a drug addict and a "pervert," as the bar's waitress eagerly informs Ore. Confronting this spectacle, Ore's attitude changes from reluctant admiration to calm superiority. He muses: "So you couldn't get rid of your fear. Instead of crawling forward into fear, when night comes around you escape into whisky, or drugs, or homosexuality."[33]

Ore turns away in disgust at this "pig" into the waiting arms of the bar girl and has his first experience of actual intercourse, an unsatisfying one. He cannot erase Minamihara's memory with indifferent sex, and so must return to his "rose colored ravine" for his final escape. Significantly, his "revelation from the emperor," which leads to his successful act of assassination, occurs the following day.

The two encounters with Minamihara are also thematically significant because they give the impression that Ore wavered at least once before setting foot on the path that leads to his eventual destruction, unlike the resolute Takeyama. This "humanization" of Ore, however, brings us back to the question of how much of a parody "Seventeen" really is, especially when we also must deal with the perplexing humanity of Minamihara. Was it really necessary in narrative terms to make Minamihara such a complete anti-hero? Even for the sake of even-handedness, such a grim portrait of a character, who in many ways can be considered the author's representative, severely blunts the presumed ideological message of "Seventeen." To some extent the portrait of Minamihara may be compared with Mishima's many self-hating portrayals of intellectuals, but it is also possible to conclude that Minamihara cannot be perfectly good, simply because Ore cannot be perfectly bad.

Undoubtedly, Minamihara is not the only character in "Seventeen" who represents Oe. From what we know of Oe through his essays and semi-autobiographical fiction, it is obvious that Ore, too, shares certain aspects of his creator's personality. Just as Takeyama in his yearning for an intense experience, his narcissism, and his passionate nature undoubtedly represents certain aspects of Mishima, so, too, does the embarrassed, lonely young hero of "Seventeen" with his burning desire to become the emperor's "beloved Seventeen" resemble a particular side of Oe.

This side is, of course, the "patriotic boy" mentioned in the introduction, who is the other side of the postwar "democratic boy" with his Western values of liberalism and humanism. Thus, the diachronic antinomies between an emperor who is the living manifestation of the "land of the gods" and an emperor who figureheads postwar democratic Japan are internalized in Oe himself and his characters. The adult Oe, who majored in French literature at Tokyo University, became a vehement anti-nuclear activist, and is a passionate espouser of relativistic humanist ideals, cannot completely break away from the golden imperial past of an absolute faith in a living god. The problem is further complicated by the fact that the emperor is the most important symbol of continuity between Oe's childhood self and his adult maturity.

This comes across most clearly in Oe's 1962 novel *The Youth Who Came Late*, quoted at the beginning of this chapter, where the protagonist spends his time regretting that he came "too late for the war" and remembering the days when he was the "child of the emperor."[34] In a crucial early scene, he also conflates his dying father with the emperor, a scene that will be echoed in Oe's 1973 novella "The Day He Himself Shall Wipe My Tears Away." Ore, of course, is too young to realize what he has "missed out on"; but he, too, is obviously conflating his father and the emperor when he calls on the emperor to take his "beloved Seventeen" unto him. It is also significant that Ore's real father is a liberal intellectual and a totally inadequate, unsympathetic father who can give the boy no help in dealing with the problems of the real world.

It is hardly surprising, therefore, that despite some exaggerated, even shocking, imagery, the final delineation of emperor worship in "Seventeen" is ambivalent. Just as Mishima's text, which initially seems to be trying to make the hero Takeyama perfect, ends up showing him up as a conceited egoist more concerned with creating a beautiful impression than with serving his country, Oe's work is conversely incapable of making his protagonist quite as loathsome as the reader might at first anticipate. For that matter, even Mishima's depiction of emperor worship has its ambivalent side. Although Takeyama and his wife write as their final message "Long live the Imperial Forces," the narrative text is much more concerned about the ecstasies and pains of sex and death than about the joys of sacrifice for the emperor.

This brings up the question of the function of sexuality in both these stories. As was seen in previous works, sexuality was one of the major forms of escape for many of Oe and Mishima's characters. In "Seventeen" and "Patriotism" it performs the same function, but with the added aspect of an ideologically based quasi-mystical experience. Of course, even in the West, the association of eroticism and religious ecstasy is not unknown; but in these two works, the sexual scenes have important narrative functions as well. Both the ecstasies of Mishima's couple and the lonely satisfaction of Ore's masturbation prefigure the final ecstasy of death. The fact that Ore's autoeroticism is lonely and sterile, while Takeyama's sexual excitement is at least as narcissistic as it is physical, still does not take away from the protagonists' genuine satisfaction.

Takao in *Outcries* "liberated" himself through rape and murder, achieving eventually the "best orgasm of his life" after his killing of the high school student; and Etsuko in *Thirst for Love* "slept peacefully" after her sexually inspired murder of Saburo. But the heroes of "Seventeen" and "Patriotism" are even more fortunate. Their sexual ecstasies have an ideological, even religious sanction. For this reason, these protagonists may be accounted among the most "successful" of either writer's "heroes of action," having achieved almost everything a romantic could yearn for, a passionate death in service of a loving deity. The fact that Ore's death, by external standards, is a pathetic, immoral farce, does not take away from him his final fulfillment, nor his final escape from a world that offers nothing.

Furthermore, the very brutality of the descriptions of masturbation in the emperor's name also suggests that sexuality is not merely an escape but an attack in "Seventeen." The critic Hirano Ken has pointed out that in the Japan of the late 1950s sex and the emperor were the last taboos.[35] By taking on both taboos at once, Oe's prose constitutes a virulent assault on Japanese social conventions. Within the bounds of the story however, Ore's pathetic equation of sexuality and the emperor remains one of the protagonist's highest satisfactions, in its grotesque way, the perfect symbol of his transcendence of the wasteland of disappointing adolescence.

And yet, in the long run, it is possible to suggest that it is the two young heroes of "Patriotism" who have had the "luckiest" escape from a humdrum existence. As Sasaki Yoshioka points out,[36] the explicit and passionate descriptions of love and death contrast with and are strongly accentuated by the quiet normality of life around them. But it is more than normality from which they escape. Although seemingly less painful than Ore's world of humiliations, the world outside their little house is not a place for two such god-like heroes. The wasteland they are leaving is that of the realities of historic time, of the onrushing events of the 1930s which would bring their country's defeat and their own decay into old age. More perfectly than any of Mishima's other works, "Patriotism," in all its claustrophobic passion, is thus an escape from historical inevitability, a rewriting of history the way it should have been.

FROM IRONY TO MADNESS: *RUNAWAY HORSES* AND "THE DAY HE HIMSELF SHALL WIPE MY TEARS AWAY"

"Seventeen" and "Patriotism" were each in their own way departures for their authors. Although Oe had been concerned with the emperor in a number of previous works, most notably *The Youth Who Came Late*, he had never before lambasted the imperial house so forcefully or with such a wealth of grotesque imagery. Conversely, until "Patriotism," Mishima's work had been virtually unpolitical with the single exception of Shunkichi's problematic conversion to the right wing in *Kyoko's House*. As it turned out, in Mishima's case "Patriotism" was the start of an important trend in the last decade of his life, the decade of the 1960s when he rediscovered Japanese tradition at the same time that many of his countrymen, especially the younger ones, were intent on negating all tradition. His final statement concerning Japan's tradition was summed up in his tetralogy *The Sea of Fertility,* the last work of fiction that he produced before his death. Of the tetralogy, *Runaway Horses,* the work that we will consider in this section, may be seen as his final fictional statement on the role of the emperor in Japanese society.

Perhaps surprisingly, the tumultuous decade of the 1960s saw Oe turning away from overtly political works, at least in fiction. Although he remained a prolific and committed essayist, the traumatic birth of his first child in 1960, brilliantly chronicled in *A Personal Matter,* focused his fiction into a more personal realm than in the previous decade. He dealt marginally with political problems in such works as the 1967 *Silent Cry;* but it was not until 1972 that he published the work which may be considered his definitive statement on the emperor and modern Japan, "The Day He Himself Shall Wipe My Tears Away." Like "Seventeen," the novella is an angry attack on fascism but, also like "Seventeen," it is not completely successful as a satire. Indeed, both *Runaway Horses* and "The Day" hark back to a prewar world of certainty, though written after a decade of enormous social upheaval, culminating in the country-wide student strikes of 1968.

Based on what at the time might have seemed like isolated historic moments, a 1936 uprising and a 1959 assassination, "Patriotism" and "Seventeen" in retrospect may be seen to anticipate some of the crucial political events that swept Japan over the next ten years, most notably the attempted appropriation of the political process by young people. Of course, from Takeyama's point of view, his actions are in service to a higher cause; but, as "Patriotism"'s title ironically underscores, he is in fact placing his own pleasures and concerns above those of the government which he technically serves. "Patriotism" not only contains almost no discourse about duty to his country, but even his reverence for the emperor supposedly in whose name he is committing suicide, is only expressed in the single sentence at the end of the couple's suicide note. The emperor is simply a quasi-religious sanction for escaping the horrors of normal life.

Even more clearly does "Seventeen" point to a growing need on the part of some Japanese youths to find something more meaningful than the American-influenced "democratic ideals" of the 1950s. If the

Freedom Voyagers of Oe's *The Floodwaters Have Come unto My Soul* are obvious spiritual descendants of the 1960s activities, Ore is in many ways the spiritual ancestor, but with the key difference that Ore is a right-wing terrorist who finds his meaning not in the "whales and trees" but in the emperor.

Indeed, for a time in the 1960s, it seemed that the symbol of the emperor had lost its ideological power. Neither threatening nor inspiring, for most radicals he was something to be consigned to the heap of broken images that constituted pre-1960s history. And yet, in famous debates between Mishima and the Tokyo University students in 1969, the very hostility shown by the students towards Mishima's valorization of the emperor indicates that this was a broken image with power to reconstitute itself.

It was Mishima, above all others, who not only kept the issue of the emperor alive, but in fact regenerated it in the mid to late 1960s in two important fictional works—"The Voices of the Hero Spirits" ("Eirei no koe") and *Runaway Horses*—and in a major essay "A Defense of Culture" ("Bunka no bōeiron"). If "Patriotism" was a single shot, then these works were an entire military offense, part of a larger fictional rediscovery of the 1930s on Mishima's part, a rediscovery that also included two plays, *The Fall of the House of Suzaku* (*Suzakuke no metsubō*) and *My Friend Hitler* (*Wagatomo Hitora*). Apparently inspired by Mishima's growing concern that Japan was in danger of a left-wing takeover, the two plays celebrate virtues that might well be called "fascistic."

Although not dealing directly with the emperor, the two plays were quite controversial when they opened, especially *My Friend Hitler*, which, despite its title, is more a glorification of Ernst Roehm and his young SS soldiers than of Hitler himself. In a thematic parallel to "Patriotism," *My Friend Hitler* pits the supposed beauty and purity of the violence of the youthful SS against the ugly manipulations of aging capitalists, exemplified in the play by the elderly Gustav von Krupp, who convinces Hitler to sacrifice his friend Roehm. The play is hardly a stridently pro-Nazi tract, but it unquestionably embraces certain of the more passionate doctrines of fascist ideology, most notably the romanticization of youthful militaristic violence.

Mishima's "Voices of the Hero Spirits" continues this fascination with youthful sacrifice but this time back on native territory. A short story full of strikingly beautiful imagery, "The Voices of the Hero Spirits" consists of what might be called a Shinto version of a seance, where a priest calls back the spirits of Second World War kamikaze pilots, only to hear them accuse the emperor of abandoning them by renouncing his divinity. "The Voices of the Hero Spirits" thus lays the ground not only for Mishima's *Runaway Horses* but also for his own suicide and the speech before it, in which he too accused the emperor of betrayal.

If Mishima began the regeneration of the emperor, it was Oe who, by taking this regeneration seriously in both essay and fiction, showed how deeply important the emperor still was to many Japanese. It is perhaps not surprising that a romantic aesthete such as Mishima, raised on prewar ideals and increasingly disgusted with the historical developments around him, should have developed an image of aesthetic absolutism which became his image of the emperor. What is more surprising is that a leftist such as Oe, who, in the early 1960s in *A Personal Matter* seemed to be turning away from his interest in the emperor and the war, should have produced a decade later a work that in many ways is obsessed with both issues. Even *Our Era,* published the same year as *A Personal Matter,* although it does contain the bizarre account of Shigeru's attempted assassination of the emperor, treats the emperor himself in a curiously detached manner—as a signifier whose main referent seems to be as something (anything) to rebel against.

Oe did not maintain this detached attitude for long. In 1972 he published "The Day He Himself Shall Wipe My Tears Away," one of his most passionate works. Partly a reaction to *Runaway Horses* and partly a reaction to Mishima's suicide and the ideology which he believed to have inspired it, Oe's novella is also a continuation, even an encapsulation of various themes and concerns that had animated Oe's own fiction from its inception. It is a complicated and controversial work, but in its themes and obsessions it makes an intriguing comparison with *Runaway Horses.* If *Runaway Horses* is Mishima's most sustained attempt to rewrite history, then "Day" is Oe's most powerful attempt to show the dangers of just such attempted rewriting.

Runaway Horses is also in some ways a complicated work, containing, as it does, two mutually reinforcing stories of political terrorism: The main narrative tells of an attempted rebellion in the 1930s, while embedded within it is a work called "The League of the Divine Wind," which chronicles a rebel group of the Meiji Period. Despite this structural complexity, however, the message in *Runaway Horses* is far more straightforward than that in Oe's "Day"; and Mishima's novel will, therefore, be examined first.

Even more than "Patriotism," *Runaway Horses* is almost a classic example of the *roman à thèse*. The novel's plot pits good against evil, with good winning a moral, if not an actual, victory in the end. The hero Isao is supposedly a reincarnation of Kiyoaki, the aesthetically perfect hero of *Spring Snow (Haru no yuki)*, the first volume of the tetralogy. Isao is a pure and virtuous young man fighting against the miasma of corruption characterizing Japan in the 1930s. He is thus the *bu* (military) to Kiyoaki's *bun* (culture), as Watanabe suggests. A superb kendoist and charismatic leader, Isao attempts to bring together a group of like-minded souls in a coup that will restore power to the emperor. He is caught and imprisoned before he can attempt the coup but is pardoned and goes off on his own to murder a financier whom he believes to be corrupt. Successful in that, he than fulfills his most precious dream of all, "at the top of a cliff at sunrise, while paying reverence to the sun . . . while looking down upon the sparkling sea, beneath a tall, noble pine . . . to kill myself."[37]

The plot of *Runaway Horses* is, in effect, a lengthy retelling of the 1960 "Patriotism"; and the protagonists Isao and Takeyama are basically the same "active hero" type. But although both die supposedly in the name of the emperor, Isao is granted the further wish-fulfilling pleasure of actually assassinating someone in his name as well. *Runaway Horses* is also complicated by the presence of a second point of view in the person of the cynically observant intellectual Honda, whose unwillingness to believe in Isao or Isao's crusade keeps the novella from being a simplistic *roman à thèse*. Still another difference is the heavy foregrounding of the "real" 1930s in this novel. While everyday life simply lapped at the corners of the world of "Patriotism," *Runaway Horses* is intent to show in explicit detail exactly how much the world had decayed from the delicate beauty portrayed in *Spring Snow*. Corrupt financiers, venal politicians, and even cowardly military men crowd the pages. It is this overt contrast indeed, conflict, between reality and the romantic world of military death, the latter signified by Isao, the emperor, and the traditional beauties and virtues which surround them, which makes *Runaway Horses* so clearly an ideological novel.

The narrative employs many redundancies of characterization to point up Isao's superiority to the wretched inhabitants of society around him. Thus, he has many of the characteristics of the ideal Japanese samurai. Isao is a kendoist, the most traditional of Japanese sports; and the text supplies a number of scenes showing his prowess with the sword, including, of course, his successful assassination. His personality is also described in terms evocative of samurai masculinity. Such words as "vivacity,"[38] "manly force"[39] and above all "purity" (which must occur virtually every ten pages in the novel) leave the reader no doubt that Isao is an ideal hero.

The text also underlines the fact that such an ideal is unlikely to exist in the real world by having Isao realize at one point that "he had become a character in a romance. Perhaps he and his comrades were on the verge of a glory that would long be remembered."[40] In fact, he and his comrades are caught soon afterwards, but the conscious elevation of the group to characters in a romance indicates that the hero of *Runaway Horses* is not to be judged by the standards of realistic fiction. Indeed, such lines as those above are intratextual echoes of that other romantic tale, "The League of the Divine Wind." The chronicle purports to be a genuine story of an uprising, but its most important function is once again of redundancy: *Runaway Horses* is not just the tale of one doomed attempt to save the Japanese spirit but of two.

From an extraliterary point of view, this redundancy works to emphasize corrupt aspects of the Japanese reality over which romantic gestures cannot prevail. In earlier works like "The Voices of the Hero Spirits," Mishima had hinted that social decay was to be equated with modernization and Westernization. Here he treats that equation explicitly and at length. It first becomes apparent in the chronicle Isao reads and gives to Honda, in which it is stated that the purpose of the league of the Divine Wind is to "protect the gods of Japan so utterly disdained by the new government."[41] Even more obviously anti-Western is the League's contempt for the "Western-style professional army with its ruthless disregard of all tradition,"[42] and their corresponding insistence on the purity of the Japanese spirit.

But it is when the text turns to describing Isao's adventures that the full magnitude of the Western contamination is revealed through Isao's words and thoughts. Thus, at one point, in response to his would-be mentor Honda's call for moderation, Isao thinks angrily, "This man understands nothing at all of the blood that flows in Japanese veins, of our moral heritage, of our will."[43] Even more blatantly, later on in the book, Isao learns the connection between Japan's moral decay and the influence of the West: "And one clouded

stream that never ran dry was that choked with the scum of humanism, the poison spewed out by the factory at its headwaters. There it
was, its lights burning brilliantly as it worked even through the
night—the factory of Western European ideals. The pollution from
this factory degraded the exalted fervour to kill; it withered the green
of the sasaki's leaves."[44]

The text goes from such high-flown abstractions to more concrete
indications of decadence, as Isao gives an impassioned speech in court
concerning the decay of modern Japan in which he covers everything
from the London Naval Conference of 1930 to the corruption of the
zaibatsu. Indeed, Mishima is so anxious to get his ideological point
across that there are moments when the narrative reads suspiciously
like a textbook of modern Japanese history.

The somewhat strained combination of romantic adventure and
textbook history in *Runaway Horses* does not always succeed in literary terms, but in ideological terms it certainly hammers the point
home. The text's use of Honda, the formerly cynical observer character of *Spring Snow,* is also effective in a more subtle way in helping get
the message across. Although Honda's role will be discussed more thoroughly later, it is important to note here that his role as a mediator
between realism and romanticism is much expanded in this novel.
Since he is a lawyer, the reader expects him to be rational and intellectual; and when he too begins to be pulled into Isao's irrational world
of violence and emperor worship, the reader's response to the narrative
inevitably changes as well. Furthermore, unlike "Patriotism" the text
allows for few potential ironies. Isao seems genuinely committed to
serving the emperor, as shown in his many impassioned speeches.

In the long run however, the text's final impression may be a subversive one after all, suggesting that such perfect service, such perfect
fulfillment is possible only in the imagination. Not only is Isao a
"character in a romance," but his final wish fulfillment of the perfect
suicide can only be achieved through the imagination. Although Isao
had dreamed of dying at sunrise, by the sea next to a noble pine, the
reality is quite different because his successful assassination attempt
leaves him no time to create his perfect death:

> Isao sat upright upon the damp earth . . .
> "The sun will not rise for some time," Isao said to himself, "And I can't
> afford to wait. There is no shining disk climbing upward. There is no
> noble pine to shelter me. Nor is there a sparkling sea."[45]

In his imagination however, Isao does achieve the perfect escape from the wasteland of the real. For, as he rips open his stomach, "The instant that the blade tore open his flesh, the bright disk of the sun soared up and exploded behind his eyelids."[46]

In many ways, *Runaway Horses* is the supreme example of a romantic call to arms, an insistence that disappointing reality can be destroyed, or at least escaped, through the correct ideology combined with the transforming powers of the imagination. If further proof is needed, we need only look at the text of Mishima's last speech before his suicide which contains many echoes of Isao's excoriation of modernity. Like Isao, Mishima had to create his own perfect death, using *Runaway Horses* and "Patriotism" as models. Indeed, in a perceptive and angry essay written soon after Mishima's death, Oe suggested that the novels' artificiality, in particular the one-dimensionality of Isao's character, is due to Mishima's desire to make the novel into a fictional paradigm of his own suicide.[47]

Whether Mishima ultimately believed in his own last words is subject to debate. What is certain is that Oe took Mishima's speech, his suicide, and the text of *Runaway Horses* very seriously. His first reaction was the essay in which he criticized the novel for its "artificiality" and accused Mishima of "insulting all those who had lived through the postwar era,"[48] especially his fellow writers who had genuinely suffered during the war. His second reaction was to write "The Day He Himself Shall Wipe My Tears Away," a fascinating and disturbing blend of satire, fantasy, and grotesque realism.[49]

"Day" is a difficult work for even Japanese to read, because of both its complicated style and its often grotesque content. The novella calls attention to its fictionality almost from the beginning by indicating the textual presence of several narrative voices inside the overall third-person narrative framework. The main narrator, who is also the primary protagonist, seems to be a playwright or author who may or may not be dying of cancer but who has, in any case, retreated to a hospital bed where, donning green goggles, he proceeds to dictate what he calls a "history of the age" to the secondary narrator. This secondary narrator, the so-called "acting executor of the will," is presumably his wife but might also be a nurse. The "acting executor" is willing to challenge the primary narrator's judgment at times; but it is only toward the end of the novella, when yet another narrator (apparently the writer's mother) appears, that we are given a very different vision of the "history of the age."

It is this "history" which is the real flesh of the story: a bizarre chronicle of the narrator's father's romantic attempt to lead an uprising on the last day of the war. The uprising, essentially an attempt to "save the emperor from himself," was to involve the bombing of the imperial palace by the father and his comrades in planes disguised to look like American jets. Only thus, the absurd argument ran, would the Japanese people finally wake up to the approaching defeat and unite together to save their country.

Obviously the uprising is a highly unlikely one, but only in its degree of absurd detail is it radically more unlikely than the planned coup of Isao and his young comrades. Its unreliability is further heightened by the manner in which the narrator relates the story, in jerky flashbacks that are constantly being interrupted with very different alternate versions by the "acting executor of the will" and by the narrator's mother. The reader is left with a confused idea of what actually happened and with strong doubts concerning the credibility or even the sanity of the narrator himself, who insists on referring to the period of war just before his father's rebellion as his "happy days." The narrator is thus attempting to escape reality in every possible way, from the action of donning the goggles which allow him to see only what he wishes, to his insane valorization of the war and, later on, of the emperor, to his attempt to recreate history through a presumably distorted retelling of history.

Even the text's stylistic complexity might itself be a reaction against Mishima; for by constantly reminding the readers that they are reading fiction, and fantastic fiction at that, the narrative subtly reprimands Mishima for his final confusion of the "word" with "action," of the fictional with the real. The father's mad rebellion, which purported to save Japan by destroying the emperor, clearly echoes what Oe considered to be Mishima's distortion of Japanese values.

The father, moreover, is not the only Mishima-esque character in the novella. The narrator himself resembles Mishima in his egocentric manipulation of reality, his erotic and narcissistic fascination with death (for example, believing himself to be dying, the narrator stares into the mirror to see whether his face has come to resemble that of a picture he owns of a Chinese man being drawn and quartered with an expression on his face "like a braided rope of agony and pleasure"),[50] and, most importantly, in his obsession with the period of history that ended in 1945.

This valorization of the "golden" time before Japan's defeat is not restricted to Mishima but is instead shared by Oe and many of his fictional creations as well. Thus, the unnamed narrator of "Day" is as close to Oe as he is to Mishima. At thirty-five the narrator is roughly the same age as Oe was when he wrote the novella, and the narrator too hails from a mountain valley in Shikoku. Whether or not he is an alter ego of the real Oe, he also shares a number of important characteristics with many of Oe's protagonists, most notably the two emotions that animate him, desire and resentment. The desire is for an escape from being thirty-five with adult responsibilities. And the resentment is towards those who seek to block his escape both physically and mentally. In particular, the narrator resents his mother, whom he feels "humiliated" his father and himself and even now, through her stubborn insistence on giving her own version of the rebellion, blocks his attempt to escape into romanticized memories.

In part, the "history of the age" is aimed at his mother, a childish attempt to make her feel guilty for all the suffering she has caused; but it is also an attempt to recover the past and rediscover his father who, by dying in the uprising, abandoned his child in order to search for an intense, transcendent experience. Now the son in his hospital bed uses words to search obsessively for that same experience which, when he finds it, will somehow unite him with his father.

The climax of the story of the insurrection, as related with increasing fervor by the narrator, is both a grotesque parody of Mishima's bloody coup and a parody of Mishima's belief in the beauty of terrorist violence. The narrator recalls his father's last day when, bleeding horribly of bladder cancer, the father is bundled into a cart by a group of soldiers who have apparently come to the valley resolved to make him the leader of their pathetic rebellion. Ultimately, they are all killed, perhaps even bombed by enemy planes. Or at least that is how the narrator remembers it. His mother, however, has a very different version, especially in reference to the father (referred to throughout, as "*a certain party*"):

> . . . and those soldiers took him and carted him off in a ridiculous wooden box with sawed off logs for wheels . . . it was a cruel business but I didn't go out of my way to interfere . . . The child, who of course had no inkling of this, he was clutching old diapers for to wipe away blood from *a certain party*'s bladder, his bayonet clanking at this side, so grim and determined he was pale . . . Well, if you're wondering whether the soldiers who took

a certain party with them really drove that truck onto an army airfield and stole fighter planes and flew to Tokyo, they did no such thing! There was a shootout at the bank entrance and *a certain party* and all the soldiers were killed, yessir![51]

His mother's words bring back the horrors of the real world in no uncertain terms, but this rational narrative voice cannot penetrate the protagonist's world of *"Happy Days."* In this crazed but intensely satisfying world, the imperial palace was indeed bombed and the emperor ultimately ascended into heaven: "Though it was inevitable that he die in a bombing once, now truly he would revive as the national essence itself, and more certainly than before, more divinely, as a ubiquitous chrysanthemum would cover Japan and all her people. As a golden chrysanthemum illuminated from behind by a vast purple light and glittering like an aurora, his Majesty would manifest himself."[52] Finally, and significantly, the narrator identifies his father with the emperor: "And *a certain party*, leaping beyond his limitations as an individual at the instant of his death, rendered manifest a golden chrysanthemum flower 675,000 kilometers square, surmounted and surrounded by, yes, a purple aurora, high enough in the sky to cover entirely the islands of Japan."[53] Thus, in a prose more purple than Mishima at his most florid, Oe's narrator envisions his father/emperor's last stand. The fragmentation of the defeat is replaced by the imaginary "aurora" which wraps the Japanese archipelago in a comforting imperial cloud.

The imagery remains exaggerated even when the text leaves the clouds for a more realistic but memorably grotesque account by the narrator of the father's last journey:

> ". . . the boy wiped, again and again, with old diapers the sticky urine and hemorrhaging blood that kept soaking *a certain party*'s abdomen and crotch. But he could not wipe around his obese, planted buttocks without help from the soldiers, and before long, the pillows on the floor between *a certain party*'s buttocks and his thighs were submerged in a pond of evil smelling blood."[54]

The contrast between such grotesque details and the previous exalted description of the "rebellion" creates a disturbingly confused impression. On the one hand, this description suggests that the narrator is tacitly agreeing with his mother's evaluation of the insurrection as a "cruel business," futile and ugly; yet, with his earlier, alternate imagery of chrysanthemums and clouds, he apparently remains committed to an insane, Mishima-esque vision of the rebellion as a glorious and ineffable moment. Oe's intended purpose may have been to contrast the romantic exaltation of clouds and auroras with the grim reality of blood and urine; but by having one narrative voice encapsulating both, he creates an ambivalent final impression.

Furthermore, despite the many overtly satirical elements in "Day," the novella still presents the same complexities that confronted the reader in "Seventeen," namely variation of tone and authorial attitude. The artistry in "Day" prevents it from being simply a one-note attack on the imperial system.[55] For example, in order to present a clear, if simplistic, contrast between the insane and rational, the mother's narrative might have been the story's rational voice; clear objective accounts from her might have shown the absurdity of her son's fevered myth-making. But in the complicated world of "Day" as actually written, the mother has her own axe to grind, an old hatred towards her husband and a contempt for her son, which comes out clearly in the passage quoted above where she calls the boy's participation in the insurrection a "cruel business," but adds "I didn't go out of my way to interfere."

Thus, as in "Seventeen," there is finally no rational center to turn to for relief from the obsessed protagonist. And it is finally the protagonist's golden vision of "the happy days" and of his heroic father that haunts the reader. In an odd way, the protagonist/narrator resembles a more hysterical Honda figure; for Honda's life, too, is given meaning by the bizarre actions of characters whom he can admire but never directly imitate.

For Oe's protagonist it is his father who, in memory, becomes the ideal alternative to any acceptance of real life. Lying on his hospital bed, the narrator explains how his "happy days" really began when his father apparently deserted the army to return to their village and hide in a dark storehouse. Liberated from conventional childhood by his father's highly unconventional behavior, the boy spent his time wandering the village, a helmet on his head, a bayonet at his side, ready to defend his father from any possible danger. An obvious echo of the boy's adventure-story existence of *Pluck the Buds,* the boy's playing at soldier is also an absurdist version of Mishima's Isao.

It is not surprising that this boy's ideal fantasy culminates in the narrator's "memory" of accompanying his father to war. It is also not surprising that the narrator is desperately trying to return to these

"Happy Days" any way he can. Somewhat like Mishima and Isao in their active seeking of the transcendental Otherness of death, the narrator of "Day" eagerly awaits death because, through it, he can finally return to his *"Happy Days."* As he puts it, "I consider that period in my life the first *Happy Days* in my thirty-five years, alongside these final *Happy Days* as I lie here dying unhurriedly but swiftly of cancer . . . Don't you agree the patient should have the freedom to choose diluted life over a long period, or concentrated life briefly?"[56]

Of course, this intense desire, too, may be parody of Mishima's suicidal desires; but it is more likely that the yearning for a "concentrated life" is a genuine one, largely because the desire for a "concentrated life" appears often in Oe's more straightforward novels and autobiographical recollections. If the idea of a concentrated existence sounds similar to, if less histrionic than, some of the yearnings of Mishima's characters, it is because Mishima and Oe are not so far apart. The Oe of 1960 who was unable totally to satirize the passionate young adolescent of "Seventeen" is, in 1973, still incapable of completely separating himself from the despairing and passionate thirty-five-year-old intellectual or the ten-year-old child soon to be expelled from his *"Happy Days."* As Nathan says of Oe, "there is also a longing, not so different in quality from Mishima's own, for the sweet certainty of unreasoning faith in a god."[57]

For both Mishima and Oe and also for their characters, the "god" is strongly identified with the emperor; and this godlike emperor is a glorious and even frightening vision. Thus, the narrator of "Day" becomes enraged with his mother when she exposes his greatest fear (which, at the same time, may be his secret desire): "he's afraid there may even be an emperor in the Japanese world after death."[58] She is referring to an occasion in his childhood when he was asked whether he would die happily for the emperor. Two decades later, he is still unable to overcome his fear and his shame that his childhood self hesitated before answering, "Yes, I'll die happily."[59]

This childish association of faith, death, and the emperor is echoed in the more exalted scene in *Runaway Horses,* quoted at the beginning of this chapter, where Isao gladly states that he will "cut open his stomach." This scene has quasi-religious tones in the notion of absolute sacrifice for a superior being; and indeed one commentator has compared Mishima's concept of the emperor to the Christian idea of God, except that this is a "God" who died in 1945.[60] Although this interpretation may be going too far, it is certainly clear that the "free-floating signifier" which is the emperor can take on immense existential weight, as it gives Isao's life and death a meaning that it would not otherwise have had.

It can also be argued, in the case of Mishima himself, that the emperor served as a convenient rationale for that which he wished to do anyway (i.e., commit suicide); but if so, it is still interesting how often in Oe's fiction as well a character's fascination with the emperor leads to death: the suicide of Ore in "Seventeen," the slow "semisuicide" of the narrator in "Day," and the death of Shigeru in *Our Era.* The obvious link here is through the emperor's association with war, but the imperial house is far more than simply a war machine. Even in degraded form, it is a "machine" that gives purpose by setting up for its servants a paradigm of physical and emotional intensity, a false paradigm, according to Oe, but a powerful one nonetheless.

The question finally remains, how important is the emperor in the works of Oe and Mishima? The emperor is significant for a variety of literary, historical, and psychological reasons. Certainly the fact that Mishima organized in the mid 1960s the so-called Shield Society to "shield" the emperor from presumed left-wing activists and finally committed suicide in the emperor's name suggests that the emperor was of paramount importance to him. And yet, although Oe's treatment of the emperor has obvious extraliterary dimensions to it, his attitude is fundamentally the more personal one while that of Mishima is in a certain way more distant, as the two quotations at the beginning of this chapter suggest. This may seem surprising in view of Mishima's suicide; but, as should be clear by now, even his fictional models commit suicide out of motives that are not totally patriotic.

Mishima's conception of the emperor contains at least one element that is totally lacking in the case of Oe, and that is the aesthetic one. This aesthetic dimension is most clearly evidenced in his long essay "A Defense of Culture" published in 1968, in which Mishima posits a mysterious emperor who is the fount of Japanese culture – the source from which Japan obtains its uniqueness and its superiority.

Mishima explains this by identifying Japanese culture with the aesthetic concept of *miyabi*, courtly refinement – and this "courtliness" is naturally related to the emperor as head of the court. (Incidentally, there is an erotic element here as well, since court culture and literature essentially raised eroticism to an aesthetic in itself.) Although complex, Mishima's argument does not seem to be much different from the familiar arguments of cultural superiority which have been popular at least since the eighteenth-century school of Motoori Norinaga and his National Learning teachings. In any case, when viewed in terms of Mishima's overall life and most importantly, his death, "A Defense of Culture" comes across as rather specious, an excuse for Mishima to attractively package his dislike of the postwar world, combined with his own philosophy of aesthetics in imperial wrapping paper.[61]

It is this aesthetic attitude towards the emperor, and, in related terms, towards violence and eroticism, that leads to suspicions that Mishima's obsession with the emperor is on a more impersonal level than that of Oe. Mishima in a sense "discovered" the emperor in his thirties with the publication of his two stories concerning the February 26 incident. "Patriotism" allowed him to explore the erotic possibilities of emperor worship, while "The Voices of the Hero Spirits" allowed him to explore its aesthetic possibilities. Indeed one scene in "Hero Spirits" where the emperor, revealing himself as a god incarnate and riding a white horse on a snow-covered field, presides over his soldiers' seppuku, is so exquisitely described that one might almost suspect that Mishima had written the story simply as a showcase for it. Nevertheless, the cries of betrayal by the "hero spirits" are also so beautifully and movingly rendered that Mishima's attitude towards the emperor remains problematic even in this story. Although the aesthetic framework in which he wrote and lived should not be ignored, it is also important to remember that the ideals he had Isao espouse in *Runaway Horses*, and the moral decay that he details throughout the tetralogy, are issues that he again took up in his last speech before committing suicide. It is also probable that the deep sense of betrayal, complained of by the "hero spirits" in "The Voices of the Hero Spirits" is one shared on some level by Mishima as well.

Indeed, if the emperor meant anything to Mishima on a personal level, it is probably in a way that is very similar to Oe's feelings, that is, as a symbol of a plethora of missed experiences, missed opportunities, missed lives, and missed "certainties," to use Nathan's expression. For Mishima, these desired Others included the impossible beauty of young death in a glorious cause while for Oe they are associated with the excitement, mystery, and potentialities of boyhood. It is significant that for Oe, the emperor is identified with a sympathetic father figure, while Mishima in *Runwaway Horses* hints at an overwhelming authority figure for whom Isao will gladly cut open his stomach. For both authors, the emperor suggests the potential for belonging to a greater whole, a transcendent unity far from the atomizing anomies of modern Japan.

Mishima through his works, his "patriotic" activities, and his suicide, attempted to unite with that entity and to transcend the writing on the wall of postwar history. Oe, over the last thirty years, has continued to confront and criticize history in his writings and to grow away from the ten-year-old boy who was content to be a "child of the emperor," and to become instead the genuine democratic humanist which the grown-up Oe wishes to be. At times his struggle to liberate himself from the emperor has been so vehement that some Japanese critics have considered him a quintessential spokesman of the anti-imperial intelligentsia,[62] and certainly his nonfiction essays have placed him squarely among the left wing.

However, as should be clear from this chapter, Oe in his fiction has been unable to maintain a simplistic attitude. Much though he might aspire to feel at home in the Western tradition of iconoclastic individualism, he still cannot escape his own imperial past and is still too deeply rooted in the traditional and communal framework of prewar Japanese society. Although in his later fiction, most notably the monumental *Game of Contemporaneity*, Oe does create a sustained attack on emperor-centered history, he does this by eliminating any conventionally interesting or sympathetic protagonists with whom the reader might identify. Instead, *The Game of Contemporaneity* presents an alternative history of Japan through concentrating on the legends surrounding a hidden Shikoku village of outsiders struggling against the "great Japanese empire." Rather than ambivalence, *The Game of Contemporaneity* shows a thoroughgoing hostility towards the emperor system suggesting that, by creating a "group protagonist," Oe is finally able to depict the issue in a more consistently black-and-white manner. *The Game of Contemporaneity*, however, has been criticized by Japanese critics for its artificiality, and it certainly lacks the emotional force of "Day."[63]

As of the writing of "Day," at least, his central protagonist, like those of Mishima, is still incapable of accepting his lonely individuality and is last seen still searching desperately for some larger protective figure, perhaps his father, perhaps the emperor:

His bayonet clanking at his side, he crawls toward the stone steps at the bank entrance where *a certain party* waits, bullet riddled and army sword held high in one hand, the other outstretched to embrace him, shot in the back and dying ... His head nothing more than a dark void now, the blood all drained away, he is no longer certain whether the person awaiting him at the top of the stone step is *a certain party*, but if he can crawl just one yard more digging at the hot ground with his bullet broken hands he will reach the feet of the person unmistakably awaiting him, whoever he may be, and his blood and his tears will be wiped away.[64]

In a chapter so full of ironies, it is ironically appropriate that the avowed left-wing humanist should have the most poignant description of the need for the emperor, rather than the man who gave his life in his name. Of course, there can be no question that the "democratic Oe" abhors everything that the emperor system stands for, especially the kind of insane actions committed in the emperor's name by someone like Mishima. While *Runaway Horses* builds up a kind of chilling logic of aesthetic fanaticism, "Day" exposes that fanaticism for the insanity it really is. Oe also understands the kind of personality that is likely to become a terrorist, and that personality is far more likely to be the lonely malcontent seen in "Seventeen" than the perfect young heroes of "Patriotism" or *Runaway Horses*.

And yet, what remains most keenly for the reader of all these works, be they by Mishima or by Oe, is the protagonists' agonizing fear of abandonment by the emperor or by history in general. Thus, the last cries of Ore are little different from the outraged cries of the voices of the hero spirits. The emperor may be used for immoral, indeed evil purposes; but, riding on his white horse weeping tears for his warriors, or standing at the top of the stairs waiting for a boy's bullet-ridden body to reach him, he remains one of the most powerful and evocative symbols of the fears and yearnings that continue to exert their power in modern Japan.

6 · The Final Quest

Mishima's four-volume *Sea of Fertility* (*Hōjō no Umi*) and Oe's *Silent Cry* are powerful and challenging works that encapsulate each author's main literary preoccupations and observations on Japanese society and modern history. Despite major differences in style and final emphasis, the works mirror each other. Both, for instance, once again contrast active and passive heroes. Both take their stories back almost a century to a glowing past at the beginnings of Japan's modernization and then return to the bleak present. Both mix genres — realism, romance, fantasy, and myth — to capture visions of the modern world and offer romantic alternatives to it. Moreover, this play of romantic genres against realism is a return to the yearned-for pastoral worlds of romantic action that appeared in both authors' first novels.

As the preceding chapters have noted, romantic alternatives to reality are important both by their presence and even more by their absence in much of the two writers' fiction. In works as diverse as Oe's *The Floodwaters Have Come unto My Soul*, or Mishima's "Voices of the Hero Spirits," the romantic and even the fantastic take considerable prominence over the mundane and the plausible. But these romantic visions of alterity were always transient, "moments at odds with reality," bounded by death or destruction, or simply by time or reality starting up again. Should we conclude, then, that reality must always win out?

The works discussed in this chapter explore that question. Although more realistic in some ways than the early pastoral visions, they contain some of the most obvious romantic, even mythic, elements found in both writers' later works. In Mishima's case, the *Sea of Fertility* tetralogy is the final rendition of what could well be called his entire mythic vision. In the case of Oe, although his writing career is still evolving, *The Silent Cry* may be considered his most complete and powerful statement on myth, romanticism, and realism thus far, especially since his more recent works veer further and further away from the realistic to create an increasingly overtly fantastic literary world. Oe's *Game of Contemporaneity*, for example, is in many ways both another attack on Mishima and a rewriting of *The Silent Cry* with much broader strokes. The prime focus of comparison here, however, will remain *The Silent Cry* because of its intriguing structural similarities to *The Sea of Fertility*.

Previous chapters traced the basic outlines of the alternative worlds both writers submit as contrasts to modern Japan. To summarize: Mishima's romantic vision of the imaginary is characterized by visual beauty, both of setting and of protagonist, and a sense of harmony between nature and the hero. In many of his later works this feeling of harmony becomes related to the protagonist's yearnings for a union with the emperor and death, although in *The Sea of Fertility*, the figure of the emperor is dealt with in only one work, *Runaway Horses*. In Oe's works, the mythic other world is largely a pastoral one, a return to nature and to childish innocence in a dream place (Africa and the sea being prime examples) that still contains potential for excitement or magic. The observer child in Oe's "Prize Stock" is an early example of the passive hero who appears intermittently in the early, romantic works of both writers and becomes an increasingly important type in both writers' fiction, realistic as well as romantic. Indeed, by the time of *A Personal Matter* by Oe and the latter part of Mishima's *Sea of Fertility*, the passive hero virtually eclipses the active protagonist. This might seem surprising in Mishima, given his avowed contempt for the intellectual and the increasing preoccupation with the hero warrior evinced in such works as "Patriotism" and "The Voices of the Hero Spirits"; yet it is really the relationship between the active and passive protagonists, and not just the hero warrior himself, that is the dynamic driving the plots of those and his other later works.

Besides this shift to passive heroes, there are other important changes in the later work of both authors. A pronounced strain of exoticism, which was less evident in his earlier fiction, runs through Mishima's tetralogy as well as a rather self-conscious preoccupation with traditional Japanese culture. Oe largely eschews exoticism, although his characters sometimes evoke an international flavor; but in *The Silent Cry* and other late works such as *The Game of Contemporaneity* he, too, burrows back into Japanese history in a somewhat self-conscious manner. Oe's history, however, tends to be held to a primitive folk level, while Mishima sticks to high culture, as in his flamboyant evocations of the aristocratic world in the Meiji period.

Finally, and of special note, *The Sea of Fertility*, *The Silent Cry*, and *The Game of Contemporaneity* all share a preoccupation with time, specifically mythic or imaginary time versus contemporary reality and real world history, a history which oppresses all the protagonists on an individual and a universal level. Where Mishima's *Sound of Waves* and even Oe's "Prize Stock" or *Pluck the Buds* took place in essentially frozen worlds of childhood set outside time, all these later works reveal a pressing awareness of history and its impact on the hero. Mythic time interweaves with real time, be it through Mishima's use of an explicit reincarnation motif in *The Sea of Fertility* or Oe's conscious juxtaposition in *The Silent Cry* of two parallel events that are, in fact, one hundred years apart.

Although Mishima is perhaps more obvious in his intention, there can be no doubt that both works explicitly set their mythic worlds, especially those of the past, at odds with the degenerate world of the present. Thus a minor character in the Oe novel will make such statements as "the valley has grown hopelessly decadent,"[1] or Mishima's *Decay of the Angel* will contrast the contemporary ugliness of the Japanese coastline with its idealized literary version in a Noh Play.

The mediator between the real and the imaginary/mythic in *The Silent Cry* and *The Sea of Fertility* is once again the hero of action, who must take the tortuous journey between real and unreal worlds. Even more than the previous pastoral works, these narratives concern journeys, indeed quests. The quests vary greatly, especially those of the active heroes. They range from the impossibly beautiful love or honor that Mishima's Kiyoaki and Isao seek to the "intensity" that Oe's hero Takashi is avowedly searching for. Another sort of quest is evident as well that is different from the earlier pastoral myths: the quest of the passive hero.

The quests of the two passive intellectuals—Mishima's Honda and Oe's Mitsusaburo—are very similar: the pursuit of truth. And the truth, should they find it, may not only set them free and give meaning to their own lives, it will give meaning to the rest of the world as well. The fact that "truth" rarely serves as a major object of pursuit in Japanese literature, which instead has usually delighted in the relativity and manipulability of "truths," only underlines the distinctiveness of Oe and Mishima's respective visions.

Of all their fiction, these two works can most legitimately be considered contemporary reinterpretations of the basic wasteland myth, that of a hero sent out from a dying land on a quest abroad to find the means of reinvigorating his country. Rather than escaping from the wasteland, they are both formally and thematically answering the question, can one transform the wasteland? Thus, *The Sea of Fertility* and *The Silent Cry* are not simply the self-centered rites-of-passage myths of the earlier stories; they are myths with a wider extent and larger social implications, since the state of the contemporary world is closely linked to the reasons behind the hero's quest.

What is the truth these heroes seek that will regenerate a dying culture? Essentially it is the truth of the efficacy of myth, the proof that the world can contain more than what the intellectual senses perceive, that myth can live and transform the mundane. Whether the heroes find such truth is another matter. In fact, *The Silent Cry* and *The Sea of Fertility* place the lushest romanticism and the bleakest realism side by side in a contest between myth and anti-myth. In this case, however, Mishima's title, *The Sea of Fertility*, is drawn from a feature on the moon's lifeless surface and hence by its irony warns, in effect, that at the end of the tetralogy the wasteland will reign supreme. If the myth and romance are to triumph, the quest will have to be achieved in Oe's work.

Within the narratives themselves a third quest is occurring, the quest for identity in the broadest sense, not just of the tortured and agonized characters, but of modern Japan itself. This identity is sought not only within the structure of the quest narrative itself, or by the individual characters, but in the overall form that the novels take. Rare in modern Japanese literature, these are genuine attempts to create mythic narratives.

The heroes embarked on these journeys are the archetypal Mishima-Oe pairings of active hero and passive observer: The active hero sets the romantic plot in motion; the passive protagonist keeps it within realistic bounds and provides intellectual commentary. Although these characters are psychologically more complicated than their predecessors, they are still overtly "romantic" and easily analyzable in terms of the mythic paradigm described by Campbell and Frye.

YOU CAN LEARN A LOT FROM LEGENDS: *THE SILENT CRY*

Turning first to Oe's *Silent Cry*, we find that it fulfills a surprising number of mythic requirements. First is its setting, which is obviously another imaginary pastoral non-place, drawn in conscious distinction to modern urban Japan. Once again, the reader returns to the remote mountain village of *Pluck the Buds* and "Prize Stock," which, although accessible to the real world, is plainly not part of it. Even for an isolated village in the Japan of the 1960s, this unnamed hamlet is a remarkably remote and bizarre community, peopled by an unusual collection of grotesques and quasi-monsters, ranging from Jin, "Japan's Fattest Woman,"[2] to the mad hermit Gii and the fearsome Chosokabe, which never actually appears, but is said to lurk at the edges of the forest. The grotesques and the village, however, all exist within the limits of plausibility, indeed very clearly within the context of the events of the late 1960s, from which they cannot entirely escape.

For the village is no longer the potentially "good" place of the pastoral works. Far more than the war, modern urban life in general has contaminated it. Although it is still a place of potential redemption, it is also structurally related to the underworld, a fact which is made even more obvious by the frequent reference to a picture of hell that hangs in the village temple and, significantly, of which the active hero has an irrational fear. As in the Campbell and Frye paradigms, *The Silent Cry* is the story of a hero's journey to that underworld where he must battle with and ultimately vanquish a variety of monsters before traveling out again. But in Oe's modern myth, this journey is ambiguous, for neither monsters nor heroes are always what they seem.

For example, although Oe never makes this explicit, students of Japanese history will know that the Chosokabe is actually not a monster at all but simply the name of the feudal clan which held the area before the Meiji restoration took over. Thus, the Chosokabe symbolizes the dark power of history that cannot be quite forgotten, an image lurking on the borders of memory and imagination. It is this dark power that the hero summons up to help him reinvigorate the wasteland/village. The hero himself, a young man named Takashi, who is the younger brother of the passive protagonist Mitsusaburo, is ultimately successful, but only by sacrificing himself.

Although he is more complex than most of Oe's heroes of action, Takashi's background and ambitions also make him the very model of a mythic hero. Forced to leave his valley home and go out into the world to seek adventure, Takashi returns with two definite quests in mind. His first might be considered an update of the rite-of-passage quest: it is a desire to find himself, to return to his roots in the remote Shikoku village where his family sprang from, and, in particular, to recapture the "intensity" that he believes his great-grandfather's younger brother experienced when he led a peasant revolt against the landlords.

Takashi's second quest is a less self-centered one and involves his dream of inspiring his native village with what he has learned from the outside world, in particular, the transforming and invigorating powers of collective violence. Of course, Takashi is a far more three-dimensional character than this mythic outline suggests; indeed one of the novels' strengths is the way it explores the underside of the charismatic hero's motivations; but another characteristic of *The Silent Cry* is its remarkably close adherence to the archetypal theme of a hero's quest to bring fruit to the wasteland.

Superimposed on this archetypal quest is another sort of quest, this one involving Takashi's older brother Mitsusaburo (Mitsu), an equally complex character although one more familiar from his various literary predecessors such as Bird and Yasuo. While much of Takashi's earlier journeys into the wilderness have occurred "offstage," for Mitsusaburo the valley itself is the wilderness, the site of his adventures and his own quest for identity and truth.

Turning first to Takashi's story, it is interesting to note that, like many heroes of fantasy, Takashi is an orphan who lost his parents at an early age. Unlike his fortunate elder brother Mitsusaburo, who was sent off for schooling in Tokyo, he was forced to remain in penurious circumstances with his half-witted sister in their uncle's house. Also similar to fantasy heroes, Takashi bears a quality of predestination: Before her death, his mother advised her imbecile daughter to stay with Takashi, "By and by, Mitsusaburo will be ugly and Takashi will be handsome. People will like Takashi and he'll lead a successful life."[3]

Perhaps because of this "special" quality, from an early age Takashi identifies himself with his most special ancestor, the aforementioned great-grandfather's younger brother, whom he perceives as a noble revolutionary. In fact, Takashi identifies to such an extent with this ancestor that he asserts, half seriously, that he is the great-grandfather's younger brother's reincarnation.

Already thus endowed with charisma and self-identified with violence, Takashi goes out into the world on a quest to prove himself in a variety of adventures. These include his apparent leadership in the 1960 student riots and a bizarre trip to America, where he joins a drama group touring the country in a series of vignettes entitled "Ours was the Shame," which purports to apologize for Japan's hostile attitude towards America during the riots. As the climax of his trip, and in a revealing sidelight on his potential for self-destruction, Takashi seeks out a black prostitute in Harlem and contracts a venereal disease.

Takashi thus participates in some of the most important incidents of the 1960s and also reflects the mixed feelings of rage, humiliation, and gratitude toward Americans felt by the postwar Japanese. In her discussion of *The Silent Cry,* Wilson points out the subconscious awareness of the American presence that frames the novel.[4] This American presence is not limited only to the recent Occupation and the security treaty riots of the 1960s; it also incorporates the arrival of Perry's black ships in 1860, the year Man'nen from which the novel's Japanese title is taken. It is America which, twice in Japanese history, has propelled Japan down a new path, a road which ultimately separated it from the old traditions of village collectivity that *The Silent Cry* and later Oe works such as *The Game of Contemporaneity* and *Letter to a Nostalgic Year* celebrate.

The American presence is not only an historical one, however. In Takashi's case, America becomes one of his first personal proving grounds. Although on a realistic level, his adventures in New York have a somewhat amateurish and comic quality to them, it is clear from his brother's unwilling envy that Takashi has become a different person on his return from America, stronger and more determined, and perhaps capable of becoming a genuine "man of violence" like his great-grandfather. The major part of *The Silent Cry* shows Takashi's attempt to establish this new persona by leading his own revolt, an event that occurs back in his home village, where he is aided by some young supporters and observed caustically by his envious older brother, the novel's narrator.

Responding imperturbably to his older brother's criticism that he is letting his imagination run wild, Takashi says simply, "'There's a lot to be learned from legends, you know.'"⁵ He stirs up the village's young men's association with exciting tales of the peasant uprising of a hundred years before. He then equates the Korean owner of the new supermarket, which is destroying the village's traditional economy, with the oppressive feudal landlords, Finally, he identifies himself with the leader of the 1860 peasant uprising and begins to "train" the young men under cover of creating the *futtoboru* or soccer team of the novel's Japanese title, which could be translated literally "Football in the Year 1860."

Takashi does not simply attempt to revive the good old days, however. He feels free to fill in the outlines of the 1860 rebellion with his own embellishments to create what he calls "a riot of the imagination."⁶ By thus superimposing the mythic world of the idealized past onto the real world of the present, he gives his henchmen an archetypal pattern to follow, at the same time making the rebellion into his own creation. So successful is he in this superimposition on the minds of his followers that one of the young men, when expelled from the group, heads out into the trackless forest beyond the valley in an apparent attempt to recreate the great-grandfather's younger brother's legendary journey to a castle town beyond the forest.

Real time and mythic time blend even more effectively when Takashi leads his followers in an attack on the supermarket, making sure that they see themselves as heroic fighters of oppression, rather than as the lawbreaking looters that they secretly know themselves to be. "Taka's riot," as it is dubbed by the townspeople, is in some ways the genuine "miracle" that it appeared they needed. For a few days, the villagers exult in a wanton celebration of excitement and communality, feeling a sense of "self-liberation."⁷ They even revive the ages-old *nembutsu* spirit dance, which had fallen prey to modernization. Not only do old legends teach; it seems they can live again, once called from the darkness of history. Although the excitement fades quickly, for a brief moment, Takashi actually succeeds in putting the villagers in touch with what he believes to be the spirit of the 1860 uprising.

As in the two pastoral Oe stories, all these events occur within a realistic framework. The characters may identify themselves with myth, but nothing explicitly supernatural actually occurs. Thus, the text makes the supermarket riot plausible by giving previous examples of the prejudices of the villagers against the Korean owner. At the same time, however, Oe has the villagers call the owner the "emperor," a title which not only suggests ironic overtones of the decadence to which the village has sunk, but also, of course, gives an archetypal mystique to a character who, as plain Mr. Paek, would have had far less mythic resonance (and incidentally hints at a major contemporary political controversy, the question of whether the "divine" emperor's ancestors were actually Korean immigrants). The attack on the supermarket becomes possible only because a snowfall fortuitously isolates the village from the rest of the world; an incident of such complete isolation is a plausible yet unlikely event in industrialized modern Japan.

Matsubara points out, moreover, that the reader never really sees the exact machinations behind the takeover of the supermarket, and this vagueness adds to its mythic quality.[8] As for Takashi himself, it is through death that he achieves genuine mythic stature; for although he has been portrayed as amazingly charismatic and lucky up to that point, he has been primarily a realistic character. The death itself is a bloody and violent one, no doubt appropriate to the "man of violence" Takashi believes himself to be. Significantly, it is Mitsusaburo who finds the corpse and reads Takashi's last defiant message, which is, "I told the truth."[9]

Takashi's death is self-inflicted, but it is a suicide of many mythic reverberations. The ostensible reasons behind it are twofold: First, he insists that he has raped and murdered a village girl and prefers to take his own life rather than be lynched by a mob. Second, he feels guilt over his incestuous relationship with his retarded sister, a relationship that led to her pregnancy and subsequent suicide. The first explanation, as Mitsusaburo points out, is particularly unbelievable, since it is highly unlikely that Takashi raped or murdered the girl. Mitsusaburo hypothesizes instead that Takashi deliberately puts himself into a false position in order to bring about his own death. If that is the case, then, is his self-destructiveness really due to guilt over his sister?

Superficially, the text seems to suggest this reasoning, but the explanation appears a bit thin. Certainly Mitsusaburo, although accepting his brother's guilt, does not believe that guilt alone would force Takashi to his death. As he points out to his brother, "though you're always playing at putting yourself in peril, you're the type who invariably has a way out at the last moment. You acquired the habit on the day that our sister's suicide allowed you to go on living without being punished or put to shame."[10] As is evident from these remarks,

Mitsusaburo's own role in goading his brother to suicide should not be ignored, though it may well be conceded that from the realistic psychological viewpoint, Takashi is indeed portrayed as too selfish to commit suicide out of guilt.

On the level of archetypal myth, however, Takashi's incest and the approaching mob violence of the villagers are peculiarly appropriate elements in the death of a mythic hero. As Girard explains in *Violence and the Sacred*, the act of incest makes its perpetrator evil and worthy to be sacrificed, and the emphasis is on the sacrifice rather than the incest. In fact, as Girard explains, the hero *must* die for the good of the community, and the incestuous act simply makes the death legitimate. Or as Girard puts it in his discussion of Oedipus, "Incest is neither a first cause nor an essential condition. Although it may initially appear to offer justification for the act of sacrifice, on a deeper level it is the act of sacrifice that justifies the incest."[11]

Knowing this, we can now understand why the "official" explanation for Takashi's death seems on one level too pat, while on another level it allows a certain subconscious satisfaction. For the purposes of the wasteland myth that Oe is retelling, Takashi must die; and, using an archetypal paradigm, Oe attaches to Takashi the stigma of incest. But the real mythic importance of Takashi's death lies in its sacrificial aspect. For whom and for what is his sacrifice?

The theme of the sacrifice of the innocent in previous chapters resonates through Oe's work on many levels from the ideological to the psychological. In a Lacanian view of the ego's development, the "sacrifice" is of the unity of the imaginary world as the ego develops autonomy and joins the symbolic order of language. In this regard, Takashi's last message, "I told the truth," is significant. Takashi has, through his death, sacrificed his romantic persona as a "man of violence" and achieved a new stature. He has been inscribed into the symbolic order, both through his brother's written account and also through his own last words. Unlike most of the active heroes profiled in this book, he has gone from action to language in his attempt to create a new world.

On a more mythic level, Takashi's sacrifice is quintessentially the hero's sacrifice for the revival of the wasteland. In the chapter on pastoral myths, it was suggested that the sacrifices in those early stories are perverted ones in that they are conducted for ideologically unhealthy reasons, rather than in a genuine attempt to prevent violence or regenerate the country. In those anti-myths, the sacrifice of the innocent heroes can best be viewed as a sacrifice of the imaginary for the sake of a highly unwholesome symbolic order, the politically suspect Word of the Father. In the case of *The Silent Cry*, however, Takashi's death can be viewed as a truly regenerative act on several levels.

On the most obvious one, Takashi serves as the villagers' scapegoat in their subsequent confrontation with the "emperor"; and, because of his death, they are allowed to go unpunished for their involvement in the riot. On a deeper level, Takashi's uprising and death serve to galvanize the village as nothing had before. Although the uprising is a material failure, at the end of the novel some signs of life appear in the community, including the election of one of the young men to the village council! Even more significantly, at the narrative's end the villagers allow Takashi to return as a "spirit" in the *nembutsu* folk dance, thus tacitly acknowledging his mythic dimensions. He has become a legend in his own right and, in doing so, has perhaps helped to inject new life into the village.

Where "Prize Stock" and *Pluck the Buds* might be called anti-myths, *The Silent Cry* represents an almost perfect example of pure myth, with the final rebirth of the hero and of the wasteland. Furthermore, Takashi does not only return as the stuff of ritual and legend, he also returns in two physical manifestations. First, he will quite literally be reborn, inside the womb of Mitsusaburo's wife, whom he impregnated before his death (and to whom he also gave "new life" through his sexual and psychological vitality), thus assuring his physical as well as spiritual continuation. Secondly, he returns inside the heart and mind of his older brother.

In contrast to his brother, Mitsusaburo's character is both more complex and more simple: complex, because he is an agonized intellectual, capable only of devious manipulation and tortuous analysis, and simple because the forces that drive him, namely passivity and jealousy, are far more easily analyzed. If Takashi is Oe's most fascinating and archetypal hero of action, then Mitsusaburo may well be his most fully realized, and most negatively presented, hero of inaction.

From Mitsuaburo's very first appearance sitting in a cesspool early one morning in an obvious attempt to return to the womb, the reader is struck by the fact that this is a character who can only act negatively if at all. Admittedly, Mitsusaburo has many reasons to be angst-ridden, among them the suicide of his best friend, his wife's delivery of a deformed baby, and her subsequent plunge into alcoholism; but it is significant that his reactions to these events are consistently escapist. He resigns his post at the university where he and his friend both taught, places his child in an institution, and, finally, climbs into the cesspool.

Given this paralytic state, it is unlikely that Mitsusaburo would ever undertake a quest involving an actual physical journey. And yet, thanks to Takashi's enthusiastic prodding, Mitsusaburo does end up accompanying his younger brother on the journey to the village, although, not surprisingly, his quest differs enormously from Takashi's grandiose dreams of finding his roots or revitalizing the village. Instead, Mitsusaburo believes that he is searching for his "thatched hut," a poetic phrase evoking the medieval prose work *Tsurezuregusa* (Essays in idleness), but actually meaning yet another place to hide from reality, although of a slightly more romantic quality than the cesspool. Being an intellectual, however, Mitsusaburo cannot ultimately quell the forces of curiosity within him; and subconsciously he begins a search for the truth and for his own identity, a hunt that will finally return him once more to the bottom of a pit.

Initially, however, Mitsusaburo's escape from the urban wasteland simply takes him to another form of wasteland, that of the village in the valley. Instead of the romantic thatched hut of his dream, Mitsusaburo must confront the disappointments of reality mixed with the ghosts of memory. For him, the valley is a place of gloom and dark memories of a ghastly childhood, haunted by a mad mother and a murdered older brother. It is not surprising, therefore, that Mitsusaburo fears the past and the forest which represents it. For him, it contains both the spirits of his dead ancestors, who may be presumed to reside there, or the openly fantastic monster of his childhood, the Chosokabe.

Unlike J in *The Sexual Human,* who is driven out of the pastoral wasteland to create his own imaginary non-place within the city, Mitsusaburo stays on in the country to fight, in a manner which is both typically intellectual and yet which also contains elements of Campbell's mythic journey. Thus, the following passage describes Mitsusaburo and his wife about to cross the "threshold" into a wilderness of adventure:

> In the very heart of the forest the bus halted without warning, as though the engine had stalled ... The obstacle ahead of the bus was a young peasant woman with a large bundle on her back and something crouched perfectly still like an animal at her feet. Staring, I saw that

it was a child squatting facing in the opposite direction . . .

The forest road, hemmed in on both sides by close ranks of huge evergreens fell gradually away from the front of the bus and the woman and the child at her feet appeared to float about a foot above the ground . . . With a vague sense of fear I was readying myself for some nameless, terrifying thing to come leaping upon us. . . .[12]

Campbell mentions the dreamlike aspects of the start of an adventure as the hero crosses the threshold[13] and this description is certainly dreamlike, if not actually nightmarish, in its eerie ominousness. The woman and child appearing at the entrance of the "very heart of the forest" seem related to the frightening presences who often guard the hero's road in Campbell's paradigm. The woman "floating" silently above the ground is like a messenger of death, while the child is, at best, an ambiguous symbol of possible rebirth—and as noted, children have very problematic associations in Oe's work.

The literal descent into the forest itself echoes Frye's theme of the hero's descent into hell or the underworld. Indeed, as the novel progresses, the forest begins to assume a terrifying power of its own, appearing to encroach on the lives of the villagers, as Takashi himself points out. Even more importantly, a descent into hell can also mean a descent into one's past, which the forest represents in full negative force.

This journey into the past is not initially a therapeutic one for Mitsusaburo. At the beginning, in fact, even the positive remnants of his youth seem to mock him. Thus, in a particularly poignant scene as they approach the valley, Mitsusaburo leads his wife to a forest spring which he remembers as having exceptionally delicious water:

As I bent down over the spring to drink from it directly, I had a sudden sense of certainty that everything—the small round pebbles, greyish blue, and vermillion and white lying at the bottom of water whose brightness still seemed to harbor the midday light . . . was just as I'd seen it before . . . And the same certainty developed directly into a feeling that the "I" bending down there now was not the child who had bent his bare knees there, that there was no continuity, no consistency between the two "I's," that the "I" now bending down there was a remote stranger. The present "I" had lost all true identity. Nothing, either within me or without, offered any hope of recovery.[14]

In the wasteland myth not only does the land dry up and lose its fertility, but men lose their sense of hope and their souls as well. In his spiritual wasteland, which Mitsusaburo projects onto the spring and forest, he has indeed lost himself. He can feel no continuity, no connection, and is therefore hopelessly alone:

> I shut my eyes and sucked up the cold water. My gums shrank, leaving a taste of blood on my tongue. As I stood up, my wife bent down in obedient imitation, as though I was an authority on how to drink from the spring. In fact, I was as complete a stranger to the spring by now as she, who had just come to the forest for the first time. I shuddered.[15]

A stranger to himself and to his own land, Mitsusaburo is the paradigm of deracinated modern man no longer even able to accept the succor of the natural world. In "Prize Stock" the spring was a life-giving element, bringing the children and the black soldier together into an ecstatic celebration of communion with nature. In *The Silent Cry*, however, the spring is a silent embarrassment to the adult Mitsusaburo; and the few apathetic children in the village seem unlikely candidates to delight in nature. Significantly, it is only Gii, the crazed hermit, who seems comfortable in the forest; and even more significantly it is Takashi, who exults in the forest's isolation, who attempts to befriend the hermit, while Mitsusaburo can only watch from the sidelines.

Dispirited by his one attempt to make contact with his past, Mitsusaburo soon goes down into the mists of the valley and enters a state of complete apathy. Steadfastly refusing to be swept along by Takashi's enthusiasm, he smugly adopts the stance of objective observer, consistently interpreting Takashi's words and actions in a negative light. Thus, when Takashi and his followers rescue a village child from drowning, Mitsusaburo is only able to think of "[w]hat would have happened if he hadn't succeeded. If the rescue operation had failed . . . Takashi as the man responsible for the carnage would inevitably have been driven down onto the lump of concrete as it swung like a weight on a line, there to smash his own head in . . . Why, I wondered with a sense of unfocused anger, had Takashi voluntarily put himself in such danger?"[16]

Not only is Mitsusaburo completely incapable of empathizing with his brother's decision to "put himself in danger," he is suspiciously eager to imagine the terrible punishment that might have been meted out to Takashi had he failed. His jealousy is, of course, of the archetypal sibling-rivalry variety; but it is also the jealousy of a passive hero who knows he can never imitate the active hero, even if he should admit to himself that he wanted to try.

Mitsu half recognizes that his critical attitude toward Takashi stems from jealousy, but for most of the novel he shows no sign of wanting to change that attitude. Instead, he feels compelled to exercise control in the one way possible for an intellectual, through words. Because *The Silent Cry* is narrated in the first person by Mitsusaburo, the reader's vision of Takashi and his rebellion is filtered through his brother's jealous language. This is even clearer in Mitsusaburo's verbal confrontations with Takashi when he tries to denigrate not only Takashi's actions, but his dreams as well. Thus, after having demolished Takashi's romantic vision of their slain elder brother, he admits, "I found a perverted pleasure in waiting for the fresh flaws that my corrections lured from Takashi's memory and shooting them down as they appeared. Suppressing a certain disgust with myself, I energetically set about stripping the heroic aura from the image of S. [their older brother], that Takashi had just built up in my wife's mind."[17]

In this instance, Mitsusaburo's immediate reason for destroying Takashi's dream brother is sexual jealousy over Takashi's influence on his wife. But his deeper reason is fear: Because Mitsusaburo cannot be a hero himself, he does not even want to be reminded of the potential for heroism in either of his brothers. Since he cannot live up to that model, he must perforce tear it down through his brutal analysis.

Mitsusaburo almost succeeds in demolishing Takashi's vision because on the level of dispassionate analysis, he is absolutely correct: Takashi is certainly foolish to put himself into unnecessary danger, and his fantasies concerning their brother or their ancestors are simply fantasies. But they are fantasies with power. Takashi has indeed "learned a lot from legends," and Mitsusaburo cannot entirely succeed in his demolition because Takashi does produce results with his successful raid on the supermarket. Of course, Mitsusaburo is quick to disparage his brother's riot as criminal and foolish, but at the same time he is both stunned and alarmed by the successful power of Takashi's violence.

In such a tense relationship, which fits the Cain-and-Abel or *Kojiki* archetype, it is not surprising that Mitsusaburo is at least partially responsible for his brother's death. After Takashi confesses to

Mitsusaburo his incestuous relationship with their sister, the elder brother's only response is that his brother is twisting the truth and that he does not really want to expiate his crime of incest, suggesting that "You're the type who invariably has a way out at the last moment."

Even when Takashi, desperate for some emotional reassurance from his brother, asks, "Mitsu, why have you always hated me so much?",[18] his brother can only reply,

> "Hated? It's not a question of what I feel, Taka. I'm simply giving you my objective opinion that even someone like you who chooses to live in pursuit of a dramatic illusion, can't keep up the critical tension indefinitely, unless, say, he actually goes insane ... All fantasies that ignore those facts are meaningless in the long run. You don't have sufficient confidence in the facts. But you're too old, Taka, to get burned up about heroic fantasies of this kind. You're not a kid anymore."[19]

Not content to refuse any hint of the romantic in his own life, Mitsusaburo must also deny it to others; and in denying it in Takashi, he effectively destroys him. Takashi's suicide is the logical outcome of the destruction of his soul, a sacrifice on the altar of his brother's objectivity. It is no wonder that Takashi's last gesture is to write, to try and appropriate the older brother's control of language and to insist that "I told the truth" in a last attempt to protect his own vision. At the same time, Takashi's death is paradoxically the means to Mitsusaburo's salvation, to his discovery of the real truth that lies behind the "facts" that up to then were all that he had valued.

While his friend's death had immobilized Mitsusaburo, his brother's death liberates him, although at first he is slow to notice this. The first sign of change occurs when Mitsusaburo becomes interested in the fate of his great-grandfather's younger brother, discovering that he had not, as previously believed, escaped to a new life after the farmer's uprising, but instead had remained concealed for the rest of his life in a hidden cellar beneath the family storehouse, only emerging once, when his leadership in a second uprising was needed. Upon making this discovery, Mitsusaburo's immediate reaction is an impulse to tell his dead younger brother the news: "In a strained voice, I heard myself call 'Taka!' into the gloom surrounding the open fireplace, but realized at once that Taka was dead and regretted his absence more keenly than at any time since he killed himself. It was he, more than anyone else, who deserved to hear the new facts about the storehouse."[20]

Mitsusaburo is wrong, however. As Matsubara says, "The discovery would not have mattered to Takashi, because to him history was nothing more than a means to create myth";[21] and it is myth and the way people perceive myth that is important. This is the "fact" that Mitsusaburo subconsciously is beginning to understand. What he really "regrets" about his brother's absence is the loss of Takashi's enthusiasm and the transforming power of his vivid imagination. Without Takashi, it is Mitsusaburo who must respond to the excitement of the discovery; and it seems that, without Takashi, he is now finally able to discover his own buried enthusiasm.

In the last phase of his quest, Mitsusaburo goes down into the cellar to spend the night with the ghosts of his ancestors. Whereas even his discovery concerning his ancestor was a typical intellectual's finding, through reading, this journey is finally a form of action. In many ways, this action both resembles and contrasts with his climb into the pit at the novel's beginning, where he attempts to escape to the womb and get away from the accusing ghost of his dead friend. This time, however, the pit, while retaining some womblike aspects, is not a place of escape but of confrontation.

Appropriately, Mitsusaburo's vision includes a trial. As he squats in the cellar, he feels surrounded by eyes—Takashi's eyes, his great-grandfather's eyes, his wife's eyes—"They would go on multiplying, I felt sure, throughout the time remaining to me, till a hundred pairs of eyes would glitter like a chain of stars in the night of my experience."[22] The trial, as I have noted earlier, is related in general to themes of betrayal and the loss of the imaginary. Thus the hero spirits of "The Voices of the Hero Spirits" accuse the emperor of betraying them by becoming human, and the narrator in "The Day He Himself Shall Wipe My Tears Away" agonizes over "abandonment" (by his father, by his emperor). For Mitsusaburo, however, it is he who has abandoned the imaginary, the romantic alternative; and his punishment is to open himself to judgment by those he has betrayed, including his ancestors.

Faithful to his still passive self, Mitsusaburo immediately thinks of escape: "[W]as there perhaps some way of letting go and retreating into a more comfortable darkness? As in a sequence of photographic stills, I saw another me slip free from my drooping shoulders as I sat hunched like a body in a buried urn and, rising crawl through the gap in the floorboards then go climbing up the steep staircase, the clothes bundling its body fluttering in the gusts of wind that blew straight up from the valley."²³ Mitsusaburo envies that other self which, escaping, will not even try to summon up the courage needed to grasp the truth that Takashi and his great-grandfather's younger brother were seeking. And yet, in admitting his lack of courage, and getting rid of that other self, he makes the crucial discovery that "just as Takashi from childhood had been fired with a sense of opposition to me, so I had been hostile to Takashi and his idol, his great-grandfather's younger brother, and had sought meaning in a placid way of life quite different from theirs."²⁴

It is this final discovery that releases Mitsusaburo. His confrontation in the pit has killed off one self, the passive escapist one; and a new self has begun to appear. When Mitsusaburo reemerges from the cellar he has become, not a man of violence, but a changed man, willing to reject a safe sinecure that has been offered to him and instead take on a potentially dangerous job in Africa. Mitsusaburo's quest for his thatched hut may have been unsuccessful, but he now has the impetus to go on searching for it in an active way. Even more importantly, on the journey through self-discovery he has stumbled on something far more valuable than the hut, his own personal vision of Takashi's truth: He can never be the kind of hero of action that his brother was, but he can understand its romantic appeal and, in his own way, find a sort of heroism within his own soul.

Of course, he could not have accomplished this without the aid of his younger brother. As Matsubara suggests, "It almost appears that Takashi's self-destruction was simply a tragic sacrifice offered up for Mitsusaburo's redemption."²⁵ Yet, the relationship between the brothers is more complex than simply victim and survivor. In many ways, as Izu points out, the two brothers can be seen as the two halves of a single self.²⁶ That this seems to be Oe's conscious intention is clear if we note his consistent identification of the two brothers with opposite types of imagery.

Aoki Mamoru has noted the use of red imagery throughout *The Silent Cry*;²⁷ and Takashi, in particular, is consistently associated with red, from the blood that he has feared since boyhood, to the hell screen that fascinates and repels him, even to the flush that rises on his face when he speaks of the 1860 uprising. Just as the black soldier was strongly linked to primitive life and nature, so Takashi's association with redness evokes a similar raw, primitive quality. Also like the black soldier, Takashi is associated with the beauty and spontane-

ous joy of the natural world, as the following scene where Mitsusaburo watches his brother run naked in the snow demonstrates:

> The essence of that moment would be drawn out indefinitely, direction in
> time was swallowed up and lost amid the steadily falling flakes just as
> sound was absorbed by the layer of snow. All pervasive time: Takashi as he
> ran stark naked was great grandfather's younger brother and my own,
> every moment of those hundred years was crowded into this one instant
> of time . . . Suddenly, Takashi gave a series of sharp grunts and rolled over
> and over in the snow. I saw that he had an erection. His penis had the same
> air of power stoically controlled and the same odd pathos as the sweating
> muscles of an athlete's upper arms.[28]

In its portrayal of a man glorying in nature and his own sexuality,
the passage not only echoes the snow scenes in *Pluck the Buds* and the
scene at the spring in "Prize Stock," but it also contrasts with the
scene described earlier, where Mitsusaburo attempts to gain new
vigor from the forest spring of his past and fails miserably. Takashi
is in touch with the past, with himself, and with nature, while Mitsusaburo throughout most of the novel is utterly cut off from all three.
Thus, in his trial in the cellar, Mitsusaburo makes peace not only
with this ghost but with history, "every moment of those hundred
years."

Oe does not let his two heroes remain simply opposite sides of the
same coin, however. Rather, he allows the new Mitsusaburo who
emerges from the pit to take in part of Takashi's sensuality and openness to nature. Mitsusaburo thus becomes the first of Oe's passive
heroes who seems, at the end of the novel, to be about to realize his
dream of adventure in Africa, the continent that represents for Oe's
heroes the antithesis of modern Japan. In fact, at the very end of *The
Silent Cry*, the reader sees Mitsusaburo envisaging "a life of sweat and
grime in Africa," but not wholly on a pessimistic level.

Part of Takashi's adventuresomeness has obviously been reborn in
Mitsusaburo. In a revealing comment in this passage, Mitsusaburo
anticipates that, once in Africa, he will be "too busy to consider what
was going on inside me."[29] For the first time in his life, Mitsusaburo
will be taking action and will no longer be allowed to fall into the pit
where ratiocination draws all action into despairing passivity.

The conclusion of *The Silent Cry* is not wholly a happy ending,
however. Despite the romantic attraction Africa holds for Mitsusa-

buro, he must still acknowledge that "working as an interpreter in Africa wasn't going to solve everything";[30] but the fact that he is still willing to try it out is close to a miracle, even though occurring within a realistic framework.

It has been suggested that there are two levels of reality in *The Silent Cry*, the "realistic" reality represented by Mitsusaburo, and the mythic reality that is opened up by Takashi's actions: The first level, according to Aoki, is that of "darkness, fear, powerlessness and death." The second level is the mythic world of "flight and action, violence and heroism, fire and the color red."[31] The impressive achievement of *The Silent Cry* is that it ultimately manages to integrate the two realities successfully without ever straining either of the component parts. Both the reader and Mitsusaburo are left with a vision of the potential for the miraculous in the real world. In later Oe novels, such as *The Game of Contemporaneity*, the legends begin to overwhelm the characters; but in *The Silent Cry*, Oe maintains the balance between the real and unreal by treating the two fundamentally opposed heroes in such a way that their still more fundamental attraction is underscored.

It is no accident that this ambitious work was written in 1967, one hundred years after the Meiji Restoration. Far more than a family saga, Oe is attempting to encompass modern Japanese history from the coming of the black ships and the destruction of the old clans, symbolized by the shadowy Chosokabe, to the security treaty riots and their poisonous aftermath, signified by Takashi's venereal disease.

The Silent Cry symbolized a new direction for Oe, towards wider scopes and more apocalyptic, more explicitly political works. But *The Silent Cry* is still perhaps his most successful effort to encapsulate Japanese history, society, and politics within a single tight narrative. The fact that the novel succeeds so well on a literary level largely results from the tension between active and passive protagonists, and it is this tension which Oe sacrifices in later works.

THE EMPTY GARDEN: *THE SEA OF FERTILITY*

Because the attraction of opposites, of rational passive hero and spontaneous active hero, is also the underlying dynamic of Mishima's *Sea of Fertility*, it is particularly apt for comparison with *The Silent Cry*. But where Oe sends his two heroes on an ultimately successful quest that makes the perils of the journey worthwhile, Mishima's final version of the quest myth suggests that the journey may be more valuable than the actual prize: His heroes discover in the end that the past cannot reinvigorate the present but can only make the present seem more hopeless by comparison. The reader who follows Mishima's heroes of action and inaction through four novels finds that the ultimate truth is emptiness, but Mishima at least provides a varied and exotic trip. Some of this exotica is undoubtedly superfluous, Mishima's attempt to play towards a popular market; but his portrait of a degenerate modern Japan is still a powerful one.

The Sea of Fertility, which covers a lot of historical ground (it begins in the Meiji period and ends in the 1970s), is held together by two threads—by the reincarnation in each book of the active hero, Kiyoaki, and by the continued presence of the passive hero Honda, Kiyoaki's friend, helper, and foil. In Honda, Mishima has created one of his most memorable, even tragic characters. A brilliant vision of human degeneration from rational cynic to unspeakable old voyeur, the portrait of Honda at the same time transcends Mishima's typical degradation of intellectuals to passive heroes, because Honda is a fully realized, three-dimensional character whose pathetic impossible yearnings are memorably articulated.

In one of the most poignant passages of the tetralogy Honda walks home after being rejected by Ying Chan, a beautiful Thai princess, and experiences a painful moment of self revelation:

> Were he young, he would have cried aloud as he walked. If he were young. But he had never cried when he was young! He had been a promising youth who thought he should use reason to bring success to himself and others instead of wasting time in shedding tears . . . His only recourse was to daydream about a different kind of self in the past. How different? It had been quite impossible to become a Kiyoaki or an Isao.[32]

This sense of "impossibility" animates both Honda's story and the tetralogy itself. *Spring Snow* and *Runaway Horses* are tales dominated by heroes of action. As such, it is not surprising to find a number of archetypally mythic elements in them, centering around the character of the heroes themselves. In fact, *Spring Snow* might well be considered an effective combination of myth and fairy tale, containing both the mysterious and beautiful aspects of the fairy tale, along with the higher seriousness of myth.

This fairy-tale aspect is most clear in its sumptuous setting. A story of aristocrats and princes, of beautiful women and exquisite landscapes, the novel offers an appealing alternative to the Japan of 1965 when it was written. Set in a time a little after the turn of the century, its otherworldly ambience makes it easily both "anti-historical," as Watanabe Hiroshi suggests,[33] and at the same time profoundly attached to Japanese history.

Mishima uses the device of a photograph of soldiers in the Russo-Japanese war to draw the reader into this other world: "This photograph, printed in sepia ink, was quite unlike the usual cluttered mementos of war. It had been composed with an artist's eye for structure . . . Both its age and the sepia ink tinged the photograph with an atmosphere of infinite grief."[34] Like the photograph, which removes all the horrors and bloodshed of war, except for a poignant tint, the novel *Spring Snow* sets the reality of modernizing Japan at a safe distance from itself, in order to explore a narrow world of beauty and grief. The "real world" still exists and will come to the fore in the later novels of the tetralogy; but in this, the most romantic of Mishima's works since *The Sound of Waves*, realism is important mainly by its absence.

The person looking at the photograph is Kiyoaki. Although hardly an active hero in the galvanizing sense that Takashi was, the protagonist of *Spring Snow* also has a quest, but his quest is a totally selfish one: He is searching for an impossibly beautiful love, a love that as in "Patriotism" is elitist, romantic, and bounded by death. Although the search for love may not be the major quest form in Western literature, it is perhaps the most important of all quests in Japanese literature, beginning at least as early as the *monogatari* (romance) tradition of the tenth century.

In fact, Mishima's novel is explicitly inspired by the eleventh-century *Hamamatsu Chūnagon monogatari* (The tale of the Hamamatsu Middle Counselor), the story of a nobleman's trip to China and his forbidden love affair with and impregnation of a Chinese imperial consort. Mishima omits the trip to China and sets his story in the nineteenth century; but the basic elements of the tale, its reincarnation theme and its pair of elegant secret lovers, whose love can only invoke imperial wrath, remain the same. Where Oe used elements of Japanese folk tales to give *The Silent Cry* not only a mythic but a primitive, ghost-story quality, Mishima borrows the pieces of a Heian monogatari to give his story an other-worldly elegance evoking the exquisite but often sinister world of the monogatari or the fairy tale.

Like a true hero of romance (and like one of Oe's heroes of action), Kiyoaki is exceptional from childhood. Sent away from his nouveau-riche family at an early age to learn manners from an aristo-cratic household, Kiyoaki, while not technically an orphan, is dis-tinctly alienated from his natural parents. In his new family, his unearthly charm and physical radiance are soon remarked. Later on, in a further fairy-tale touch, at Kiyoaki's initiation-into-adolescence ceremony, the previously shrouded moon suddenly appears from behind the clouds as he gazes into a basin of water to read his future.

Yet, as was the case with Takashi, all these good omens apparently come to nothing. Kiyoaki's beauty, indeed his very commitment to beauty, eventually bring about his downfall. Like Takashi, who wants to live his life "intensely," Kiyoaki early on knows what he wants. As *Spring Snow* explains, "The only thing that seemed valid to him was to live for the emotions."[35] The problem for Kiyoaki lies in achieving this ambition.

Since Kiyoaki's quest is one of the emotions, there is no need for him to set forth on a literal journey, as the archetypal hero does; but it is interesting to note a number of images with mythic resonances to them that appear at various symbolic "thresholds" throughout the novel. Thus, in the scene where the reader is first introduced to Satoko, the girl who will become Kiyoaki's great love, the gloomy omen of a dead black dog found beneath a waterfall intrudes itself. Although the incident may also suggest Mishima's tendency to ren-der in an ugly way certain traditionally beautiful Japanese scenes, it seems more likely here in this fantasy setting that the dog is simply a reminder that darkness and evil may lurk in the most beautiful places, while the use of natural imagery in general also may have asso-ciations with Shinto.

Although there is no concretely realized threshold for Kiyoaki to cross in his journey of the emotions, there is a dream barrier for him to penetrate. This obstacle appears only after Kiyoaki discovers that Satoko, whom he has hitherto rejected, is now promised to an imperial prince and must henceforth be regarded as inviolate. Now that Satoko is unavailable to him, Kiyoaki has found the perfect realization of his quest for an impossible love, and it is significant that the moment he hears of her betrothal a vision appears before him of "a darkened cor-ridor long and wide and at the end a door fastened with a small pad-lock of solid gold . . . And suddenly, with a noise like the grinding of teeth, it opened of its own accord, a metallic rasp echoing in his ears."[36]

Although the Freudian implications of this vision are obvious, this sinister but beautiful corridor may also be viewed as the threshold at the opening of an adventurous journey. That the allure of this journey is due to its underlying association with death is made clear when Kiyoaki contemplates his transgression of having slept with the betrothed Satoko and thinks, "I've dared to betray his Majesty. There's nothing more to do but die . . . a thrill went through him but whether of joy or dread he could not tell."[37] Although it must be stressed that Kiyoaki's wooing of Satoko is completely realistic (although confined to the almost unreal elitist world of aristocrats and imperial princes), with a little exaggeration of certain details, the balance could easily tip over to fantasy. Thus Kiyoaki's friend Honda in this novel takes on the aspect of the hero's faithful helper, as he guides Kiyoaki to his many secret rendezvous with Satoko; and Satoko's elderly female servant, Tadeshina, who is willing to manipulate and maneuver for the young couple, has a sinister, almost witchlike quality.

Aided by these two characters, Kiyoaki initially succeeds in his quest and plunges into a passionate love affair with Satoko. Naturally, the fact of the legal and social impossibility of the union dictates that it must be short-lived. In the novel's tragically romantic ending, the pregnant Satoko is forced to have an abortion before fleeing to a nunnery, while Kiyoaki contracts pneumonia after waiting outside the temple gates in the snow and dies at the age of twenty. Unlike Takashi, whose child will live and whose existence signals a hope for the future, Kiyoaki does not reinvigorate the wasteland of modernizing Japan in any obvious way with the exception of the invigorating effect his life has on Honda. Overall, however, the very nostalgic romanticism of Kiyoaki's life itself creates an image of a more gracious age and serves as a positive contrast to the growing shadows of industrialization spreading across twentieth-century Japan.

Again, history plays an important role in these novels. In *Spring Snow*, Kiyoaki appears to be unconsciously striving to do what Takashi successfully accomplished, to connect with an early, more intense age of Japanese history and bring it to life once more. If Kiyoaki does not totally succeed, his radiant beauty and the incandescent passion of his love affair have at least illuminated Honda's prosaic mind, showing him a vision of fertile beauty if not fertility itself. As a later volume of the tetralogy has Honda reflect, "this Kiyoaki's life gave meaning to Honda, having flowered with a beauty that Honda's itself would never attain."[38] Kiyoaki also conforms to the mythic hero type in one other important area: He returns after death, in this case through reincarnation.

Kiyoaki is first reincarnated as the Isao of *Runaway Horses,* discussed above in Chapter Five. It is Honda who makes the identification and is forced to accept it after recognizing three telltale moles on Isao's breast, calculating that the right amount of time has lapsed between Kiyoaki's death and Isao's birth, and matching certain incidents involving Isao with dreams recorded by Kiyoaki in a diary. The text both demands that Isao and Kiyoaki be linked and makes clear that the two characters are distinct. As Hasegawa points out, Isao's purity contrasts with Kiyoaki's elegance.[39] Where Kiyoaki's character harks back to the elegant Heian period of early Japanese history, Isao is obviously meant to embody the more martial side of premodern Japan, to the point that the young man consciously patterns his planned uprising on an 1875 rebellion (an interesting note of similarity to Takashi).

Yet, despite Kiyoaki's and Isao's differences, it is more important for purposes here to remember that they are united in being the antithesis of Honda. The fact that one is aesthetic and the other military should not obscure the point that they are also both active heroes characterized by passion, spontaneity, and imagination, all three of which qualities directly contrast to the character of the passive intellectual Honda. It is also important to note that the Honda in *Runaway Horses* is far less helpful to Kiyoaki's reincarnation than he was to Kiyoaki, ultimately, in fact, setting himself in direct opposition to Isao's quest.

Admittedly, Isao's quest is a far more violent and perhaps more problematic one than that of Kiyoaki since it involves murder and suicide. Viewed in mythic terms, however, it becomes, if anything, more of a selfless quest than the erotic/aesthetic obsessions of Kiyoaki. In realistic terms, Isao's quest is a terrorist one, the assassination of a number of Japan's military and industrial elite in the hope of inciting a countrywide rebellion, to be followed by his own suicide. In Isao's eyes, however, and from a mythic viewpoint, his quest is simply an attempt to reinvigorate the corrupted wasteland through martial valor and violence, rather than through passion and beauty.

Like Takashi, although without Takashi's complex motives, Isao is willing to sacrifice himself in order to bring the energies of the past into the degenerate present, hence his fascination with the 1875 uprising. Other significant similarities between the two heroes also exist. First, as was the case with Takashi, there is no specific textual moment when Isao crosses the threshold to adventure. By the time he first appears in the novel, he has already made his initial forays onto the path of heroism and, also like Oe's hero, has successfully developed a group of followers who are attracted by his charisma and enthusiasm. Although a far less complicated or guilt-ridden figure than Takashi, Isao is also animated by a vision of violence and the intensity of that vision sends him to his death.

Despite the fact that Isao is in many ways a less interesting character than either Takashi or Kiyoaki, he certainly belongs squarely within the mythic tradition. In *Runaway Horses*, however, realism and mythic romanticism confront each other in the form of the passive hero Honda's initial cynicism toward, followed by gradual acceptance of, Kiyoaki's reincarnation. The reader becomes increasingly dependent on Honda to interpret the fantastic events, because Isao is almost always presented through Honda's focalization.

Indeed, the focus increasingly shifts to Honda in *Runaway Horses* and the mythic elements in the story tend to cluster around the encounters between the fascinated but still skeptical Honda and Isao, who is unconscious of the fact that he is presumably a reincarnation of Kiyoaki. It is really in this novel that Honda begins to take the first steps on his own quest. In *Spring Snow*, he was still the passive observer, watching and occasionally abetting the unfolding drama of Kiyoaki's love. In *Runaway Horses*, however, Honda actually crosses the psychological threshold and becomes an active searcher for the truth that he hesitantly believes is being revealed to him in Kiyoaki's apparent reincarnation.

Because Honda is becoming a far more important character, it seems that the most fantastic elements in the story can exist only when Honda is there to affirm them. For example, in an early scene where Honda meets Isao underneath a sacred waterfall and discovers that Isao is probably Kiyoaki's reincarnation, it is clear that this is Honda's crossing of the threshold into another world. The text prepares the way by describing Honda's feelings of awe and anticipation as he climbs up a sacred mountain where, unknown to him, he will encounter Isao. Just as Mitsusaburo must go into the forest, so Honda's journey into the unknown includes nature as well: "The Iwakura—the seat of the gods—had suddenly appeared at the end of the steep slope in front of them. Its circumference marked by sacred rope . . . since ancient times, this mass of rock had defied comprehension, had never submitted to the general order, its bulk an awesome lump of pure chaos."[40]

It is important to note that this non-place, divided from the real by the Shinto rope, is associated with the imperial house, the "seat of the gods." But it is Honda, not Isao, who feels the beauty and mystery of the natural setting surrounding him and the potential of the supernatural which has "never submitted to the general order." This feeling of mystery culminates in his discovery of the supremely mysterious symbols of Kiyoaki's reincarnation, the three moles on Isao's chest. Like Mitsusaburo who must literally descend into the pit and confront and accept the ghosts surrounding him, so Honda must begin to accept the possibility of the fantastic within the real world. As befitting his apparently more tolerant attitude to the active hero, Honda is less hesitant to accept the power of the irrational than was his counterpart in Oe's novel.

Furthermore, the incidents that follow his revelation about Isao wrap Honda in an otherworldly aura that helps to undermine his faith in rationalism. Thus, Honda spends the next morning at a shrine festival where he watches a ritual dance by young women attendants holding lilies: "As Honda looked on, he felt a kind of intoxication overcoming him. He had never seen such a beautiful ritual. The effects of his sleepless night made the spectacle begin to blur and the lily festival he was now watching started to merge with the kendo match he had seen the previous day.[41]

Just as time in *The Silent Cry* merged back and forth from mythic to real, the possible and the impossible are beginning to blur in Honda's mind, as is clear in the following scene where he lies awake in the predawn darkness, the day after meeting Isao:

The window was beginning to whiten . . . As he gazed at the pagoda, hardly more than a shadow in a corner of the grey sky, Honda felt as if he had awakened only to fall into another dream, like a man who thinks that he has escaped from one kind of irrationality to find himself in the midst of another, even more pervasive . . . Suddenly the thought struck him that it was not just a matter of Kiyoaki returning to life. Had not Honda himself risen from death? From the death manifested by a chilled spirit, a rigorous order like a file jammed with thousands of entries, by the tedious refrain, "Youth is gone."[42]

Contrary to such Oe heroes as Yasuo in *Our Era* or the narrator of "The Swimming Man," who submitted themselves to the "destructive element" of reality, Honda is increasingly willing to "fall into" the dream world of the imaginary. The above scene is perhaps the best statement summing up the effect of the active hero on the passive one in any of Mishima's work. Like Takashi, Kiyoaki, through his death and presumed return, restores the sense of possibility to the passive hero who in both cases has resigned himself to a life of dreariness. It may remind us of Campbell's description of the hero: "he is the champion of things becoming rather than of things become."[43] He animates both life and narrative.

But if Honda has ceased to simply be, his path towards becoming is not an easy one; and his role vis-à-vis Kiyoaki's reincarnation is at best ambiguous. Unable to be either Isao's accomplice or his companion as he was Kiyoaki's in *Spring Snow*, Honda is forced to watch on the sidelines as Isao awkwardly attempts to stage his revolt. It is only at the last minute, when he successfully defends Isao against the charges of treason, that he is actually able concretely to participate in Isao's life. Unfortunately for Isao, his successful defense stymies Isao's real quest, which was to die for his country. By rejecting Honda's gesture of help and committing suicide, however, Isao renders void Honda's efforts to help him. The last the reader sees of Honda in *Runaway Horses,* he also seems to have come to the conclusion that his efforts were valueless: "He had risked everything in coming to Isao's rescue and today he had at last won his gamble. Honda wondered, though, why he felt such a sense of futility."[44]

And yet, in light of the problematic relationship between passive and active hero that occurred in *The Silent Cry,* Honda's motives necessitate closer examination. Although it would appear that Mishima wishes his reader to see Honda's disappointment as genuine, it is at least interesting to speculate that this disappointment stems from another motive, jealousy. Whether consciously or not, Honda in *Runaway Horses* works very hard to ruin the moment that Isao had lived for, to die for the emperor's cause. Of course, Honda would insist that he does this from the desire to save an otherwise doomed young man, surely the most rational of motives. Honda, however, behaves very much the way the adults did in the two earlier pastoral myths of Oe, or in the way that Mitsusaburo does in *The Silent Cry.* Essentially, he is trying both to control the hero of action and to deny him the validity of his dreams.

The impulse to control and destroy becomes even more apparent in the last two novels of the tetralogy, as does Honda's other quest, for the "truth" about reincarnation. Honda is not a wholly despicable character, however. Along with his impulse to control the hero of action is his pathetic desire to participate in the imaginary world that the hero of action brings to life. That these impulses are somewhat contradictory provides the basis for the tension in the latter half of *The Sea of Fertility*.

It is in the third volume of the tetralogy, *The Temple of Dawn*, that Honda actively sets forth upon his quest; and it is appropriate that this search should begin with an actual physical journey, in this case to the overtly exotic and mysterious lands of Southeast Asia. Where *Spring Snow* led the reader into its world by means of a photograph and *Runaway Horses* spent its first chapter describing Honda's prosaic 1930s environment, *The Temple of Dawn* plunges its readers into an unreal land from its very first line, "It was the rainy season in Bangkok."[45]

Into this exotic tropical world steps Honda, arriving in Bangkok to provide legal consultation. What follows is, for a novel, a tolerably lengthy description of Bangkok's scenery and history, culminating in detailed descriptions of some of its famous temples. At first, the mysterious beauties of the city fail to touch Honda, apparently because he is emotionally exhausted, his passion drained from his failure to save Isao some years before. Thailand itself, therefore, fails to excite him.

What does seduce Honda into once more entering the world of irrational passions is the appearance of the person who is apparently the second reincarnation of Kiyoaki, a little Thai princess named Ying Chan. In complete accordance with the generally unreal quality of the Southeast Asian setting, Honda's encounter with the princess is the most blatantly fantastic incident in the entire tetralogy. Honda's first meeting with Isao had a definitely mysterious quality to it, but it still had a plausible base. His meeting with the Princess, on the other hand, can only be the product of magical forces. It is not simply that she is a princess in an exotic land; she is either mad or preternaturally gifted, because she swears that she is Kiyoaki's reincarnation.

Honda has heard about the princess; and as he goes to meet her, he is sure that he is about to encounter Kiyoaki once again. In the following scene the fantastic atmosphere intensifies slowly but steadily:

"As Honda approached his goal and, despite the joy that he knew was metaphysical, he felt as though the sound of his footsteps was that of the sharp claws of the jungle beast stalking its prey with drooling fangs. Yes, he had been born for just this pleasure."[46]

Once again, Honda is using Kiyoaki, or rather what Kiyoaki represents to him—life, excitement, rebirth—as the object of his quest. But underneath that quest, as the text makes clear when describing Honda's "metaphysical" joy, is the intellectual's quest for knowledge. Certainly, Honda wishes to meet Kiyoaki again, but he is even more desirous of simply obtaining the knowledge that Kiyoaki exists. He does not really care about the princess herself.

Thus, although he finds his meeting with her somewhat startling, because she appears to recognize him and begs him to take her back to Japan, he also finds it intellectually satisfying, because he has established that she is indeed Kiyoaki and Isao's reincarnation. The princess represents both "life" and "knowledge" in a truly delightful form. It is not surprising, therefore, that the text describes Honda's later memories of the encounter in terms of moments of intense aesthetic and intellectual pleasure:

> Segments of such sunny instants would suddenly well up, at times forming a momentary portrait of the little princess . . . the time was aglow, the air in the garden was filled with the humming of bees and the mood of the strolling ladies was cheerful too. The essence of the moment was like coral, beautiful and exposed. Yet, in those moments, the princess's innocent, unclouded happiness and the series of agonizing and bloody events of her former two lives were combined like the clear and rainy skies of the distant jungle they had seen on their way to the park.[47]

In this passage, particularly the last line, we have the key to Honda's fascination with reincarnation, and that is the satisfying notion of beauty and violence meshing together to create a situation of which only he has knowledge. Again, Honda cares little about the young princess herself. In fact, he leaves her in Bangkok with little regret and goes in quest of further knowledge.

His quest takes him to India where he experiences a rather cerebral rite of passage. While in Benares, watching corpses being thrown into the river, Honda suddenly realizes that, "What seemed heartlessness was actually pure joy. Not only were samsara and reincarnation basic . . . but they were actually accepted as a part of nature."[48]

True to his passive character, he has made this profound discovery through watching. For another discovery Honda will have to work much harder, but this one, too, will ultimately be achieved through watching. The quest for the second discovery occupies the second half of *The Temple of Dawn;* and it takes place in postwar Japan, a far less appealing or exotic place than Bangkok.

In fact, from this point on, the tetralogy becomes increasingly realistic, providing relatively fewer of the fantastic elements that appeared in the first two books, perhaps because Mishima is attempting to prepare the way for the final revelation that fantasy is nonexistent in the degenerate postwar world. If there is any element of the fairy tale at all in the latter half of *The Temple of Dawn,* it is from the dark side of the fantasy.

Instead of shining temples of Bangkok and the childishly innocent little princess, Honda, now grown rich and old, surrounds himself with grotesques: an aging writer dreaming of lechery; a voyeuristic woman poet; a cynical, wealthy lesbian and her debauched nephew; and a couple of decaying aristocrats. Honda has not simply accepted the wasteland, he now revels in it. But once again, Kiyoaki's presumed reincarnation sends him on another quest for knowledge.

This time, Honda's search for knowledge is an ugly one. Although its ultimate object is to give Honda one more proof of reincarnation, its immediate object is sensual knowledge. Honda wishes to see whether the grown-up Thai princess, recently arrived in Japan, has the three telltale moles on her body. To do so, he must either seduce her or have her seduced by someone else in a way that he can see her nude. Honda's sensual quest is an inappropriate one for a passive hero, as he himself is aware: "Falling in love was a special privilege given to someone whose external sensual charm and internal ignorance, disorganization, and lack of cognizance permitted him to form a kind of fantasy about the other. It was a rude privilege. Honda was quite aware that since his childhood he had been the opposite of such a man."[49]

In fact, however, in this novel Honda begins to take on some of the characteristics of the active hero in that he physically attempts to achieve his quest. While Takashi bequeathed to Mitsusaburo the will to life, Kiyoaki and his reincarnations give Honda the zeal to seek, if not to create. Eventually, Honda does achieve his goal, but through typically voyeuristic means. Although unable to seduce her himself, he at least manages to witness a scene where Ying Chan makes love to another woman and sees the three moles that identify her as the genuine reincarnation of Kiyoaki and Isao.

While she may be the legitimate reincarnation of the two heroes of action, Ying Chan's character is a disappointing contrast to them. Although in her beauty and sensuality she suggests ripeness and fertility, within the myth of the wasteland hers is a barren sensuality, since as a lesbian, she is unlikely to bear children. She does have the spontaneity and physical presence associated with the heroes of action; yet, overall, she is a somewhat lesser hero of action, although Honda is still extraordinarily attracted to her.

In this regard it is significant that Mishima makes Ying Chan a woman and that Honda attempts to seduce her. Although Honda rationalizes that he is in love with Ying Chan, it is clear from the way he thinks about her that the actual impulse behind the seduction is the desire for control. While Honda was able to hide his jealousy of Kiyoaki and Isao, with Ying Chan he is finally given the opportunity to affect a hero of action through physical rather than intellectual force. Had Honda been able to possess her as he so ardently desired, he might finally have felt himself both part of and superior to that active kind of personality.

Mishima does not allow Honda such total fulfillment. Instead, Honda succeeds only in his quest for knowledge, permitted to see the moles on the princess's chest but once again denied the opportunity to partake in the life and excitement that he senses in the heroes of action. The quintessential voyeur, he fulfills his quest by spying on a sensuality that is forever denied him.

Nor is his quest for complete control fulfilled in the last volume of the tetralogy, *The Decay of the Angel*, which describes both Honda's most fervent attempt to dominate a hero of action and his final attempt to discover the truth, an exercise which ends in disappointment. Indeed, in this novel, Mishima finally reveals to the reader what we may have suspected all along, that he is creating not myth but anti-myth and that the quest on which he has sent his heroes can end only in a return to the wasteland with no further hope of succor. *The Decay of the Angel* retains some romantic touches, but these serve largely as ironic contrast to the tawdry drama of decay that the narrative relates.

That degeneration is the novel's main theme is immediately evident from its title, which has both Buddhist and literary associations, since its refers to a famous Noh drama, *Hagoromo,* which concerns an angel's near-fatal visit to earth and subsequent joyful return to heaven. Mishima uses this ethereally beautiful drama, not to suggest the mythic qualities inherent in the real world, but to emphasize what the contemporary world has lost.

Thus, early on in the novel, Honda makes what turns out to be a momentous journey in which he visits the pine grove where *Hagoromo* is said to have taken place. Instead of the idyllic scene that readers of the play would expect, however, Honda finds only the appalling detritus of modern life: "In the sand along the breakwater a great litter of garbage lay scoured by the sea winds. Empty Coca-cola bottles, food cans, paint cans, nonperishable plastic bags, detergent boxes, bricks, bones."[50]

The fragments of modern life that Honda sees are all that the latter half of the twentieth century is capable of producing, at least in Mishima's nihilistic vision. This time, then, Mishima refuses to ground his novel in an exotically magical setting. If fantasy is allowed to creep in at all in *The Decay of the Angel,* it is largely through the medium of the characters' dreams and delusions. Thus, soon after Honda returns from viewing this ugly scene, he dreams of a fantasy pine grove, magically free of twentieth-century debris, where angels "disport themselves" above the grove. Watching them, he is "filled with a clean happiness" and discovers among them, Isao, Kiyoaki and Ying Chan.[51] Even in dreams, however, such romantic beauty cannot endure; or perhaps even more significantly, Honda does not allow it to last:

> Honda presently came to find the constant motion irritating and even unbearable. He was still watching, as if from beneath a giant deodar in a park. A park of humiliation. Automobile horns in the night. He watched on and on, reducing everything to a common element, the most sacred and sordid of things ... In deep depression Honda opened his eyes and tore away the dream, as a man swimming in from the ocean might tear away clinging seaweed and fling it down on the shore.[52]

This passage, while of course referring obliquely to Honda's future humiliations when he is arrested for voyeurism in a public park, is also important because it encapsulates the entire action of *The Sea of Fertility.* The park of humiliation is also the wasteland of modern Japan, the empty garden that Honda will find at the novel's end. For, at the end of the tetralogy, "the most sacred and solid" are indeed reduced to a "common element." Moreover, it is Honda who does the reducing, tearing away the seaweed of fantasy to reveal the ugliness of reality. It is Mishima's ironic final twist in this last novel to place Honda exactly in the footsteps of the resplendent Kiyoaki and have him retrace Kiyoaki's last quest, but with very different results.

As in the first three novels, an apparent reincarnation of Kiyoaki appears as a foil to Honda (and vice versa), but this time the gap between the heroes of action and inaction is far less. In fact, as Honda himself realizes, in many ways Honda and Toru, the presumed reincarnation, are one and the same. They are both unappealing mixtures of active and passive hero, and in the course of the novel they degenerate even further.

For Toru, too, is a watcher and a manipulator; and although he is eventually moved to violence, it is of a conscious, calculated sort, very different from the spontaneous fires that animated Isao. Similarly, his sensual predilections are so cold and offhand that they bear little relation to the erotic obsessiveness of Kiyoaki or the earthy sensuality of Ying Chan. Finally, Toru has one more vital dissimilarity to the other three: he does not die, he is a false incarnation.

Not only is Toru radically unlike the three earlier incarnations of Kiyoaki, he also suggests poignant contrasts to some of Mishima's other heroes of action of the genuinely romantic type, especially Ryuji of *The Sailor Who Fell from Grace with the Sea* and Shinji of *The Sound of Waves*. Like these two genuine heroes, Toru is young, good-looking, and strongly linked to the sea; but the differences between their relation to the sea and Toru's are extremely illuminating. It is not simply that Toru's sea, far from being the exotic wonderland of Ryuji's dream or even the marvelous natural force that dominated Shinji's life, has degenerated into liquid junk, but rather that Toru's own involvement in the sea is not that of the active, heroic sort.

No sailor or fisherman, Toru is simply an observer at a signal station, his job being to watch the sea and signal ships. And it is his cold intelligence that controls his attitude toward the sea, a far cry from Ryuji's romantic imagination or even Shinji's spontaneous enjoyment of the ocean's moods. Given Mishima's pessimistic final message to the world, it is perhaps fitting that his final novel should have as its protagonists two men who are fundamentally voyeurs.

Toru, then, is a realistic, not a romantic character; but it is still possible that such passivity might be appropriate, at least at the beginning of a fairy tale, in that it would allow for greater contrast when the character begins to shed his lethargy and adopt a more heroic stance. However, when Toru is in fact offered a place in a real-life fairy tale, he does not change into an active hero. Instead, his passive observer's personality remains unchanged, except that it grows more vicious. If Toru has a quest, it is simply a vulgar imitation of Honda's, to manipulate and control the life around him.

Toru's fairy tale begins when Honda, returning for a second look at the pine grove, discovers him at his signal station. Seeing that the boy has the three moles that he believes signal Kiyoaki's reincarnation, Honda abruptly offers to adopt him and make him his heir. In actuality, Honda does not expect Toru to outlive him since, as Kiyoaki's reincarnation, he ought to die at twenty. What Honda does want is finally to have the opportunity of total control over a hero of action, and to have the delectation of superior knowledge over the unaware hero.

Ironically, Toru too has a similar quest: He wishes to control and exploit Honda and anyone else who wanders into his orbit. Consequently, what could superficially have been a sentimental romance of an old man providing for a young boy becomes instead a tense drama of mutual manipulation. Unlike Honda, Toru does not even have the urge to merge with the people he attempts to control as if, having no life force himself, he feels no need to obtain it through participating in others' lives. Rather, he prefers to remain above them. In his own way, he is perhaps even more of a voyeur than the lecherous Honda. It is Honda, however, who is arrested for peeping at couples in a park and declared mentally incompetent; and for a brief time, it appears that it is Toru who will win out.

But Toru's quest is ultimately foiled by his discovery of why he was adopted. Unable to bear the truth that he has been adopted simply to be Honda's pawn, Toru attempts suicide by taking poison. Instead of dying, however, he loses his sight, surely the worst of fates for someone whose whole life had revolved around watching. Toru's blindness also anticipates the novel's bleak ending with its final disavowal of romanticism, since he can no longer view the sea, the one romantic icon with which he was genuinely associated. It is also interesting to contrast his blindness with the inner vision that concludes the more optimistic *Runaway Horses*. Isao's sea may be technically absent but it exists in his romantic mind's eye.

It is fitting that Toru took no part in the dream dance of the angels that Honda envisioned early on in the story. On one level, they, at least, are left inviolate; and it is up to the reader to decide whether they are false or not. It is for Toru to play out the part of the decaying angel whose five signs of degeneracy according to Buddhist doctrine are that "the flowered crowns wither, the robes are soiled, sweat pours from the armpit, a fetid stench envelopes the body, the angel is no longer happy in his proper place."[53]

By the end of the novel, Toru is suffering from all these signs, plus one more, his blindness. Astonishingly, Mishima accomplishes this essentially fantastic transformation with a good deal of plausibility, by basing it on Toru's despair after his failed suicide (although the motivation for his suicide attempt is rather weak). Blinded and helpless, Toru becomes completely passive and allows himself to be cared for by his paramour, a madwoman who covers him with dead flowers and wraps him in a dirty robe. As always, the reader is dependent on Honda's observation for an assessment of the hero; and through his eyes, we see how far Mishima's conception of youth has changed since the glorious days of Kiyoaki and Isao:

> Toru's heels looked up from the skirt of his kimono. They were white and wrinkled as those of a drowned corpse ... The kimono had gone quite limp. Sweat drew clusters of yellow clouds at the neckline.
> Honda had for some time been aware of a strong odor ... Toru had lost his fastidiousness.[54]

In every aspect, then, Toru shows the five signs of the decay of the angel. He has failed in his quest to control and must spend the rest of his days dependent on Honda's money and his sweetheart's bizarre ministrations.

But it is Honda's quest and its success or failure that really dominates the novel, and, ultimately, the entire tetralogy as well. He has perhaps finally succeeded in his first quest, his desire to control Toru; but that success is largely fortuitous, since it is based on Toru's despair rather than on any action by Honda. In any case, his very triumph over Toru moves Honda's second quest for the truth of reincarnation onto shaky ground. He may dominate Toru, but what good does that do if Toru is only a false incarnation?

Confronted by the possibility that the entire notion of a cycle of rebirths was false, Honda's probing analytical mind cannot rest. Honda is still unsure of the truth, despite his mystical experience in India; and, facing death, he turns to the aged Satoko, now the abbess of the Gesshuji temple, for help. Determined to follow in Kiyoaki's footsteps on the day of his death when he waited outside the temple, Honda travels to the temple on foot and alone.

This journey is perhaps the most genuinely heroic of any of Honda's quests, because he deliberately puts himself through great physical suffering to accomplish it. An old man leaning on a stick, Honda struggles up the mountain road in fits and starts, in a scene which effectively conveys the various states of hope, fear, and anticipation in a character searching for confirmation of the existence of another reality beyond the mundane. Mishima evokes the summer heat, the pain of the climb, and the illness of an old man with great economy.

At times, "overcome by heat and fatigue," Honda almost gives up, "beginning to doubt that in fact he could reach the mountain gate."[55] The journey is both agonizing and beautiful: "The smell of summer grasses filled the air. Pines were thick along the road. Leaning on his stick he looked up at the sky."[56] After passing through a marsh, the road becomes easier; but at the top of the mountain, Honda suddenly feels "reluctant to reach his destination."[57] Having conquered his fear and stepped inside the temple, however, he is overwhelmed by a sense of peace and serenity. It seems that his last quest may end successfully after all. In true mythic fashion, Honda has sought out a religious guide who will finally tell him the truth.

Such a romantically satisfying ending might have been appropriate for *The Sound of Waves* but, in this last novel of Mishima's, the fairy tale has ended. When Honda finally sees Satoko, she insists that she never knew Kiyoaki and indeed insinuates that Kiyoaki never existed. If Kiyoaki never existed, then Honda begins to doubt his own existence: "If there was no Kiyoaki then there was no Isao. There was no Ying Chan, and who knows, perhaps there has been no I."[58] Finally, alone in the garden, he realizes that "he had come to a place that had no memories, nothing."[59]

In *The Sea of Fertility*, the truth does not emancipate, it blinds and destroys. The passive hero's quest has led him to a garden of denial, a place not of mythic time but of anti-time. And the truth that he has discovered is that myth cannot animate reality because there can be no myth. Where Mitsusaburo finally discovers that legends, whether true or not, are the stuff that give life meaning, Honda is "liberated" from any such childish fantasy. He knows now that there is only the wasteland of the real. The novel's last line, with its images of heat and emptiness, bears this out: "The noontime sun of summer flowed over the still garden."[60]

In *The Sea of Fertility*, then, Mishima in a sense "sets up" the reader by providing a brilliant fantasy world for the first three-quarters of the work, only to prove it all a lie. Oe's turn in *The Silent Cry* is the obverse: He uses his suspicious, passive hero to undercut the myth until the very end, when he has to accept it. In this regard, the importance of mythic time must again be mentioned. Mishima's initial use of reincarnation sets a highly visible symbol of continuity and mystery against the increasing degeneration of modern life. That Kiyoaki is believed to have been reborn as Isao and Ying Chan implies the potential continuation of the fairy-tale beauty of *Spring Snow* into the dreary materialism of the postwar world.

Mythic time and the hero of action are inextricably linked, because it is the hero who activates the myth. Consequently, it is extremely important that Honda finally comes to a place of no memories. Without memories, which combine the imagination with a sense of the past, there can be no life and there can be no myth.

In contrast to Mishima's empty, sun-filled garden is Oe's gloomy forest, full of ghosts and monsters. But life exists in the forest and not in the garden. In Oe's work, the power of the past is shown as essentially liberating. He uses the theme of reincarnation, too; but in Oe's novel it is the characters (such as Takashi) who *choose* to be reincarnated: they are not unconscious pawns of a mysterious fate. And the pattern of the past can be emancipating, offering possible models for the contemporary world, rather than presenting the hero with a rigid either/or situation.

The Silent Cry has its dark sides as well. Collective violence and sacrifice are still nihilistic ways to bring about redemption, while Mitsusaburo's forthcoming journey to Africa has an artificially upbeat quality to it, similar to the rather forced "happy end" of *A Personal Matter*. But in the mysterious power of the forest and the legends that encompass it, regeneration still seems possible; and it is this potential power which comes increasingly into play in Oe's later works.

7 · Mishima, Oe
and Modern Japan

The Silent Cry and *The Sea of Fertility* revolve around a variety of quests, the most all-encompassing of which is the quest for identity. Both Mitsusaburo and Honda are asking the same questions: "Who am I?" and "Where do I belong?" In some respects, their creators are also asking these questions about themselves at the same time that they explore them in their fiction. On another level, however, these works also reflect the quest for identity on the part of a nation. Since 1868, Japan's history has been a quest for "Who am I?" and "Where do I belong?" Throughout both their writings and their lives, Oe and Mishima have attempted to answer these questions, in ways that few other writers have dared to try, at least in not so comprehensive a manner.

Mishima answered the question in the elite imagery and language of the imperial house, while Oe answers it in the earthy tones of the communal village where an emperor is finally, if provisionally, overthrown. Mishima delved into his country's aristocratic and warrior past to find heroes worthy of admiration, while Oe went back into a personal and folk past for his equivalent models. Both *The Sea of Fertility* and *The Silent Cry* limn a Japan corrupted by the poison of Western humanism referred to contemptuously in *Runaway Horses*, degraded by the urbanization signified by the supermarket in *The Silent Cry*, and emasculated by the loss of that most archetypal myth, the myth of the divinity of the imperial house and Japan as the "land of the gods," a myth in which most Japanese no longer believe but are still uncomfortable about completely dismissing.

It is perhaps for this reason that Mishima's dramatic suicide touched such a nerve in the Japanese psyche. It was not that his death signaled a major resurgence of postwar militarism, as initially feared. Rather, Mishima's choice of the most traditional form of suicide, following directly on his speech in front of the Self-Defense Forces in which he blamed the emperor for abandoning the nation and accused modern Japan of degeneracy and decadence, came at a time when most Japanese seemed to have safely put these issues behind them. Mishima's actions awakened uncomfortable memories of a painful past; even worse, they stimulated uncomfortable speculations about the materially rich but spiritually impoverished present.

Japan in 1970 had recently completed a decade of double-digit economic growth so successful that even the Japanese themselves were asking whether they might be "economic animals." At the same time, the country had just gone through the mass demonstrations and protests of the late 1960s, in which students at the most elite universities denounced not only their teachers but the entire social system that supported them. The "Mishima Incident," as journalists labeled his suicide, thus occurred at a fragile moment in postwar Japanese history. Mishima's forlorn call for a Showa Restoration embarrassed and disturbed even those who found it pathetic; it became the occasion for an enormous outpouring of critical soul-searching for some and violent denunciation for others.

In all this mass-media turmoil, Mishima's literary reputation was almost lost. Tanaka Miyoko succinctly captured the impact from the writer's death when she wrote:

> Because of his final moments, Mishima Yukio, the writer, was refigured, crowded out of the territory of literature and forced to stake a claim in every territory of Japanese intellectual thought: politics, society, culture and religion. The incident was a shock, awakening people from the tranquil sleep of economic prosperity. Inevitably people were panicked and excited; driven by impatience, they swarmed to take aim at this mysterious death in opinions, analyses, and comments which tried to explain the dangerous enigma.[1]

Those who staked a claim in Mishima were a varied and not always admirable group, especially the sensation mongers who titillated the public by "confessions" about their alleged relationships with him. Even more respectable scholars ignored his writing to concentrate instead on his presumed pathology. In particular, the question of his homosexuality in relation to emperor worship was addressed from all sides. Even years after the "incident," a group of reputable scholars still allotted as much time to a discussion of Mishima's presumed homosexuality and how it might have affected his politics as they did to his art.[2]

Much of this reaction is inevitable. Mishima's life was colored with flamboyance, his death even more so; but it is unfortunate that his literary skills should have been overshadowed by his personal eccentricities to the point that some critics have even mentioned the development of a "Mishima legend."[3] Recently, however, both in Japan and in the West, that reputation seems to be on the upswing, as more scholars and critics are returning to his fiction to find more than the self-indulgent ravings of a right-wing fanatic. Not only was Mishima a complex and sophisticated writer, the concerns which animated him, although distinctive, were ones that also had resonance within Japanese society.

Thus, the problem of the emperor system is still an important one, and one that is not limited to either Oe or Mishima, as the flurry of articles appearing during the Showa Emperor's illness and demise made clear. Eto Jun, for example, in a moving meditation in *Shokun*, compared the passing of the Showa era with that of the famous death of the Meiji Emperor, an event which stimulated a time of national self-reflection.[4] On a less literary level, Inose Naoki and Yamaguchi Masao recently examined the imperial house system in relation to its mysterious dealings with financial empires, Tokyo construction conglomerates, and the entertainment industry. They mention, for example, the inexplicable popularity of the 1986 film, *Yukiyukite shingun* (The emperor's naked army marches on), about a man who spends his life fanatically obsessed with the events of the Second World War and who, in a grotesque echo of Oe's band of incompetent terrorists in *Our Era*, makes a half-hearted attempt at harming the emperor.[5] Even the many intellectuals who excoriate the emperor system cannot ignore the fact that it is one of the last and most visible symbols of continuity between the different worlds of prewar and postwar Japan.

It remains for the living Oe to have the last word on this subject, at least as far as this study is concerned. While Mishima attempted to answer the problem of Japanese identity in the imagery around the imperial house, Oe has turned increasingly to his rural roots for his own solution. His answer, however, is still highly conscious of

Mishima's emperor-centered response. In 1980, Oe published *The Game of Contemporaneity,* a novel which, in many ways, is his comprehensive response to *The Sea of Fertility.* It is also a long and complex attempt to explore again the question of national identity. Where "The Day He Himself Shall Wipe My Tears Away" was an emotional and highly colored attack on the dangerous militarism of *Runaway Horses* and the equally dangerous insanity of Mishima's suicide, Oe's novel is a coldly reasoned, even abstract, fictional response to the entire ideological structure that was the background of *The Sea of Fertility.*

While *The Sea of Fertility* privileged an elitist sensibility to create what Oe would consider as the establishment view of Japanese history, *The Game of Contemporaneity* sees Japanese history from the margins. The particular margin Oe uses is a familiar one to his readers, a village deep in a forest in Shikoku. In other ways, however, the work is a major departure for Oe. Rather than hinging on a conventional narrative structure, the novel revolves around a series of legends surrounding the village, legends that highlight the marginal, outsider status of the community's inhabitants. Thus, the story of the village's creation shows the founders as a group of exiles with fantastic powers, who are led by the Destroyer, the leader who blasts open a mass of evil-smelling rock to create a hidden "cosmos" in a remote Shikoku valley. These fantastically endowed founders, according to Oe, are the equivalent of the gods who, according to traditional Japanese mythology, were expelled from Japan at the time the sun goddess Amaterasu, the assumed progenitrix of the imperial family, arrived. Reduced to demon status, these outsider gods lurk in the woods protecting their hidden village, a place which the narrator refers to as "the village = nation = minicosmos."

Other legends make clear the hostile relationship between the village and the "center," which by the nineteenth century has become the "Great Japanese Empire." The most famous is the story of what the villagers call the "Fifty-Day War," in which for fifty days the village battles with and almost triumphs over the Imperial Japanese Army, using a variety of sometimes fantastic devices such as the mazes mentioned above in the Introduction. The final defeat is ultimately unimportant. The war itself is never recorded in the outside world's annals, thereby proving once again the villagers' fundamentally marginal status.

Much of *The Game of Contemporaneity* revolves around such successful efforts to humiliate and trick the central imperial power structure. For the purposes of this study, the most significant such incident is one in which the village's Shinto shrine is turned to satirical use. Significantly named the Mishima shrine, it is, of course, part of the imperial institution. Thus, when the village is occupied by the military during the Second World War, the authorities expend great effort to ensure that the shrine receives proper reverence and they plan an important shrine ritual which the entire village is expected to attend. Their scheme is ruined, however, when the shrine's priest, who is also the narrator's father, appears to perform the rite dressed in a thoroughly outrageous manner.

As the narrator recalls,

> My father's costume was one of such elaborateness that even our childish eyes could tell that it must have required a great deal of preparation. My father who equals the priest was wearing a dishevelled vermillion-dyed hempen wig, and a goblin mask dyed the same vermillion . . . [T]he large shoes which covered his feet were of red and black hemp like the feet of a beast. Other than that, my father, the priest, was completely naked and his entire body was engraved with vermillion crests. However, his penis was encased in a vermillion sheath and from his buttocks a stick of the same color protruded, while his hips were encircled by the string that tied the two together.

The village children dissolve into laughter at this bizarre sight, and the solemn ceremony is ruined, although the narrator insists that he has no idea whether his father had expected that outcome or not. As Wilson points out, festive laughter and japery are the weapons of choice for these marginals who cannot take on the Great Japanese Empire in any other fashion.[6] In writing *The Game of Contemporaneity,* Oe follows the narrator's father in doing a grotesque parodic dance around the most sacred institutions of imperial Japan, especially the emperor system that Mishima avowedly revered.

The novel has other echoes of Mishima as well: As in *The Sea of Fertility,* death and rebirth form one of the novel's continuities. In this case, the rebirth belongs to the Destroyer, who at the novel's end may have been reborn to again take on the Greater Japanese Empire. Far more than *The Sea of Fertility,* however, *The Game of Contemporaneity* contains strong elements of the *roman à thèse,* particularly in its highlighting of a collective "good" hero, the village, against the "bad" protagonist, the Japanese empire. This is not to say that the villagers are presented in a simplistic, positive light; they too have the violent and amoral aspects found in the collective heroes of *The Flood-waters Have Come unto My Soul* and *Pluck the Buds, Shoot the Kids*. But, also as in these books, no doubt exists that, in the end, the outsiders are better than the evil establishment.

Still, *The Game of Contemporaneity* differs radically from such earlier works and from *The Sea of Fertility* in that it almost completely deemphasizes the role of individual protagonists. Contrary to Mishima's romantic glorification of individual characters such as Kiyoaki and Isao, Oe deliberately allows the legends to overwhelm his characters. Thus, although like Oe's other passives heroes the narrator of *The Game of Contemporaneity* has the characteristics of a bystander and intellectual, he lacks the individual characteristics that made such characters as Yasuo and Bird memorable, if not lovable, personalities. Instead, the narrator consciously inscribes himself into the symbolic order of the "Word of the Father," referring to himself consistently and repeatedly as the historian of the village, the role that his father assigned to him in his childhood.

Interestingly, this "Word of the Father" is in itself an alien language, for the father is not a native of the village. It is as if the folk history that Oe wants to describe is so inchoate that it can only belong to the discourse of the imaginary. Turning it into language requires an outsider's intelligence. Not only is the father an outsider, so are the narrator and his siblings, products of their father's liaison with a traveling entertainer. Living in the farthest part of the valley, they are thus the epitome of the marginals, although their interaction with the village provides part of the novel's structure.

Besides the narrator and his mysterious father, the most important member of the family is the narrator's younger sister to whom he addresses the series of letters that constitute the narrative of *The Game of Contemporaneity*. Even more than the narrator, the sister is a largely iconic character; she is known mainly for the role that their father has imposed on her as the Destroyer's "vestal virgin." The Destroyer himself is both the shadowy central figure of all the legends purveyed by the narrator and a potentially real character, whose incarnation could conceivably reanimate the village. Thus, at the novel's end, the narrator's final letter envisions the resurrected Destroyer, who has now grown to the size of a dog, cradled in his sister's lap, waiting for the day when the marginals will rise again.

Whether they finally will or not, or even whether the sister and the Destroyer actually exist, are problems that Oe leaves for the reader to deal with. Indeed, *The Game of Contemporaneity* is quite a problematic work. Although the novel created an initial sensation, some critics took it to task for the artificiality of its legends. Oe himself has referred to it in conversation as *"shippaisaku"* (failure); and although this opinion is subject to disagreement, the novel may not accomplish everything it sets out to do.

For example, although Oe in his essays insists on the redemptive power of the grotesque and of festive laughter, the actual incidents chronicled in the work are often more shocking or disgusting than comical. Far from being a utopia, this marginal village seems to contain as much violence and discrimination as the central power structure that it opposes. For example, the narrator relates the story of the crazed woman who holds some of the village children hostage, only to be captured and gang-raped before she is murdered.

Even more tellingly, in this supposedly unhierarchical village where at one point everyone is forced to change houses, the Destroyer still exerts a commanding and central influence. Even if Oe destroys the imperial gods, he must install something else in their place. The tradition of dependence has changed its object but it has not disappeared.

In this regard the problematic role of the "father = shrine = priest" is important. It is he who brings order out of chaos by forcing his son to become the historian of the village and his daughter to become the caretaker of the Destroyer. It is as if Oe, almost despite himself, is still searching for some final word from an all-powerful father figure. The fact that the narrator, in the long run, does not even know whether the Destroyer really exists also suggests a fundamental uncertainty about the power of legends. Like Honda hesitating outside the temple, he does not know whether the garden is empty. Unlike Mishima, however, Oe at least leaves the final answer up to the reader.

This brings me to a last question concerning Oe, Mishima, and their impact on Japanese readers in the 1990s. How important are Oe and Mishima to a Japan that is increasingly made up of a generation of *shinjinrui* (new people), who prefer to read *manga* when they read at all? Obviously, such a question is difficult to answer with any finality.

Among intellectual circles, they are both still popular, as is evidenced by the many journal articles still devoted to their works. Oe's new books continue to be greeted with much interest on the part of both mass press and critical commentary. But Mishima's romantic, apparently elitist response to the problem of Japanese identity may seem increasingly irrelevant to a younger postwar generation. At the same time, Oe's complex, obsessive novels may appear too difficult and too folk-oriented for the new young urbanites.

Even today, however, the questions that both writers asked are fresh and pertinent ones. Thus, Oe's *Game of Contemporaneity* can be viewed as part of a general literary and public interest in a return to rural values. Ironically, one former Japanese prime minister assumed office with a call to create new *furusatos* (home towns) throughout Japan, in response to the overcrowding and urban blight of Tokyo.

In the long run, it will be interesting to see for what particular aspects of their work are Oe and Mishima remembered. My own guess is that they will be remembered for the elements that they had in common, their revulsion from contemporary society and their powerful and intense visions of alternatives to that society. Even more memorable, if perhaps more surprising, is another common element, their brilliant depictions of marginal and outside characters. In a society which values conformity and docility above all else, Oe and Mishima wrote about violently antisocial characters. Mishima may have wanted to privilege the elite, but ultimately he is far closer to Oe than either author would be likely to believe. Long after the empty shadows of Isao or Takeyama have faded from memory, the half-contemptous, half-pathetic narrator of *Confessions of a Mask* or the stuttering, ugly Mizoguchi of *Temple of the Golden Pavilion* will take their place next to such distinctive creations as Bird in *A Personal Matter* or the juvenile delinquents of *Pluck the Buds, Shoot the Kids* as emblems of another side of modern Japan.

These notably antiheroic protagonists are not the only memorable aspects of Oe and Mishima's literature, however. It is the romantic visions of alterity with which they are combined that make both writers' works so distinctive and important. Such romanticism is important both in purely literary terms for the powerful and beautiful imagery each writer created, and, in extra-literary terms, for the ideological message their works transmit.

Romanticism has often been linked with fascism in the West, and certainly Mishima's self-righteous young officers in "Patriotism" or "The Voices of the Hero Spirits" or even Oe's confident young juvenile delinquents in *Floodwaters* seem to be disturbingly close to ideological fanatics. And yet these disquieting creations are always more than simple ideological icons; their very confidence is thought-provoking to the careful reader. Oe's and Mishima's romanticism has always been undercut with healthy doses of skepticism even when their characters remain one-sided. Thus, Honda's garden is an empty one at the end of *The Sea of Fertility,* while Oe's forests continue to be places of darkness as well as new life.

In their consistent interest in the radical, the extreme and the apocalyptic, Oe and Mishima are, like other Romantic writers before them, "writers of crisis," as Harold Bloom says of Wordsworth and Freud.[7] Their works profile a country and a people in agonizing turmoil that still seeks for some outside escape. In this regard, they are far from being typical mainstream writers in the sense of the self-involved Japanese Naturalists who resigned themselves to exploring only the claustrophobic inner world. But if Oe and Mishima are exceptional writers in modern Japanese literature, they are certainly not insignificant ones. In twentieth-century Japan where conformity and resigned acceptance are placed among the highest of social values, their memorable outsider characters and their even more memorable visions of escape are an extraordinary and important literary legacy.

Notes
References
Index

Notes

INTRODUCTION

1. Oe Kenzaburo, *Dōjidai gēmu*, p. 385.
2. Mishima Yukio, *Confessions of a Mask*, trans. Meredith Weatherby, p. 15.
3. Fukushima Akira, "Oe bungaku no shinteki kōzō," *Eureka* 6.3:114 (1974).
4. Edward Fowler, *The Rhetoric of Confession: Shishōsetsu in Early Twentieth Century Japanese Fiction*, p. 26.
5. In fact, one of Mishima's earliest and most famous works, *Confessions of a Mask*, is largely based on his own life, although its effect is very different from the more sentimentally confessional novels of the Naturalists. But his later works veer sharply away from the use of autobiography. Oe's use of his personal past is even more extensive and more complex, leading to a narrative structure which he himself styles as a form of "double deconstruction": Oe Kenzaburo, *Shōsetsu no takurami chi no tanoshimi*, p. 181.
6. For example, a special edition of the literary magazine *Kokubungaku* devoted to the question "what was Mishima Yukio" ("Mishima Yukio to wa nan de atta ka") contained a group discussion on his novel *Confessions of a Mask* in which a full third of the talk concerned the author's homosexuality rather than the protagonist's: *Kokubungaku* 26.9:7–16 (1981).
7. Kataoka Keiji, *Oe Kenzaburoron*, pp. 210–216.
8. Mishima Yukio, "Shūmatsukan kara no shuppatsu: Showa no ninjū jigazō," *Mishima Yukio zenshū*, vol. 27, p. 48.
9. Oe Kenzaburo, "Sengo sedai no imēji," *Oe Kenzaburo Dōjidaironshū*, vol. 1, p. 8.
10. Oe Kenzaburo, "Boku jishin no naka no sensō," *Oe Kenzaburo Dōjidaironshū*, vol. 1, p. 53.
11. Samuel Hynes, *The Auden Generation*, p. 21.
12. Michiko Wilson, *The Marginal World of Oe Kenzaburo*, pp. 3–9.
13. For more information on the Naturalists, see Fowler, *Rhetoric of Confession*; Irena Powell, *Writers and Society in Modern Japan*, pp. 22–59; and Kato Shuichi, *A History of Japanese Literature*, vol. 3: *The Modern Years* (New York: Kodansha International, 1983), pp. 158–170.
14. Fredric Jameson, *The Political Unconscious*, p. 104.
15. Tom Moylan, *Demand the Impossible: Science Fiction and the Utopian Imagination*, p. 31.
16. Rene Girard, *Deceit, Desire, and the Novel*, pp. 270–271.
17. This attitude is best summarized by Northrop Frye in *Anatomy of Criticism* (p. 193) as

"the search of the libido or desiring self for a fulfillment that will deliver it from the anxieties of the reality but will still contain that reality." As for the term *romantic* itself, it is an extraordinarily slippery one, with echoes of everything from medieval tales and nineteenth-century poetry to the aforementioned Japanese Romanha; but I use it here in its wider sense to indicate "an extraordinary and improbable tale of adventure," the definition given by J. A. Cuddon in his *Dictionary of Literary Terms*. Along with this "adventure plot" goes a certain type of highly colored imagery and characterization (as Frye puts it, p. 195, "subtlety and complexity are not much favored") which can be found in varying degrees in both writers' work.

18. Mishima Yukio and Oe Kenzaburo, "Gendai sakka wa kaku kangaeru," in *Gunzō* (September 1964) as reprinted in *Mishima Yukio zenshu*, suppl. (hōkan) vol. 1, p. 349.

19. Ibid., p. 355.

20. Ibid., p. 370.

21. Fukushima Akira, p. 112.

22. Doi Takeo, *The Anatomy of Dependence*, passim. See esp. p. 34, where Doi discusses the different kinds of loyalty felt toward the father and the emperor.

23. H. D. Harootunian, "The Ideology of Cultural 'Totalism' in Mishima: The Economy of Expenditure and Loss," unpub. paper, p. 2.

24. For a discussion of the relation between the Imaginary and the Symbolic in Lacan, see Malcolm Bowie, *Freud, Proust and Lacan: Theory as Fiction* (Cambridge: Cambridge University Press, 1987), esp. pp. 113–133. For a discussion of the Symbolic Order and the Word of the Father, see Juliet Flower MacCannell, *Figuring Lacan: Criticism and the Cultural Unconscious* (London: Croom Helm, 1986), p. 134.

25. Yamanouchi Hisaki, *The Search for Authenticity in Modern Japanese Literature*, p. 172.

26. Susan Suleiman, *Authoritarian Fictions: The Ideological Novel as a Literary Genre*, pp. 2–23 and passim.

27. Henry Scott Stokes, "Last Samurai: The Withered Soul of Postwar Japan," *Harpers* (October 1985), p. 59.

1. THE LOST GARDEN: BEGINNINGS OF A MYTHIC ALTERNATIVE

1. Matsubara Shinichi, *Oe Kenzaburo no sekai*, p. 67.

2. Isoda Koichi, "Oe, Eto ni okeru dentō to kindai," *Kokubungaku* 16.1:85 (1971).

3. In a broad definition of *pastoral* that is particularly appropriate to the three narratives discussed in this chapter, Cuddon says that it "displays a nostalgia for the past, for some hypothetical state of love and peace which has somehow been lost. The dominating idea and theme of most pastoral is the search for the simple life away from the court and town, away from corruption, war, strife, the love of gain . . . In a way it reveals a yearning for a lost innocence, for a pre-Fall paradisal life in which man existed in harmony with nature. It is thus a form of primitivism . . . and a potent longing for things past."

4. Jerome Bruner, "Myth and Identity," in Henry Murray, ed., *Myth and Mythmaking*, p. 285.

5. Joseph Campbell, *The Hero with a Thousand Faces*, p. 30.

6. John Nathan, *Mishima: A Biography*, p. 121.

7. In modern Japanese literature nothing quite compares to this form of purity testing, although such early heroes as Yamato Takeru in the *Kojiki* are forced to undergo tests of strength and cunning; but is does call to mind some classic Western myths, such as the Arthurian legends. See, for example, Charles Moorman, "Myth and Medieval Literature: Sir Gawain and the Green Knight," in John B. Vickery, ed., *Myth and Literature*, pp. 177–179.

8. Mishima Yukio, *The Sound of Waves*, trans. Meredith Weatherby, pp. 75–76.

9. See Nathan, *Mishima*, p. 121.

10. Mishima, *Sound of Waves*, p. 6.

11. Ibid., p. 65.

12. Jameson, p. 112.

13. Ibid., p. 213.

14. Oe Kenzaburo, "Prize Stock," in his *Teach Us to Outgrow Our Madness*, trans. John Nathan, p. 165.

15. Fukushima Akira, p. 110.

16. Oe, "Prize Stock," p. 113.

17. Ibid., p. 123.

18. Ibid., p. 145.

19. Ibid., p. 146.

20. Ibid., p. 155.

21. Ibid., p. 165.

22. Ibid., p. 161.

23. Ibid., p. 163.

24. Shinohara Shigeru, *Oe Kenzaburoron*, p. 67.

25. Oe Kenzaburo, "Hakuruberi Finu to hiro no mondai," *Oe Kenzaburo dōjidaironshū*, vol. 7 (Tokyo: Iwanami Shoten, 1981), pp. 40–62. For discussions in English, see John Nathan, "Introduction," to Oe Kenzaburo, *Teach Us To Outgrow Our Madness*, pp. xii–xiii; and Wilson, *Marginal World*, pp. 33–35. Oe's basic point is that Huck is a genuine existential hero who chooses his own fate, whether it is "to go to hell" or to be willing to live outside the dictates of society. Huck is also, of course, an outsider, already rejected by society, an "embattled cultural hero," as Wilson, following Oe's argument, terms him.

26. Oe Kenzaburo, *Memushiri kouchi*, in *Oe Kenzaburo zensakuhin*, vol. 1, p. 207. All translations mine.

27. Ibid., p. 208.

28. Ibid., p. 270.

29. Ibid., p. 269.

30. Ibid., p. 279.

31. Mishima, *Sound of Waves*, p. 77.

32. Oe, *Memushiri*, p. 298.

33. Ibid., p. 319.

34. Suleiman, p. 112.

35. Ibid., p. 107.

36. Wilson, *Marginal World*, p. 12.

37. Oe, "Prize Stock," p. 168.

2. THE WASTELAND OF SEX

1. Oe Kenzaburo, "Afterword," to *Warera no jidai*, p. 272.

2. Mishima Yukio, *Mishima Yukio vs. Todai zenkyōtō*, p. 24.

3. Oe Kenzaburo, quoted in Matsubara Shinichi, p. 113.

4. Michel Foucalt, *Herculine Barbin*, quoted in Catherine Belsey, "The Romantic Construction of the Unconscious," in Francis Barker et al., eds., *Literature, Politics, and Theory*, p. 60.

5. This paradigm is, of course, not limited to Japan. Werner Fassbinder's film *The Marriage of Maria Braun*, for example, uses a prostitute's life to trace the development of postwar Germany.

6. Tony Tanner, *Adultery in the Novel*, p. 91.

7. Tayama Katai, quoted in Jay Rubin, *Injurious to Public Morals*, p. 99.

8. Oe Kenzaburo, quoted in Matsubara Shinichi, p. 173.

9. Oe Kenzaburo, quoted in Shinohara Shigeru, p. 134.

10. Oe Kenzaburo, *Warera no jidai*, p. 8.

11. Ibid., p. 30.

12. Mishima Yukio, *Confessions of a Mask*, p. 163.

13. Ibid., p. 138.

14. Oe, *Warera no jidai*, p. 6.

15. Mishima, *Confessions*, p. 199.

16. Victor Brombert, "The Intellectual as Impossible Hero," in Victor Brombert, ed. *The Hero in Literature*, p. 253.

17. Oe, *Warera no jidai*, p. 36.

18. Mishima, *Confessions*, p. 158.

19. It is also interesting to note the narrator's fascination with the Christian martyr St. Sebastian, whose image as a beautiful, sacrificial youth became the object of a homoerotic cult among European writers during the First World War, the war that sacrificed more Western young men than any other. For a discussion of the St. Sebastian cult, see Paul Fussell, *The Great War and Modern Memory*, pp. 270–286.

20. The relationship between the war and *Confessions* is much discussed by those Japanese critics who prefer to see the book as more than simply an autobiographical homosexual manifesto. In "Sei Sebasuchin no kao," one of the best essays on the subject, Hanada Kiyoteru argues that the metaphor of the mask itself signifies a kind of protest against the war, a time when those who opposed the war "appropriated prudent attitudes and, donning a variety of masks, strolled composedly among the wild animals" (*Nihon gendai bungaku*, no. 23, p. 257). Hanada thus explains the mask's contempt for normal sentimentality as an intelligent reaction to the emotional excesses of the war, an explanation which is unintentionally ironic, considering the manner of Mishima's suicide.

21. Oe, *Warera no jidai*, p. 268.

22. Mishima, *Confessions*, p. 252.

23. Ibid., pp. 252–253.

24. Mishima Yukio, quoted in Yoshida Hiroo, "Kamen no kokuhaku," *Kokubungaku: 37.15:114 (1972).

25. Mishima Yukio, Kagi no kakaru heya," in his *Kagi no kakaru heya*, p. 234.

26. Ibid., p. 235.

27. Ibid., p. 229.

28. Ibid.

29. Ibid.

30. Ibid., p. 235.

31. Ibid., p. 240.

32. Ibid., p. 235.

33. Ibid., p. 247.

34. Ibid., p. 248.

35. Ibid., p. 263.

36. Ibid., p. 264.

37. Ibid., p. 266.

38. Ibid.

39. Ibid., p. 274.

40. Ibid., p. 266.

41. Ibid., p. 263.

42. Ibid., p. 264.

43. Tanaka Miyoko, "Mishima bungaku no josei." in Hasegawa Izumi et al., eds., *Mishima Yukio kenkyū*, p. 176.
44. Ibid., p. 174.
45. Oe Kenzaburo, "Oyogu otoko," in his *Reintsuri o kiku onnatachi*, p. 217.
46. Ibid., p. 216.
47. Ibid., p. 235. It is also interesting to note that the OL's sexual adventures have occurred *outside* Japan, in exotic "non-places" noted for heat and passion.
48. Ibid., p. 265.
49. Ibid., p. 269.
50. Ibid., p. 287.
51. Ibid., p. 249.
52. Ibid.
53. Ibid., p. 250.

3. CRIES IN THE WASTELAND: SEXUAL VIOLENCE

1. Mishima Yukio, quoted in Kubota Mamoru, "Ai no kawaki," *Kokubungaku* 37.15:116.
2. Matsubara Shinichi, p. 173.
3. Oe Kenzaburo, *Sakebigoe*, p. 19.
4. Matsubara Shinichi, p. 170.
5. Ibid.
6. Oe, *Sakebigoe*, p. 7.
7. Ibid., p. 30.
8. Ibid., p. 22.
9. Ibid., pp. 22–23.
10. Ibid., p. 23.
11. Shinohara Shigeru, p. 164.
12. Oe, *Sakebigoe*, p. 95.
13. Shinohara Shigeru, p. 164.
14. Oe, *Sakebigoe*, p. 97.
15. Kubota Manoru, p. 117.
16. Matsumoto Tooru, "Mishima Yukio ni okeru erochizumu," *Kokubungaku:* 41.2:25 (1976).
17. Mishima Yukio, *Thirst for Love*, trans. Alfred H. Marks, p. 27.
18. Ibid., p. 42.
19. Ibid., p. 39.
20. Ibid., p. 51.
21. Ibid.
22. Ibid., p. 37.
23. Ibid., p. 29.
24. Ibid., p. 32.
25. Ibid., p. 109.
26. Ibid., p. 111.
27. Ibid., p. 113.
28. Ibid., pp. 114–115.
29. Ibid., p. 199.
30. Ibid., p. 197.
31. Ibid., p. 125.
32. Oe, *Sakebigoe*, p. 7.
33. Mishima Yukio, *Madame de Sade*, trans. Donald Keene, p. 103.
34. Ibid.

35. Ibid., pp. 40–41.
36. Ibid., pp. 103–104.
37. Ibid., p. 73.
38. Ibid., p. 29.
39. See Tanner, notes to pp. 153–155.
40. Mishima, *Madame de Sade,* p. 102.
41. Ibid., p. 52.
42. Yamanouchi, p. 168.
43. Oe Kenzaburo, *Seiteki ningen,* in *Oe Kenzaburo zensakuhin,* vol. 6, p. 30.
44. Ibid., p. 62.
45. Ibid., pp. 62–63.
46. Of course, modern Japanese literature in general tends to skimp on characterization of minor characters; but it seems to me that, perhaps owing to their ideological content, Mishima's and Oe's works thus far discussed are particularly notable in this regard.
47. Mishima Yukio, "Patriotism," in his *Death in Midsummer,* trans. Geoffrey W. Sargent, p. 107.
48. Ibid.
49. Frye, *Anatomy,* p. 33.
50. Oe Kenzaburo, *A Personal Matter,* trans. John Nathan, p. 111.
51. Ibid., p. 110.
52. Ibid., p. 112.
53. Ibid., p. 113.
54. Ibid., p. 118.
55. A particularly interesting discussion of this phenomenon can be found in Bram Dijikstra, *Idols of Perversity: Fantasies of Feminine Evil in Fin de Siècle Culture.*
56. Himiko is also one of the few female characters in Oe's works to have a fully developed vision of an alternative world, her so-called "parallel universes," where negative occurrences in the real world are all corrected.
57. Mishima Yukio, "Subarashi gijutsu, shikashi . . . Oe Kenzaburoshi no kakioroshi *Kojinteki na taiken,*" in *Mishima Yukio zensakuhin,* vol. 31, p. 313.
58. Gwen Boardman Petersen, *The Moon in the Water: Understanding Tanizaki, Kawabata, and Mishima,* p. 217.
59. Ochiai Kiyohiko discusses this tendency in "Erochizumu," *Kokubungaku:* 43.10:72 (1978).
60. Mishima Yukio, *Forbidden Colors,* trans. Alfred H. Marks, p. 34.
61. Petersen, p. 240.
62. Mishima, *Thirst for Love,* trans. Alfred H. Marks, p. 35.
63. Mishima, "Kagi," p. 236.
64. Tanaka Miyoko, "Mishima bungaku no josei," p. 174.
65. Ibid., p. 186.
67. Mishima Yukio, *Five Modern No Plays,* trans. Donald Keene (Tokyo: Tuttle Books, 1980), p. 151.
68. Matsubara Shinichi, p. 118.
69. Ian Buruma, *Behind the Mask,* p. 60.
70. Torture itself has been a part of Japanese aesthetics, at least since the kabuki theater began to highlight various forms of painful death. It is probable that Mishima was influenced by this tradition when he described the mask's dreams of a "murder theater" in *Confessions of a Mask.*
71. Oe Kenzaburo, *Reintsuri o kiku onnatachi,* p. 15.

4. IN SEARCH OF THE GARDEN

1. Nathan, "Introduction," p. xiii.
2. Girard, *Deceit,* p. 269.
3. Noguchi Takehiko, *Mishima Yukio no sekai,* p. 213.
4. Mishima Yukio, cited in Masao Miyoshi, *Accomplices of Silence: The Modern Japanese Novel,* p. 9.
5. Tanaka Miyoko, "Mishima Yukio ni okeru yuibi to shiseishin," *Kokubungaku* 37.15:35 (1972).
6. Nancy Wilson Ross, "Introduction" to Mishima Yukio, *The Temple of the Golden Pavilion,* p. vii.
7. Masao Miyoshi, p. 160.
8. Girard, *Deceit,* p. 286.
9. Mishima Yukio, *The Temple of the Golden Pavilion,* trans. Ivan Morris, p. 21.
10. Ibid., p. 7.
11. Ibid., p. 8.
12. Girard, *Deceit,* p. 14.
13. Mishima, *Golden Pavilion,* p. 3.
14. Ibid., p. 35.
15. Ibid., p. 57.
16. Ibid., p. 38.
17. Ibid., p. 40.
18. Watanabe Hiroshi, "Mishima Yukio ni okeru ishiki to sonzai," *Kokubungaku* 37.15:26 (1972).
19. Mishima, *Golden Pavilion,* p. 25.
20. Ibid.
21. Ibid., p. 46.
22. Ibid., pp. 92–93.
23. Petersen, p. 261.
24. Mishima, *Golden Pavilion,* p. 216.
25. Ibid.
26. Ibid., p. 256.
27. Ibid., p. 24.
28. Nakamura Mitsu, "Kinkakuji ni tsuite," in Shirakawa Mashiko, ed., *Mishima Yukio: Hihyo to kenkyū,* p. 229.
29. Sato Yoshimasa, "Umi," *Kokubungaku* 43.10:66 (1978).
30. Mishima Yukio, *The Sailor Who Fell from Grace with the Sea,* trans. John Nathan, p. 17.
31. Ibid., p. 19.
32. Ibid., p. 16.
33. Ibid., p. 15.
34. Ibid., p. 16.
35. Ibid., p. 111.
36. Ibid., p. 109.
37. Ibid., p. 43.
38. Ibid., p. 110.
39. Sato, p. 65.
40. Although John Nathan's translation for this scene has the boys "tugging" (pp. 135–136) at Ryuji, the character actually used by Mishima in the Japanese text represents "towing" and is thus an echo of the novel's Japanese title, which means literally "Towing/Glory in the Afternoon."
41. Mishima, *Sailor,* p. 144.

42. Oe Kenzaburo, *Warera no jidai*, p. 51.
43. Ibid., p. 47.
44. Ibid., p. 113.
45. Ibid., p. 114.
46. Ibid., p. 137.
47. Ibid., p. 145.
48. Ibid., p. 146.
49. Ibid., p. 213.
50. Toshizawa Yukio, "Jiko kyūsai no imēji," in Nihon bungaku kenkyūkyozai sosho series, *Abe Kobo/Oe Kenzaburo*, p. 188.
51. Wilson, pp. 7–8.
52. See Suleiman, pp. 101–148, for a detailed analysis of "the structure of confrontation in French novels of the 1930s.
53. Suleiman, passim, esp. pp. 120–126.
54. Suleiman, p. 101.
55. Suleiman, p. 103.
56. Oe Kenzaburo, *Kōzui wa wagatamashii ni oyobi*, vol. 4 of *Oe Kenzaburo zensakuhin* (2nd collection), p. 8.
57. Ibid., vol. 4, p. 115.
58. Ibid., vol. 4, p. 116.
59. Ibid., vol. 5, p. 61.
60. Ibid., vol. 5, pp. 61–62.
61. Ibid., vol. 4, p. 97.
62. Ibid., vol. 4, p. 55.
63. Ibid., vol. 5, p. 201.
64. Ibid., vol. 5, p. 184.
65. Suleiman, p. 141.
66. Rene Girard, *Violence and the Sacred*, p. 302.
67. Isoda Koichi, "Teroru no gūwa," *Eureka* 6.3:80 (1974).

5. DEATH AND THE EMPEROR: THE POLITICS OF BETRAYAL

1. Mishima Yukio, *Runaway Horses*, pp. 186–187.
2. Oe Kenzaburo, *Okurete kita seinen*, p. 34.
3. Harootunian, p. 17.
4. Mishima Yukio, *Kyoko no ie*, p. 130.
5. Ibid., p. 544.
6. According to David Titus, the emperor in 1980 was a very remote figure to most young people, who felt, at best, affection (*shitashimi*) towards him and more likely apathy. See David A. Titus, "The Making of the 'Symbol Emperor System' in Postwar Japan," *Modern Asian Studies* 14.4:550 (1980).
7. Oe Kenzaburo, quoted in John Nathan, "Introduction," p. xiii.
8. Wakamori Taro, *Tennosei no rekishishinri*, p. 24.
9. Hashikawa Bunzo, quoted in Harootunian, p. 2.
10. For a further account of this incident, the so-called "Shimanaka Incident," see Nathan, *Mishima*, pp. 184–186.
11. See Suleiman, pp. 64–100, esp. her discussion of the novel of apprenticeship in relation to the *roman à thèse*.
12. Mishima "Patriotism," p. 93.
13. Ibid.
14. Ibid., p. 94.

15. Ibid., p. 95.
16. Ibid., p. 97.
17. Oe Kenzaburo, "Sebunchin," in *Oe Kenzaburo zensakuhin*, vol. 3, p. 266.
18. Ibid., p. 293.
19. Ibid., pp. 293–294.
20. Mishima, "Patriotism," p. 111.
21. Ibid., p. 94.
22. Ibid., p. 112.
23. Ibid., p. 111.
24. Ibid.
25. Oe, "Sebunchin," p. 301.
26. Mishima, "Patriotism," p. 107.
27. Oe Kenzaburo, "Seiji shōnen shisu," *Bungakkai* 1:42 (1961).
28. Ibid., p. 47.
29. Oe Kenzaburo, quoted in Matsuzaki Haruo, *Demokuratto no bungaku*, p. 36.
30. Oe, "Sebunchin," p. 266.
31. Oe, "Seiji shōnen shisu," p. 23.
32. See, for example, Matsubara Shinichi, p. 36.
33. Oe, "Seiji shonen shisu," p. 24.
34. Oe, *Okurete kita seinen*, p. 34.
35. Hirano Ken, Supplement (hōkan) to *Oe Kenzaburo zensakuhin*, vol. 4, p. 12.
36. Sasaki Yoshioka, "Aru hazo no nai zettai e, *Eureka* 8.11:173 (1976).
37. Mishima Yukio, *Runaway Horses*, p. 126.
38. Ibid., p. 25.
39. Ibid., p. 42.
40. Ibid., p. 260.
41. Ibid., p. 73.
42. Ibid., p. 74.
43. Ibid., p. 119.
44. Ibid., p. 292.
45. Ibid., p. 418.
46. Ibid., p. 419.
47. Oe Kenzaburo, "Shishatachi no saishū na buijion to warera ikinobitsuzukeru mono," in *Oe Kenzaburo dōjidaironshū*, vol. 3, p. 235.
48. Ibid., p. 241.
49. For discussions of how Oe's awareness of Mishima, his coup attempt, and his emperor-centered fiction dominate "Day," see Nathan, "Introduction," p. xxii; and Wilson, p. 81. For an example of a Japanese critic's taking Oe to task for his "hysterical" reaction to Mishima, see Kawanishi Masaaki, *Oe Kenzaburoron: misei no yume*, p. 154.
50. Oe Kenzaburo, "The Day He Himself Shall Wipe My Tears Away," in his *Teach Us To Outgrow Our Madness*, trans. John Nathan, p. 11.
51. Ibid., p. 97.
52. Ibid., p. 99.
53. Ibid., p. 100.
54. Ibid., p. 92.
55. In *Marginal World*, Wilson draws on her reading of Oe's essay "Shishatachi saishū na buijion" and on his later essays and fiction (e.g., *The Game of Contemporaneity* of 1980) to argue that "Day" is a "masterpiece of parody" (p. 74). Although I agree that much of "Day" is parodic and indeed brilliant, my own reading of this intense and angry text is that its very intensity, culminating in the novella's final paragraph, unintentionally undermines the satire. When Oe does tone down his anger and intensity to create a more

reasoned fictional attack on emperor-centered history in *The Game of Contemporaneity*, the result is a loss of literary excitement, although the text itself remains more intellectually consistent.

56. Oe, "Day," p. 67.
57. Nathan, "Introduction," p. xxii.
58. Oe, "Day," p. 104.
59. Ibid., p. 95.
60. Oki Hideo, "Mishima Yukio ni okeru kami no shi no kamigaku," *Eureka* 8:11:66–67 (1976).
61. Mishima did not always see the emperor in aesthetic terms. In the debate with Tokyo University students in 1969, he made the argument that the prewar imperial house was the closest thing to real democracy, because of the familial nature of the system (the students were dubious). See *Mishima Yukio vs. Todai Zenkyōto*, pp. 65–66.
62. Hashikawa Bunzo and Noguchi Takehiko, "Dōjidai to shite no Showa," *Eureka* 8.11:139 (1976).
63. See Yamada Yusei's summary of critical reaction to *Dōjidai gēmu* in *Kokubungaku* 28:8:111–114 (1984).
64. Oe, "Day," pp. 109–110.

6. THE FINAL QUEST

1. Oe Kenzaburo, *The Silent Cry*, trans. John Bester, p. 90.
2. Ibid., p. 50.
3. Oe, *Silent Cry*, p. 19.
4. Wilson, p. 49.
5. Oe, *Silent Cry*, p. 66.
6. Ibid., p. 197.
7. Ibid., p. 191.
8. Matsubara Shinichi, p. 258.
9. Oe, *Silent Cry*, p. 244.
10. Ibid., p. 240.
11. Girard, *Violence*, p. 107.
12. Oe, *Silent Cry*, p. 41.
13. Campbell, p. 82.
14. Oe, *Silent Cry*, p. 58.
15. Ibid.
16. Ibid., pp. 129–130.
17. Ibid., p. 74.
18. Ibid., p. 241.
19. Ibid., p. 242.
20. Ibid., p. 258.
21. Matsubara Shinichi, p. 256.
22. Oe, *Silent Cry*, p. 269.
23. Ibid.
24. Ibid., 270.
25. Matsubara Shinichi, p. 248.
26. Izu Toshihiko, "Man'en gannen no futoburu," *Kokubungaku* 16.1:141.
27. Aoki Mamoru, "Kegare no imeji," *Eureka* 6.3:83 (1974).
28. Oe, *Silent Cry*, p. 146.
29. Ibid., p. 274.
30. Ibid., p. 272.

31. Aoki Mamoru, p. 83.
32. Mishima Yukio, *The Temple of Dawn*, trans. E. Dale Saunders and Cecilia Segawa Seigle, pp. 262–263.
33. Watanabe Hiroshi, *Hojo no umiron*, p. 89.
34. Mishima Yukio, *Spring Snow*, trans. Michael Gallagher, p. 3.
35. Ibid., p. 5.
36. Ibid., p. 160.
37. Ibid., p. 361.
38. Mishima, *Runaway Horses*, p. 41.
39. Hasegawa Izumi, "Shinwa ka kindai shōsetsu ka," in *Kokubungaku* 10:130 (1978).
40. Mishima, *Runaway Horses*, p. 35.
41. Ibid., p. 47.
42. Ibid., pp. 43–44.
43. Campbell, p. 243.
44. Mishima, *Runaway Horses*, p. 407.
45. Mishima, *Temple of Dawn*, p. 1.
46. Ibid., p. 31.
47. Ibid., p. 43.
48. Ibid., p. 61.
49. Ibid., p. 244.
50. Mishima Yukio, *The Decay of the Angel*, trans. Edward Seidensticker, p. 11.
51. Ibid., p. 30.
52. Ibid., pp. 32–33.
53. Ibid., p. 57.
54. Ibid., p. 230.
55. Ibid., pp. 235–236.
56. Ibid., p. 237.
57. Ibid., p. 239.
58. Ibid., p. 246.
59. Ibid., p. 247.
60. Ibid.

7. MISHIMA, OE, AND MODERN JAPAN

1. Tanaka Miyoko, "Mishima Yukio kenkyūshi," *Kokubungaku* 45.3:205 (1980).
2. See, for example, the *zadankai* between Miyoshi Yukio, Noguchi Takehiko, Matsumoto Tooru, and Tsuge Teruhiko, "Mishima Yukio no sakuhin o yomu," *Kokubungaku* 26.9:14–16 (1982).
3. In a *taidan* between Nakagami Kenji and Yomota Inuhiko, the two discuss how Mishima has become a figure somewhat like Yoshitsune, the historical warrior around whom many legends were developed. Appropriately, Yomota mentions Oe's fiction, in particular as being responsible for developing the "legend": "Tensei, monogatari, tennō: Mishima Yukio o megutte," *Kokubungaku* 31.8:23 (1986).
4. Ichimura Shinichi and Eto Jun, "Tennō," *Shokun* 19.12:27 (1987).
5. Yamaguchi Masao and Inose Naoki, *Mikado to seikimatsu*, pp. 186–188.
6. Wilson, pp. 123–125.
7. Harold Bloom, "The Internalization of Quest Romance," in Harold Bloom, ed., *Romanticism and Consciousness: Essays in Criticism*, p. 7.

References

Aoki Mamoru. "Kegare no imēji," *Eureka* 6.3:82–83 (1974).

Belsey, Catherine. "The Romantic Construction of the Unconscious," in Francis Barker et al., eds. *Literature, Politics and Theory.* London: Methuen, 1986.

Bloom, Harold. "The Internalization of Quest Romance," in Harold Bloom, ed., *Romanticism and Consciousness: Essays in Criticism.* New York: W. W. Norton, 1970.

Brombert, Victor. "The Intellectual as Impossible Hero," in Victor Brombert, ed., *The Hero in Literature.* New York: J. B. Lippincott, 1960.

Buruma, Ian. *Behind the Mask.* New York: Pantheon Books, 1984.

Bruner, Jerome. "Myth and Identity," in Henry Murray, ed., *Myth and Mythmaking.* Boston: Beacon Press, 1969.

Campbell, Joseph. *The Hero with a Thousand Faces.* Princeton: Princeton University Press, 1973.

Chiba Nobutada. "Okurete kita seinen," *Kokubungaku* 36.8:98–102 (1971).

Cuddon, J. A. *A Dictionary of Literary Terms.* New York: Penguin Books, 1986.

Dijikstra, Bram. *Idols of Perversity: Fantasies of Feminine Evil in Fin de Siècle Culture.* New York: Oxford University Press, 1986.

Doi, Takeo. *The Anatomy of Dependence.* Tokyo: Kodansha, 1977.

Fowler, Edward. *The Rhetoric of Confession: Shishōsetsu in Early Twentieth Century Japanese Fiction.* Berkeley: University of California Press, 1988.

Frye, Northrop. *Anatomy of Criticism.* Princeton: Princeton University Press, 1957.

——. *The Secular Scripture: A Study of the Structure of Romance.* Cambridge: Harvard University Press, 1976.

Fukushima Akira. "Oe bungaku no shinteki kōzō," *Eureka* 6.3:107–115 (1974).

Fussell, Paul. *The Great War and Modern Memory.* New York: Oxford University Press, 1975.

Girard, Rene. *Deceit, Desire and the Novel.* Baltimore: Johns Hopkins University Press, 1965.
——. *Violence and the Sacred.* Baltimore: Johns Hopkins University Press, 1977.

Hanada Kiyoteru. "Sei Sebasuchin no kao," in Tanaka Miyoko, ed., *Nihon gendai bungaku,* no. 23: *Mishima Yukio.* Tokyo: Kadokawa Shoten, 1980.
Harootunian, H. D. "The Ideology of Cultural 'Totalism' in Mishima: The Economy of Expenditure and Loss." Unpublished paper given at University of Indiana, Conference on Mishima Yukio, Bloomington, Indiana, May 1987.
Hasegawa Izumi. "Shinwa ka kindai shosetsu ka," *Kokubungaku* 43.10:119–131 (1978).
Hashikawa Bunzo. "Nakamasha no me" in Shirokawa Mashahiko, ed., *Hihyō to kenkyū: Mishima Yukio.* Tokyo: Haga Shoten, 1974.
—— and Noguchi Takehiko. "Dōjidai to shite no Shōwa," *Eureka* 8.11:123–143 (1976).
Hirano Ken. Supplement (hōkan) to *Oe Kenzaburo zensakuhin,* vol. 4. Tokyo: Shinchōsha, 1966.
Hynes, Samuel. *The Auden Generation.* New York: Viking Press, 1972.

Ichimura Shinichi and Eto Jun. "Tennō," *Shokun* 12:26–39, 1987.
Isoda Koichi. "Oe, Eto ni okeru dentō to kindai," *Kokubungaku* 16.1:83–89 (1971).
——. "Teroru no gūwa," *Eureka* 6.3:73–81 (1974).
Izu Toshihiko. "Man'en gannen no futoboru," *Kokubungaku* 16.1:138–143 (1971).

Jameson, Fredric. *The Political Unconscious.* Ithaca: Cornell University Press, 1981.

Kataoka Keiji. *Oe Kenzaburoron.* Tokyo: Rippushobo, 1973.
Kawanishi Masaaki. *Oe Kenzaburoron: misei no yume.* Tokyo: Kodansha, 1979.
Kokubungaku 26.9 (1981). Special Edition: "Mishima Yukio to wa nan de atta ka."
Kubota Mamoru. "Ai no kawaki," *Kokubungaku* 37.15:116–117 (1972).

Lacan, Jacques. *Ecrits: A Selection.* New York: Norton, 1977.

Matsubara Shinichi. *Oe Kenzaburo no sekai.* Tokyo: Kōdansha, 1967.
Matsumoto Tooru. "Mishima Yukio ni okeru erochizumu," *Kokubungaku* 41.2:23–29 (1976).
Matsuzaki Haruo. *Demokuratto no bungaku.* Tokyo: Shin Nihon Shuppansha, 1981.
Mishima Yukio: Works in Translation
——. *After the Banquet.* Trans. Donald Keene. New York: Berkley Medallion, 1975.
——. *Confessions of a Mask.* Trans. Meredith Weatherby. Tokyo: Tuttle Books, 1981.

——. *Decay of the Angel.* Trans. Edward Seidensticker. New York: Pocket Books, 1975.

——. *Five Modern No Plays.* Trans. Donald Keene. Tokyo: Tuttle Books, 1980.

——. *Forbidden Colors.* Trans. Alfred H. Marks. New York: Berkley Medallion, 1968.

——. *Madame de Sade.* Trans. Donald Keene, New York: Grove Press. 1977.

——. "Patriotism," in his *Death in Midsummer.* Trans. Geoffrey W. Sargent. New York: New Directions, 1966.

——. *Runaway Horses.* Trans. Edward Gallagher. New York: Pocket Books, 1973.

——. *The Sailor Who Fell from Grace with the Sea.* Trans. John Nathan. New York: Berkley Medallion, 1975.

——. *The Sound of Waves.* Trans. Meredith Weatherby. New York: Alfred Knopf, 1956.

——. *Spring Snow.* Trans. Michael Gallagher. Tokyo: Tuttle Books, 1972.

——. *The Temple of Dawn.* Trans. E. Dale Saunders and Cecilia Segawa Seigle. New York: Pocket Books, 1975.

——. *The Temple of the Golden Pavilion.* Trans. Ivan Morris. Tokyo: Tuttle Books, 1981.

——. *Thirst for Love.* Trans. Alfred H. Marks. New York: Perigee Books, 1980.

Works in Japanese

——. "Eirei no koe," in *F 104.* Tokyo: Kawade Bunko, 1981.

——. "Gendai sakka wa kaku kangaeru," *Mishima Yukio zenshu,* suppl. vol. 1. Tokyo: Shinchōsha, 1976.

——. "Kagi no kakaru heya," in his *Kagi no kakaru heya.* Tokyo: Shinchōsha, 1982.

——. *Kyōko no ie.* Tokyo: Shinchō Bunko, 1979.

——. *Mishima Yukio vs. Todai zenkyōtō.* Tokyo: Shinchōsha, 1969.

——. "Shōsetsu to wa nanika," *Mishima Yukio zenshū,* vol. 33. Tokyo: Shinchōsha, 1976.

——. "Shūmatsukan kara no shuppatsu: Showa no nijū jigazō," *Mishima Yukio zenshū,* vol. 27. Tokyo: Shinchōsa, 1976.

——. "Subarashi gijutsu, shikashi . . . Oe Kenzaburo Shi no kakioroshi *Kojinteki na taiken,*" *Mishima Yukio zenshū,* vol. 31. Tokyo: Shinchōsha, 1976.

——. "Suzakke ie no metsubo," in *F 104.* Tokyo: Kawade Books, 1981.

——. "Waga tomo Hitora," in *Sado kōshaku fujin / Waga tomo Hitora.* Tokyo: Shinchōbunko, 1979.

——. "Watashi no eien no josei," *Mishima Yukio zenshū,* vol. 27. Tokyo: Shinchōsha, 1976.

Miyoshi, Masao. *Accomplices of Silence: The Modern Japanese Novel.* Berkeley: The University of California Press, 1974.

Miyoshi Yukio, Noguchi Takehiko, Matsumoto Tooru, and Tsuge Teruhiko, "Mishima Yukio no sakuhin o yomu," *Kokubungaku* 26.9:6–37 (1981).

Moorman, Charles. "Myth and Medieval Literature: Sir Gawain and the Green Knight," in John Vickery, ed., *Myth and Literature.* Lincoln: University of Nebraska Press, 1966.

Moylan, Tom. *Demand the Impossible: Science Fiction and the Utopian Imagination.* New York: Methuen, 1986.
Murray, Henry, ed. *Myth and Mythmaking.* Boston: Beacon Press, 1969.

Nakagami Kenji and Yomota Inuhiko (taidan). "Tensei, monogatari, tennō: Mishima Yukio o megutte," *Kokubungaku* 31.8:18–44 (1986).
Nakamura Mitsu. "Kinkakuji ni tsuite," in Shirakawa Masahiko, ed., *Mishima Yukio: Hihyō to kenkyū.* Tokyo: Haga Shoten, 1979.
Nathan, John. "Introduction" to Oe Kenzaburo, *Teach Us to Outgrow Our Madness.* New York: Grove Press, 1977.
———. *Mishima: A Biography.* Tokyo: Tuttle Books, 1981.
Noguchi Takehiko, *Mishima Yukio no sekai.* Tokyo: Kōdansha, 1968.

Ochiai Kiyohiko, "Erochizumu," *Kokubungaku.* 43.10:71–78 (1978).
Oe Kenzaburo: Works in Translation
———. "The Day He Himself Shall Wipe My Tears Away," in his *Teach Us To Outgrow Our Madness.* Trans. John Nathan. New York: Grove Press, 1977.
———. *A Personal Matter.* Trans. John Nathan. Tokyo: Tuttle Books, 1979.
———. "Prize Stock," in his *Teach Us To Outgrow Our Madness.* Trans. John Nathan. New York: Grove Press, 1977.
———. *The Silent Cry.* Trans. John Bester. Tokyo: Kōdansha, 1967.
Works in Japanese
———. "Boku jishin no naka no sensō," *Oe Kenzaburo dōjidaironshū* vol. 1, Tokyo: Iwanami Shoten, 1981.
———. *Dōjidai gēmu.* Tokyo: Shinchōsha, 1979.
———. *Kaku no taika to "ningen" no koe.* Tokyo: Iwanami Shoten, 1982.
———. "Kurai kawa, omoi kai," *Oe Kenzaburo zensakuhin,* vol. 2. Tokyo: Shinchōsha, 1978.
———. *Kōzui wa wagatamashii ni oyobi, Oe Kenzaburo zensakuhin* (Second Collection), vols. 4 and 5. Tokyo: Shinchōsha, 1978.
———. *Memushiri kouchi,* in *Oe Kenzaburo zensakuhin,* vol. 1. Tokyo: Shinchōsha, 1966.
———. *Okurete kita seinen,* in *Oe Kenzaburo zensakuhin,* vol. 4. Tokyo: Shinchōsha, 1966.
———. "Oyogu otoko," in his *Reintsuri o kiku onnatachi.* Tokyo: Shinchōsha, 1982.
———. *Reintsuri o kiku onnatachi.* Tokyo: Shinchōsha, 1982.
———. *Sakebigoe,* in *Oe Kenzaburo zensakuhin,* vol. 5. Tokyo: Iwanami Shoten, 1981.
———. "Sebunchin," in *Oe Kenzaburo zenskuhin,* vol. 3. Tokyo: Shinchōsha, 1966.
———. "Seiji shōnen shisu," *Bungakkai* 1:8–48 (1961).
———. *Seiteki ningen,* in *Oe Kenzaburo zensakuhin,* vol. 6. Tokyo: Shinchōsha, 1966.
———. "Sengō sedai no imēji," *Oe Kenzaburo dōjidaironshū,* vol. 1. Tokyo: Iwanami Shoten, 1981.
———. "Shishatachi no saishuteki na buijion to warera ikinobitsuzukeru mono," in *Oe Kenzaburo dōjidaironshū,* vol. 6. Tokyo: Iwanami Shoten, 1981.

——. *Shōsetsu no takurami chi no tanoshimi.* Tokyo: Shinchōsha, 1985.

——. "Tero wa utsukushiku ronriteki ka," *Oe Kenzaburo dōjidaironshū,* vol. 3. Tokyo: Iwanami Shoten, 1981.

——. *Warera no jidai.* Tokyo: Shinchōsha, 1963.

Oki Hideo, "Mishima Yukio ni okeru kami no shi no kamigaku," *Eureka* 8:11:65–71 (1976).

Petersen, Gwen Boardman. *The Moon in the Water: Understanding Tanizaki, Kawabata, and Mishima.* Honolulu: The University of Hawaii Press, 1979.

Plath, David. *Long Engagements: Maturity in Modern Japan.* Stanford: Stanford University Press, 1980.

Powell, Irena. *Writers and Society in Modern Japan.* Tokyo: Kōdansha, 1983.

Ross, Nancy Wilson. "Introduction" to Mishima Yukio, *Temple of the Golden Pavilion.* Tokyo: Tuttle Books, 1981.

Rubin, Jay. *Injurious to Public Morals: Writers and the Meiji State.* Seattle: University of Washington Press, 1984.

Sasaki Yoshioka. "Aru hazu no nai zettai e," *Eureka* 8.11:170–174, (1976).

Sato Yoshimasa. "Umi," *Kokubungaku* 43.10:62–70 (1978).

Shinohara Shigeru. *Oe Kenzaburoron.* Tokyo: Toho, 1974.

Suleiman, Susan. *Authoritarian Fictions: The Ideological Novel as a Literary Genre.* New York: Columbia University Press, 1983.

Tanaka Miyoko, ed., *Nihon gendai bungaku,* no. 23: *Mishima Yukio.* Tokyo: Kadokawa Shoten, 1980.

——. "Mishima Yukio kenkyūshi," *Kokubungaku* 45.3:205–213 (1980).

——. "Mishima bungaku no josei," in Hasegawa Izumi et al., eds., *Mishima Yukio kenkyū.* Tokyo: Yuubun shoin, 1970.

——. "Mishima Yukio ni okeru yuibi to shiseishin," *Kokubungaku* 37.15:33–38 (1972).

Tanner, Tony. *Adultery in the Novel.* Baltimore: Johns Hopkins University Press, 1979.

Titus, David A. "The Making of the "Symbol Emperor System" in Postwar Japan," *Modern Asian Studies* 14.4:529–578 (1980).

Toshizawa Yukio. "Jiko kyūsai no imēji," in Nihon bungaku kenkyūkyōzai sosho series, *Abe Kobo/ Oe Kenzaburo.* Tokyo: Yuseido, 1974.

Wakamori Taro. *Tennōsei no rekishishinri.* Tokyo: Kobundo, 1973.

Watanabe Hiroshi. *Hōjō no umiron.* Tokyo: Banbi Bunko, 1972.

——. "Mishima Yukio ni okeru ishiki to sonzai," *Kokubungaku* 37.15:21–26 (1972).

Wilson, Michiko. *The Marginal World of Oe Kenzaburo.* New York: M. E. Sharpe, 1986.

Wolfe, Peter. *Yukio Mishima.* New York: Continuum Publishing, 1989.

Yamaguchi Masao and Inose Naoki. *Mikado to seikimatsu*. Tokyo: Heibonsha, 1987.

Yamanouchi, Hisaki. *The Search for Authenticity in Modern Japanese Literature.* Cambridge: Cambridge University Press, 1980.

Yoshida Hirō. "Kamen no kokuhaku," *Kokubungaku* 37.15:114–115 (1972).

Yourcenar, Marguerite. *Mishima: A Vision of the Void.* New York: Farrar, Strauss and Giroux, 1986.

Index

DATE DUE			
JUN 07 '93			
JAN 18 '9			
APR 21			
DEC 0 8 1994			
DEC 0 8 1997			
MAR 3 0 1998			